MW00478561

Betrayal of the Innocents

His argument might be true but not valid because it's based on anecdotes. He gives no evidence to suggest that the abuse was widespread. I'm prepared to believe the argument, but I find it unconvincing.

Beyond question:
1.) Clerical authoritarianism
2.) Numerous inadequately trained priests
3.) Absentee fathers, children tied to mothers

Betrayal of the Innocents

Desire, Power, and the
Catholic Church in Spain

Timothy Mitchell

PENN

University of Pennsylvania Press

Philadelphia

Copyright © 1998 University of Pennsylvania Press
All rights reserved
Printed in the United States of America on acid-free paper

10   9   8   7   6   5   4   3   2   1

Published by
University of Pennsylvania Press
Philadelphia, Pennsylvania 19104-4011

Library of Congress Cataloging-in-Publication Data
Mitchell, Timothy (Timothy J.)
Betrayal of the innocents : desire, power, and the Catholic Church in Spain /
Timothy Mitchell.
    p.   cm.
Includes bibliographical references and index.
ISBN 0-8122-3453-7 (cloth : alk. paper). — ISBN 0-8122-1659-8 (pbk. : alk. paper)
1. Sexual misconduct by clergy—Spain—History.   2. Catholic Church—Spain—
Clergy—History.   3. Anti-clericalism—Spain—History.   4. Spain—Church history.
I. Title.
BX1583.M58   1998
282′.46′0904—dc21   98-15214
                                                                           CIP

Contents

Acknowledgments   vii

Introduction: Authoritarian Sexuality in Spain   **1**

1. Institutionalized Sexual Predation   **10**

Celibate Supremacy and Symbolic Violence   16
Motherhood and Priesthood   22

2. The Anticlerical Imaginary, 1808–1901   **32**

Doña Perfecta: The Harm That Good Women Do   43
La Regenta: The Psychology of Priestly Desire   48
Electra: Galdós and the Anarchists   55

3. Spanish Sexual Politics, 1901–1939   **63**

The Sacred Family Order Under Siege   72
"The Plan Was to Kill You All"   86
A Woman Can Be the Enemy   93

4. The Guardians of Morality   **104**

Men and Women Under Franco   115
Spain in Recovery   124

Notes   133
Bibliography   155
Index   177

Acknowledgments

I completed my investigation of men and women under Franco thanks to a 1996 award from the Scholarly and Creative Activities Enhancement Program at Texas A&M University. Cultural psychology research was carried out with the help of a 1995 grant from the Program for Cultural Cooperation Between Spain's Ministry of Culture and United States' Universities. Hispanic anticlericalism research was launched with the help of Marcelo DeSautu. I salute Steven M. Oberhelman for his decisive leadership of the Department of Modern and Classical Languages at Texas A&M and for his ongoing support of interdisciplinary research endeavors. For their astute advice or encouragement I am grateful to Philip K. Bock, Richard D. Critchfield, David T. Gies, David D. Gilmore, Robert W. Kern, Stephen J. Miller, Pepe Rodríguez, Edward F. Stanton, Eduardo Urbina, and Susan Verdi Webster. Four years of effort finally came to fruition because of the perseverance and moral courage of Patricia Smith at the University of Pennsylvania Press. This book is dedicated to her.

Introduction: Authoritarian Sexuality in Spain

> A friar and a nun have more to fear from the
> very people they live with than from all the
> demons put together.
> —Saint Teresa of Avila

This is the first book to assess the long-term consequences of clergy sexual activity for an entire culture. In recent times, priests charged with abuse have captured headlines and bankrupted dioceses all over the United States. But these cases have not exacerbated class conflict, threatened the stability of the government, despoiled national folklore, obsessed several literary generations, or led to the murder of thousands of priests. Spain has seen all of this and more. To put it another way, what we find in Spain is a psychohistorical depth to the problem of clergy sexual abuse that is lacking in the United States, along with a legacy of Church power unlike anything in American experience. Both acquired their current form in the context of a late-feudal social order and a seemingly endless supply of laboring serfs or commoners servicing the psychic and physical needs of their social betters. Spain's special devotion to the Virgin Mary was part of the problem rather than the solution: the extreme idealization of the maternal instinct created special dangers for Spanish women Catholics and special risks for their children, and was intimately connected to the dynamics of priestly power and desire in Spain.

These dynamics can be traced to the great socioeconomic upheavals of the third century C.E., when Jesus Christ's message of love and optimism was nearly drowned out by small but vocal groups of sexually pessimistic Christian fanatics. Their radical body-fearing and antimarital concepts derived from "the Stone Age of religious consciousness,"

Most scholars don't credit her argument

complains theologian Uta Ranke-Heinemann,[1] but such a formulation neglects their historical novelty and political utility. There was identity-constructing method in the seeming madness of the cult members, a keen desire to distance themselves from mere Stoic restraint, on the one hand, and the family-growth policies adopted by exiled Jews on the other. The Manichaean core doctrine that most inspired the radicals was the refusal to help the world last one second longer than necessary via sexual reproduction. Severe forms of asceticism were added to this, since they were a handy substitute for martyrdom in non-persecutory epochs and an excellent way to induce prophetic and trance-like states.[2]

Authoritarian sexuality per se is the legacy of the political compromise engineered by Augustine and backed by Roman arms, whereby the zeal of this radical, mostly urban, family-despising minority was permanently, albeit uneasily, reconciled with the ancient inertia of the fertility-minded majority. As Fredric Jameson explains, "what confronts any institutionalized political body—whether the Catholic Church or the Communist Party—is the requirement of making a large place for all those ordinary humans who are not saints and cannot live by extremes and absolutes, and also of ideologically expelling those groups whose extremism and absolutism risk alienating this or that fundamental component of their larger social and class compromise."[3] The apostate Augustine repudiated Gnostic, Donatist, Arian, and every other form of extrainstitutional Utopian activism, but he did hasten to co-opt "the terrain of the fallen body itself as a field of ideological struggle." By making sexuality "the mode of explanation rather than the thing to be explained," Augustine orchestrated the withdrawal of creative energies from political praxis and simultaneously sketched out "the space of a new inwardness . . . a foolproof area for the organization of a check that always infallibly brings into being the very object it is supposed to search for." As Michel Foucault put it in his final New York lecture,

the means of the spiritual struggle against libido do not consist, as with Plato, in turning our eyes upwards and memorizing the reality we have previously known and forgotten. The spiritual struggle consists, on the contrary, in turning our eyes continuously downwards or inwards in order to decipher, among the movements of the soul, which ones come from the libido. . . . It requires a permanent hermeneutics of the self.[4]

Relentless self-scrutiny thus comes to be seen as not just one technology of the self but *the* technology of the Self, a genuine psychohistorical rupture, a new Western subjectivity instituted by wary hypervigilance of that unruly fallen body.

This approach can be challenged in at least three ways. First, in many early sexual extremists and desert saints we find not a self but a borderline disintegration of it, a proximity to psychosis accompanied by frequent and unbearable auditory or visual hallucinations. Antony of the Desert was the classic exemplar of a chaste man tyrannized by visions of cavorting nymphs (and a favorite subject of fin-de-siècle painters for that very reason).[5] In truth it was a frightening return of the semiotic in Kristeva's sense, the darkside of the *chora* where a subject is most threatened with annihilation, where the Oedipalized symbolic system has broken down or was never imposed in the first place.[6] Like suicidal members of the on-line "Heaven's Gate" cult of California, many cenobites of the wilderness excised their sex organs in a last-ditch effort to forestall total psychic collapse. If Foucault's famous "technologies of the self" were in reality closely allied with technologies of self-mutilation, then the hermeneutic paradigm becomes vulnerable to subsumption into a more complete sociopolitical or psychological paradigm, like fanaticism or malignant narcissism.[7] In any event, the Fathers of the Church agreed with the maimed hermits that physical arousal is the root of all evil, and therefore they sanctioned symbolic castrations like chastity, perpetual virginity, and celibacy.

Second, significant breeding populations of the ancient world were in the thrall of their Great Mothers (the glaringly absent Others in Foucauldian thought). Augustine's canny theological maneuvering paved the way for the conversion of large numbers of lower-class pagan families whose own masochistic impulses had previously found expression in the Cybele cult. According to sociologist Michael P. Carroll, the teeming masses of newly converted landless day laborers changed the face of Christianity forever:

> If we grant that the father-ineffective family was common among the Roman proletariat, and that such a family structure does produce in sons a strong but strongly repressed desire for the mother, then we would expect that the sudden absorption of the Roman proletariat into the Church during the great transformation of the fourth century should produce in the Church an increased emphasis upon masochism (in Church art, in clerical practice, and so on) and the appearance within the Church of a cult centered around a mother goddess disassociated from sexuality.[8]

Henceforth, Carroll argues, masochistic Marianism would be most common in the Latin Catholic countries of the northern Mediterranean whose family or extended family structures both strongly elicit and strongly repress desire for the mother. The Madonna is linked to brutal punishment and the loss of organs in several Italian legends. One medieval Spanish legend tells of a priest who severed his own hand because a woman had kissed it; the Virgin Mary miraculously restored it so he could say Mass. Another folk legend features a pilgrim who castrates himself to atone for a sin of fornication; the Virgin intervenes to save the man's life but the offending organ is not restored.[9] In this study I employ a post-Freudian view of Marian masochism that completes Carroll's fine work. The point here is that we are dealing with a long tradition of flesh mortification whose function was not to improve introspection but to block it.

This leads to a third difficulty with the whole concept of deriving Western subjectivity out of the anxious examination of libidinal pulsations: it tends to forget other psychic mechanisms that work in a contrary direction—intrapsychic "technologies" like splitting, dissociation, disavowal, and so on. Indeed, the hard-won gain in subjectivity was immediately offset by a new kind of psychic vulnerability. Foucault credits the self produced by authoritarian sexuality with more coherence than it has in its most notorious exemplars—abusive priests, who furnish living proof that archaic demands can be acted out behind the very back, so to speak, of the "introspective" ego.

Authoritarian sexuality is by its very nature dualistic, polarizing, and schismogenetic. Wary hypervigilance may usher in a new form of subjectivity, but it is a poor and myopic one; it freezes subjects at a relatively low developmental level of the psyche. A genuine "hermeneutics of the self" is the exception and in a religious context it belongs only to the exceptional, people like Teresa of Avila or Ignatius of Loyola, both of whom made progress only *after* abandoning their punitive superegos to achieve mature, nondespotic object relations.[10] A spiritual self worthy of the name only comes with the emergence of schemata that transcend the sadomasochistic fantasies of the Desert Fathers.

Disavowal prevailed over insight in the sexuality of men and women studied under the groundbreaking Authoritarian Personality project (1950). The Adorno group found that extremely prejudiced or prefascistic individuals exhibited a moralistic rejection of sexuality accompanied by an underlying disrespect or resentment toward the opposite sex, "typically combined with externalized, excessive psuedo-admiration," and occasional bouts of promiscuity.[11] Women were passive-aggressive, men exploitative and manipulative; dichotomous and depersonalized attitudes toward sex abounded, with men typically dividing women into "pure" and "low" categories. Authoritarianism studies have been reinvigorated in recent years: "Despite the flaws in the research, the theoretical and methodological controversies, and, at times, a decline of interest in the subject, the concept of authoritarianism remains vital," scholars conclude.[12] It is now clear to all that there is such a thing as left-wing authoritarianism. Anti-Semitism, thought by the Adorno group to be the paradigm prejudice, is now seen in terms of an entire constellation of "-isms," each with its own convoluted mechanisms and fantasy structures, each with its own "ideology of desire," to use Elisabeth Young-Bruehl's phrase.[13] Pathology paradigms are obsolete. Young-Bruehl concludes that "many people have prejudices *instead of* the conventional forms of various pathologies." Prejudices and their target groups are to be understood in terms of psychic configurations that are determined socially and politically through the medium of the family; they may wax and wane or shift to different target groups over time. Young-Bruehl seconds George Devereux's observation that the "others" of the hysterically prejudiced represent the family "displaced downward."[14] As it happens, such splitting strategies are more common in cultural milieus that equate sexuality with shameful depravity. The anxiety-relieving goal of prejudice is to locate a race or social class "on whom to set *down* a burden—a burden of desire and self-reproach."[15]

Were the original sexual despots of the early Church prejudiced? Did they hate and fear and desire their designated Others? Affirmative. The means of the spiritual struggle against libido were the continual turning of the eyes downward not just on oneself but on everyone else as well. It worked: for many hundreds of years, the victims of the ideology of prurient discipline I call authoritarian sexuality have been all too willing to see themselves as naturally unworthy and untrustworthy, greatly facilitating their governability. In dealing with the real-world consequences of Catholic sexual morality, it becomes exceedingly hard to distinguish technologies of the self from those of domination, as Foucault well knew.

* * *

Although authoritarian sexuality was first formulated in Roman-controlled areas of Africa and in the desert monasteries of Syria and Palestine, it was the key Roman province of Hispania that was destined to supply the space and the bodies for its fullest development. In 300 C.E. the Spanish Council of Elvira imposed celibacy on the clergy—some 150 years before it became mandatory in other parts of the declining and falling empire.[16] In the early 700s the Visigoths of Hispania reenacted the fate of the Hispano-Romans they had conquered, except this time the local lords were the barbarians and the Islamic invaders were the materially advanced ones. The last Christian king came to be blamed by all for the disaster. Rodrigo's crime had been sexual in nature (the seduction of another nobleman's daughter), and so was the expiation: the so-called Last Goth climbs into a tomb with a live serpent and allows it slowly to eat "the part that most deserves it, that which was the origin of my great misfortune."[17] Thus the canonical history of Spain begins with an act of self-mutilation, perpetrated on the fallen body of the king himself.

As authoritarian sexuality develops over the centuries, projection and scapegoating will be its dominant psychosocial *technologies*. Spanish anthropologist Manuel Delgado argues that Spain's violent folk rituals are inseparable from Catholicism's "lavish repertory of images and attitudes centered almost obsessively on the annihilation of anyone or anything that symbolizes the social enemy." That includes the well-known attempts by Spanish Christians to eliminate Spanish Jews, Spanish Muslims, and Spanish Lutherans. Eventually the social enemy role would be filled by the priests themselves; in 1936 they would be classified as dangerous hypersexual beings and slaughtered en masse, often with the same techniques used to destroy bulls, cocks, hogs, geese, and Judas-effigies in hundreds of patronal festivals the length and breadth of Spain. For Delgado this simply confirms the endemic instability and continual oscillations of his country's "tense" religious system:

> Spanish traditional religious culture — over and beyond its numerous geographical or temporal variants — has always been a magnificent example of a "tense" system, that is, of a system based on a strong ritual pressure that tyrannizes social life at large and subjects individuals to an intense, barely tolerable psychological jarring, always on the verge of turning into rebellion against the order of things that the rites impose so despotically.[18]

In Delgado's description of a cybernetic ritual system that paradoxically maintains homeostasis through regular outbreaks of antistructure, we find a parallel to the psychodynamics of authoritarian sexuality itself. A Latin American priest and psychologist named Alvaro Jiménez argues that priests who pretend to an "ambiguous chastity" are simultaneously stepping on the gas while they slam on the brakes as hard as they can — "a psychological absurdity that can give rise to severe stress and serious personality disorders."[19] Vices lurk behind authoritarian bulwarks of virtue. In his study of abusive priests Father A. W. Richard Sipe found a continual oscillation between overcontrol and loss of control, sex condemned and sex indulged, with even the sharpest pangs of guilt unable to forestall the urge to transgress.[20]

It would be reasonable to hypothesize that traditional Spain's "tense" ritual system was either put in motion or wound tighter by priests locked in their own double bind. In all likelihood we are dealing with the Spanish version of "authoritarian schismogenesis," the birth and growth of a polarized and divisive consciousness whose influence over Spanish culture can scarcely be exaggerated.[21] Anthropologist Julio Caro Baroja contended that much of Spanish culture had been shaped by such projective/persecutory beliefs and behaviors.[22] Spaniards of many social classes coincided in their righteous eagerness to identify and punish culprits. It was a moral code that maintained itself in large part through

slander, shaming, and rituals of public mockery, as described so well by
anthropologist David D. Gilmore.[23] The moral code worked, obviously,
but it crippled spiritual development in the long run.[24]

Obligatory vows of celibacy in the context of a shaming culture or
institution did not and do not prevent large numbers of religious personnel from engaging in sexual activities of all kinds, many of them not
consensual. Instead, the vows ensure that suffering will be eroticized,
shame voluptuous, and forbidden love the only kind that arouses. Without forgetting for a moment that there are abusive ministers in all creeds
and denominations, we must recognize that certain qualities peculiar
to the ministerial development of Roman Catholicism are especially
conducive to exploitative events. Following Father Richard Sipe, these
include the unrealistic nature of the demand for perfect celibacy, the
"absurd" equation of sex and sin, the denial or rationalization of abuse,
and the awesome power over people obtained via the sacrament of confession.[25] Their own physical bodies constitute the first site of battle;
when the battle is lost, the priests' corporate body often shields them
from the consequences of defeat.

One could cite thousands of specific examples of clerical "loss of control." At first it is striking to note how very little the specific acts change
over the centuries, the fondling, the groping, the fixations, the frenzy—
all the same, generation after generation. I have included only enough
examples to show the pattern. The sins of any one father are an easy
target. More merit accrues to the revelation of the iceberg, the transhis-
torical ideology of discipline and desire in which transgression is not an
unfortunate anomaly but a functioning part of the system. Not the behaviors themselves but their *inevitability* turns out to be the more striking
realization.

Scholars mining the dusty archives of the Inquisition knew about the
epidemic of clergy abuse but did not gauge the long-term consequences
of this victimization for the people of Spain. Now that well-constructed
statistical studies of exploitative events are available, we are in a position to make the attempt. A new view of Spanish culture is suggested by
research like that of Barbara McLaughlin, director of Hospital Ministry for the Catholic Archdiocese of Miami. Her analysis of one hundred
victims confirmed that, following abuse, "Catholics had a much more
negative experience of spirituality," demonstrated by declining church
attendance and an inability to trust priests.[26] Can we find evidence
of devastated spirituality among Spanish Catholics of earlier times? In
abundance, as I discuss in Chapter 1. There is nothing in America that
can compare with the extremely widespread and deeply rooted Spanish
wariness of the Church that clergy abuse engendered. Add to this the
numerous writers or demagogues who challenged the celibate/sexual

check him out

power system a hundred years ago—with ammunition provided by the system itself. Novelist Vicente Blasco Ibáñez built his career by portraying priests as "sexually-perverted sadists" (his phrase), which only served to goad them into reactionary conspiracy and repeated affirmation of dysfunctional moral dogmas. What priests considered vocations were seen by their opponents as a type of trance that impelled credulous Spanish Catholic families to surrender at least one of their offspring to a seminary or a convent. (Even today, women of Spain give birth to over 10 percent of the Church's total personnel—prelates, priests, deacons, monks, friars, nuns, and missionaries.) And that is why historically the clerical-anticlerical dispute was envisioned and expressed, by both sides, in the acrimonious terms of a custody battle. In Chapter 2, I sketch the growth of the anticlerical "industry" in nineteenth-century Spain and analyze three remarkable literary works that portray Spanish youths as virtual hostages of ultra-Catholic mothers and predatory priests.

As will be seen in Chapter 3, the Spanish Civil War (1936–1939) was partly motivated by accusations of sexual misconduct among the clergy. Anarchist and other leftist publications were obsessed with the issue, and took to the mass distribution of priest-baiting pornography as part of a planned destruction of Catholicism itself. This was the unfortunate outcome of a modernizing and even educational erotic discourse that was initially so promising (I provide an overview of novels and musical comedies). It is as if the anti-Catholic discursive spaces unwittingly opened up by sexual authoritarianism had remained secretly "contaminated" with the original anxiety, hence always on the verge of relapse into schismogenetic schemata of shame, rage, and vengeance. In 1931 the liberal leader Manuel Azaña compared his anticlerical program to "a surgical intervention on a patient without benefit of anesthesia and who in flailing about in his own pain might complicate the operation and make it mortal; I don't know for whom, but mortal for someone." [27] Read in hindsight these words seem frivolous, prophetic, and criminal all at once. When war broke out, leftist leaders organized, participated in, or tolerated the systematic slaughter of priests and nuns all over Spain. Catholics in every country were justifiably outraged, and Franco had been handed an invaluable propaganda weapon. To what extent the priests sowed the seeds of their own destruction with abusive practices is one of the questions this book seeks to answer. In the manner of a cultural chaologist, I measure the magnitude and direction of the socio-psychological forces that led to this virulent outbreak of antistructure.

If ever there was a political regime that wished to found itself upon "family values," it was Francoism. The Generalissimo and his followers, including a plurality of Spanish women, believed that the breakdown of monogamy had led directly to the political crises of the 1930s. They agreed that to have a stable social order men had to be domesticated, and that "compulsory marriage" (Wilhelm Reich's phrase) was the way to do it. It has been suggested that so-called National Catholicism was the functional equivalent of Nazi racial policy in terms of political usefulness.[28] This does not mean that notions of Castilian racial superiority were not important, especially to the army, but it does mean that ultraconservative Catholicism was the principal glue holding disparate groups of the regime together, binding their children via the educational system, reproducing authoritarian sexual paradigms in each new generation.

The defenders of any status quo are always committed to sweeping as much under the rug as possible, but in Franco's Spain the denial was eerily similar to that of a dysfunctional family system. The psychogenesis of the priesthood, Eugen Drewermann notes, is entirely dependent on the suppression of any doubts regarding the good intentions of the father, no matter what his real behavior might have been.[29] A thousand years of covert implementations of power inside the absolutely paternalistic celibate/sexual system prepared the way for the Francoist model of government: corporative, secretive, manipulative, exploitative, and hysterical in Young-Bruehl's sense. In Chapter 4 I discuss Franco's restoration of sexual anxiety after the civil war: film censorship, rigid gender roles, prostitution, the Sección Femenina, and what I call authoritarian gynecology. As will be seen, the great burst of perversity that finally flowered under Franco was a logical, indeed inevitable result of Church-sponsored prurient discipline. In the final section I discuss the steps being taken by Spaniards today to override the ancient scripts and compulsions of authoritarian sexuality.

Chapter 1
Institutionalized Sexual Predation

If we had to judge by the folkloric record alone, we would have to conclude that Spaniards remained loyal to Catholicism not because of but
in spite of the clergy. Hundreds of proverbs and sayings express popular anxieties about sexual and economic exploitation by priests, monks,
abbots, and friars. There are far more proverbs dealing with sexual predation or concubinage than with any other clerical vice. A tiny sampling:

"Al fraile no le hagas la cama, ni le des a tu mujer por ama"
(Don't make a friar's bed or let your wife be his housekeeper)
"Vivir junto al cura es gran locura"
(It's great madness to live next door to the curate)
"Ni por lumbre a casa del cura va la moza segura"
(A girl is not even safe going to the curate's house for fire)
"Si yo dijera no quiero, no quiero, no fuera yo amiga del crego"
(If I said I don't want to, I don't want to, I wouldn't be the priest's girlfriend)
"Por la verdad murió el gallo"
(The rooster died for the truth)

This last proverb commemorates a noisy rooster who was killed by
a priest creeping into his neighbor's house for purposes of adultery.
Add to the proverbs the many medieval legends that graphically depict clerical sexual misconduct. A small sampling from Harriet Goldberg's *Motif-Index of Medieval Spanish Folk Narratives*: "Hermit gets drunk,
rapes woman, kills her, is captured and executed," "Monk distracted by
thoughts of fornication neglects duty to pray," "Fire pours from throat of
dead priest who seduced the young woman he had baptized" (V465.1.1.1.
through V465.1.2.); "Priest who had sex with god-daughter dies after
seven days; fire rises from grave consuming it totally" (T427.1); "Devil
transforms priest's concubine into mare" (Q493.2); "Hypocritical cleric
participates passively in sexual acts with widow; exculpated because he
did nothing actively" (K2058.4). "Woman tricked into offering self to
God by deceitful priests in service of seducer" (K1315.1); "Priest must

give up fornication; in exchange pains are cured by saint's prayers" (T334.1.9). Golden Age scholar Maxime Chevalier cites a story in which a stallion owned by the count of Ureña fails to mate with some mares; the aristocrat counsels his men to throw a Franciscan friar's habit onto the stallion to achieve the desired result.[1]

Spanish scholar Manuel Bernal refers to the "cruel delight" and "intimate satisfaction" expressed by stories or proverbs in which a lust-obsessed clergyman is ridiculed or punished, as in "El cura de Cantarcillo, primero fue toro y después novillo" (The priest of Cantarcillo, first he was a bull then a bullock), which refers to a priest "brutally castrated by the brother of the girl whose favors he sought."[2] Scholars of several nationalities agree that Spain's anticlerical *Refranero* (proverb corpus) possesses unusual degrees of hostility and violent urges. Although an earlier generation of French Marxist critics traced the rage to economic causes, Bernal finds their reasoning insufficient; he believes that popular hostility toward men of the cloth was motivated by a keen sense of betrayal.

In any case it is clear that the more comfortable economic status of clergymen enabled them to seduce with greater success. To judge by the *Refranero*, rare was the clergyman who did not have a concubine, mistress, or kept woman (*barragana* or *manceba*). Numerous proverbs express envy of the priest's mistress, who doesn't work but always has plenty to eat. Other sayings deal with the offspring of such liaisons, the so-called *hijos de cura*, a social issue in Spanish communities to this very day. Many of these children were (and are) the product of a pious wife's adultery with a local priest; most husbands preferred to cover up and give the child their own name to prevent being branded a cuckold. It is a commonplace of Iberian folklore that when a priest refers to his "nephew" or "niece" he is really talking about his own out-of-wedlock child. Still other proverbs excoriate the lust of *beatas* (pious laywomen) and describe in graphic language what these women were hiding underneath their crucifixes and scapularies.[3]

The Protestant revolt finally goaded the Church to take repressive action against its sinful ministers at the Council of Trent convened in 1545. The council fathers decided to abolish concubinage ("the supreme disgrace") and reimpose chastity on each other. As Stephen Haliczer writes,

In their zeal to do this, they embarked upon one of the most daring experiments in sexual repression in all of human history. But in spite of more rigorous education and training, the demands of celibacy proved too great for many priests, and with ordinary sexual and social outlets having been largely circumscribed, the confessional was left as the only place where they could make contact with women and talk with them personally and intimately. By sharply repressing the sexual activity of the clergy and placing their moral conduct under the control of episcopal officials, and by insisting that priests demand an exacting and detailed accounting of sins, the Church itself had created the objective conditions for solicitation in the confessional.[4]

In historical retrospective it would seem that the older, more biologically natural vice of concubinage was the lesser evil, compared to the perversions that would sprout in the post-Tridentine Church.

The cases of *solicitantes* (clergy accused of using the confessional to procure sex for themselves) occupy an entire wing of the extant archives of the Spanish Inquisition. In examining them it is vital to recall that not all Spanish clergy were created equal. Members of the *alto clero*, or high clergy, were erudite, well-heeled, well-educated, at home with royalty or aristocrats; in fact, many church dignitaries hailed from noble families. They occupied the most prestigious positions in cathedral bureaucracies and the Holy Office of the Inquisition. Historian Bartolomé Bennassar claims that at the highest levels, Spain's prelates and bishops "were frequently remarkable men who shunned the vices of their clergy and of their parishioners. There can be no doubt on this point, for different sources are in almost perfect agreement."[5] The high clergy used the Inquisition to watch over and repress the more undisciplined members of the low clergy who, judging by the extant files and documents, were much more likely to use their confessionals to foist themselves upon women, men, girls, and boys.

The Catholic Counter Reformation introduced a new type of confessional "intended to be a protection for the public," with a wooden grille rather than curtains to separate priest and penitent, but the new confessional design was slowly adopted.[6] Grille or no grille, the confessional was routinely abused by the lower clergy for several hundred years, both for solicitation and subsequent cover-up, but this is abuse understood only in the most scandalous, literal-minded way. We are hard-pressed not to see the ritual of confession itself as an abuse of power inseparable from the maintenance of authoritarian sexuality. The high clergy *would* be implicated in this subtle form of meta-abuse: men like the Jesuit Tomás Sánchez of Córdoba (1551–1610), author of a sophisticated and explicit sex manual designed for use by confessors in dealing with the sexual problems of their penitents. For confession to be complete, it had to include "description of the respective positions of the partners, the postures assumed, gestures, places touched, caresses, the precise moment of pleasure—an entire painstaking review of the sexual act in its unfolding."[7] Hence the rhyme that made the rounds of Spain's seminaries for centuries: "Si quieres saber más que el Demonio, lee a Sánchez en *De matrimonio*" (If you want to know more than the devil himself, read Sánchez's book on marriage).[8] The same Counter Reformation prelates that introduced a newly designed, "safer" confessional box were also intent on increasing the frequency of confession and the degree of detail necessary for cleansing and absolution. As Foucault poetically put it, "According to the new pastoral, sex must not be named imprudently, but its aspects, its correlations, and its effects must be pursued down to their slenderest ramifications: a shadow in a daydream, an image too slowly dispelled, a badly exorcised complicity between the body's mechanics and the mind's complacency: everything had to be told." [9] As we can well surmise, confessors of the time were better placed than anyone else in society to study every nuance of human sexuality. Small wonder that the most daringly detailed and licentious novels of Spain's Golden Age — "full of dubious encounters, incests, and perversions" — were penned by Don Juan Pérez de Montalbán, an erudite notary of the Inquisition who was widely admired for his scrupulously celibate lifestyle.[10]

Altogether, charges were brought against nearly five thousand *solicitantes*, hardly the extent of the problem inasmuch as the Inquisition often limited its intervention to cases in which confessors were suspected of expounding heterodox views about sexuality that were at variance with the pessimism of the early church fathers. In the city of Seville alone, some 695 people were processed by the Inquisition during the seventeenth century for holding more "enlightened" views of sex (hence the appellative *alumbrados*), even though these views were often utilized in a benighted way — to facilitate seductions.[11] In 1563, a very large number of Sevillian beatas began to accuse their confessors of sexual misdeeds; twenty inquisitors and another twenty notaries were hard-pressed to sort out the accusations. Though not a nun, the typical Spanish beata made private vows of celibacy, wore distinctive clothing, and suffered herself to be guided by a "spiritual father" — her confessor priest. Many beatas were impoverished widows or women who had not found a husband; they joined together in special houses known as *beaterios* for mutual security, often taking care of orphans and performing other praiseworthy charitable acts. Still other beatas were women of the middle and upper classes who sought spiritual stimulation without the rigors of convent life. These enthusiastic daughters were much preferred by alumbrado priests interested in exploring new forms of sensual spirituality. The saintly forty-six-year-old Father Gaspar de Lucas, for example, prior of San Bartolomé and a descendant of Jews, was banished by the Inquisition in 1590 for ejaculating while massaging the breasts of thirty-six-year-old Mari Romera during confession. Father Gaspar had also experienced these "pollutions" with other beatas of the same locality — and some of the women confessed to the Inquisition that they had experienced pollutions themselves.[12]

In a celebrated case early in the Golden Age, a Franciscan monk systematically sought out pious women for carnal commerce in an attempt to breed prophets; many nuns and beatas participated willingly in the project. As late as 1780 a Sevillian beata was executed for having seduced several priests. A more typical punishment was a public flogging (up to two hundred lashes). Ironically, in one of Spain's last outbreaks of sexual heresy, that of the *molinosistas* of Murcia, a large number of women had been persuaded by their spiritual brothers to submit willingly to whipping (accompanied by groping), the better to attain the desired state of absolute passivity and annihilation of the will. The ringleader in that case was Father Francisco Soler, who was "quite deaf but possessed of a highly developed sense of touch, as his numerous female followers well knew."[13] In the meantime, the cardinal's nephew had seduced a mentally unbalanced woman inside one of the chapels of the cathedral itself. In 1741 all of the women were sent into exile and Father Soler, having already died in the dungeons of the Inquisition, was burned at the stake in effigy.

Historian Henry Kamen argues that the relentless antisexuality of some confessors' manuals "can fairly be seen as an attempt to conjure away a problem which was very much also a clerical one." Father Ortiz Lucio's manual of 1598 maintains that "the priest who while hearing confession hears vile things and because of this suffers a natural emission of semen, does not sin if it is involuntary." A widely used confessors' manual by the Jesuit Francisco Arias had advised clerics that "they must guard their eyes not only from too much looking at women, but should also take care not to look with liberty at the beauty of boys of a tender age." The records of the Inquisition and other Church courts contain numerous cases of clergy accused of pedophilia. Kamen maintains that homosexual crimes were "comparable in frequency" to heterosexual ones.[14]

The most celebrated cases of the late Golden Age involved the Mercederian order of Valencia. Fray Manuel Arbustante, a doctor of theology and regent of the convent of La Merced, was brought to trial in 1685 for sodomizing or fellating practically every member of the convent, as well as boys entrusted to the friars by local families:

What is most remarkable is the fascination that he exercises over the novices, a fascination that explains his success as a seducer; at least eight had yielded to his advances, and perhaps all save three of the religious of the convent. "The boys say [writes the Inquisitor] that he must have bewitched them, for they doted and swarmed about him like dragonflies; then he seemed like an angel to them, whereas now he appears to be a demon." A letter from the general of the order confirms that Fray Manuel had caused scandal in the convents in which he previously resided—Orihuela, Jativa, Sardinia—with activities of the same kind.[15]

In other words, the order had simply transferred the abusive cleric from one convent to another—a "solution" that continues to be applied in our day. Fray Manuel's eloquence in defending himself at his trial resulted in a light sentence—two years' exile. But soon a bigger fish fell: the provincial of the Mercederian order itself in Valencia, Fray Juan Velasco Risón, who had forced the boys into homosexual acts and forbade them to confess to anyone other than himself.

By the late sixteenth century the Inquisition had established firm control—not over the exploitative priests but over the Spanish publishing industry. Anticlerical *refranes* disappeared from printed collections of proverbs but continued underground at increased levels of invective and rage. Perennially prone to hasty generalization, Spanish folk groups came to identify curates and friars as evil incarnate. Caro Baroja points out that popular anticlericalism of the fifteenth, sixteenth, and seventeenth centuries was that of believers.[16] In every century, it seems, Spanish peasants have strongly felt the right to hate the clergy while remaining Catholic. But as Bernal concludes, the picture that emerges from folkloric sources like the *Refranero* is that popular piety in Spain was superficial, lacking in true religious sentiment, characterized both by cynicism and by attempts to manipulate divine power through superstitions.[17] In my view, these are all signs of religious alienation and spiritual devastation.

There are still others. Blasphemy has been so common and widespread in Spain that it has attracted the attention of leading anthropologists.[18] For Spanish philosopher José Ortega y Gasset, blasphemy was a chief symptom of what he termed "Spanish hysteria" (*histerismo español*)—the other signs being lack of imagination, inability to make historical progress, and "spiritual weakness."[19] In blasphemy a long legacy of cultural and individual frustration boils over into formulaic rage. In one of the most Catholic countries in the world, blasphemous oaths are a routine aspect of daily life; their perverse mixing of holy persons or things with excrement is the aspect that most disconcerts foreigners. All over Spain, many men and women need only feel mild annoyance to say "me cago en Dios" or "me cago en la Hostia."[20]

Humor constitutes yet another way to express popular exasperation with the Church. Anticlerical clichés and jokes continue to this day and take special aim at clerical sexual activity. According to anthropologist Stanley Brandes, "Most men believe that priests are just like other men. In particular, they think that priests are imbued with the same sexual desires and passions as other men, and that they hypocritically preach the repression of these natural impulses though they often become dominated by them."[21] Jokes about hypocritical celibates may let off steam, but the laymen of southern Spain have not escaped the gravitational pull of authoritarian sexuality—not even the laymen of the lower classes who most prize themselves on their machismo. In my view, their hyper-phallic fantasies are a simple transmutation of the sexual fatalism of the early church fathers, Augustine in particular. The lower-class men of southern Spain have been thoroughly "Augustinian" in their obsession with genitalia, depersonalization of women, and split-off idealization of the Virgin Mary.[22] The Andalusian gusto for blasphemy is not genuinely liberating either, though it may be cathartic to insult the supreme idol of paternal punishment.[23] The amazing persistence of superstition in Andalusia is also related to centuries of neglect by the Church.[24]

Possibly as a result of the intensified sexual predation of the Golden Age, hundreds of minor specialized cults arose all over Spain in the seventeenth and eighteenth centuries, five hundred in Madrid alone from 1702 to 1807. Known variously as *cofradías, hermandades,* and *congregaciones,* they were community associations of laypersons organized around venerated icons, with relatively little input from the clergy. The historian Bennassar rejects the inference that the cofradía phenomenon was "proof of a continuing intense religiosity; to me it proves the existence of a bigoted devotion rather than an enlightened faith or a faith of works."[25] Is it a mere coincidence that the era of abuse and meta-abuse discussed above coincides with the phenomenal growth of neighborhood religious associations that maintain only formal contacts with representatives of the Church?

Celibate Supremacy and Symbolic Violence

In spite of the documented history of clergy sexual abuse during the Golden Age, some historians are still committed to the view that Spanish priests were "puritanical." It is risky to use this word out of its own psychohistorical context. Puritanism arose in England as a fanatical drive to eradicate the remaining elements of Catholicism and "popery" in the Church of England; it was iconoclastic and antihierarchical, introspective and Bible-oriented. But the Spanish clergy were hierarchical and notably ultramontane (loyal to the papacy), wholly committed to sacred icons and outwardly luxurious liturgies, and, as is well known, little inclined to read the Bible even though excellent translations were available. Their sex phobia was matched by a proclivity for sins of the flesh, as denounced by members of their own guild. In the sixteenth-century *Guía del cielo*, Fray Pablo de León wrote in referring to lust that "this damned sin is so great among us that the entire church is hellbound." Saint Teresa of Avila herself was scandalized by the degree of immorality in monasteries and convents, affirming that "a friar and a nun have more to fear from the very ones in their convents than from all the demons put together."[26]

The closest thing one can find to "puritanism" in the Catholic Church is the Jansenist heresy that took root in certain Dutch and French minds of the seventeenth century; it was actually an attempt to bring about a return to the rigorous antisexual pessimism of Augustine. The most zealous proselytizer for Jansenism was Blaise Pascal, and his favorite targets were members of the Spanish high clergy in general and the Jesuits in particular. Pascal took aim at Spanish Jesuits like Father Escobar (1589–1669), the alleged author of the notion that the purity of one's intentions justifies acts that would normally be considered immoral and even illegal.[27] The Jansenists had rigorist minds and old-fashioned self-torturing consciences: "When Pascal died at thirty-nine, a hairshirt with little iron hooks was found on his body. Pascal had worn it to punish himself for the tiniest faults. The geniality and wit of Pascal's letters that enabled him to make his Jesuit opponents look ridiculous obscure the fact that on questions of sexual morality the 'lax Jesuits' were closer to the truth than he was."[28] In any case, Spanish clerics were (in)famous in northern Europe, not for their "puritanism" but for their ability to find justifications for reducing or mitigating the penance assigned in the confessional.

The celibate/sexual power system, the confessional ritual that reinforces it, and jesuitical casuistry—whether practiced by actual Jesuits or not—are all so far from puritanism that to introduce the word at all risks evoking an inappropriate set of schemata in readers. Historians cannot show that Spanish priests and friars were at any time characterized by scrupulous decorum in matters sexual, nor that the lower clergy (the prime source of Golden Age solicitantes) was eventually reformed, disciplined, and given better training. Instead they document the opposite, abundantly; members of the lower clergy rarely received proper guidance or training from their superiors. Historian José Sánchez tells us that the gap between the higher and lower clergies widened still more during the eighteenth century, all over Europe.[29] The miserable economic and moral situation of Spain's lower clergy was recorded by Francisco de Goya in numerous grotesque caricatures made at the end of the eighteenth century. Lest any doubt remain, three recent studies amply document the prevalence of sexual predation from the confessional in early modern Spain.[30]

One more crucial distinction needs to be made. From a psychohistorical point of view, Puritan and Calvinist minds were characterized by obsessional thoughts and behaviors; their emphasis on work and systematic calculation would play an important role in the rise of modern science. But authoritarian sexuality as it evolved in Spain, from the Middle Ages through the Golden Age to the middle of the twentieth century, is better understood in terms of an underlying *hysterical* configuration. I am not using the word "hysterical" in either its classic or its vulgar definitions, but in the sense newly developed by Dr. Elisabeth Young-Bruehl:

This is a different type of defense than obsessional splitting of idea from affect, experience from emotion. Hysterical people are not unemotional or rigidly in control; they are—so to speak—half-emotional, or half-aware of their emotions. Hysterical characters feel themselves to be more refined and less sexual than the people against whom their prejudices are directed. And it is always crucial to them that their others be lower, which means designated as the coarse ones, the more sexual ones. The classification keeps the hysterical characters separated from their own sexuality—it is assigned elsewhere, either to their own split-off self or to the objects of their prejudice, or both. . . . Hysterical prejudices are conducted in the medium of dominance and submission, masters and slaves, and the characters of hysterics are themselves hierarchical: hysterical characters have intrapsychic masters and servants quarters, double lives.[31]

Most Americans will tend to associate this description with the society of the antebellum aristocratic South. But racism is not the only type of hysterical prejudice. Young-Bruehl makes it clear that, in societies with little or no racial differentiation, many forms of classism or class prejudice function in structurally similar ways and respond to the same psychic needs. "Hysterical" ideologies of desire arise in the context of societies that are both rigidly stratified and yet dependent for their functioning on a constant, day-to-day mixture of social classes. Young-Bruehl echoes anthropologist Ralph Linton in noting that the incidence of hysterical symptomologies is greater in cloisters, convents, monasteries, and schools, with their specific forms greatly influenced by the prevailing culture.[32] Spanish psychiatrist Fernando Claramunt called the clergy victimization of beatas a "psychic epidemic." But again, overtly hysterical phenomena should not blind us to the underlying hysterical ideology of desire, its prejudices, and its protective institutional frameworks. Spain's "golden age" of clergy sexual abuse cannot be separated from the dialectic of domination within a highly stratified religious establishment, with control of sexuality as the chief stakes in the ongoing friction between higher and lower echelons of the clergy. "If anything," says historian Haliczer, "by focusing attention on the confessional as a venue for sexual activity, the Inquisition may have eroticized confession."[33] Sexual authoritarians never understood that they alone were responsible for the structures of abuse they were so intent on rooting out; the elaborate codification of solicitation and its punishments (whose loopholes were often well known by abusive clergy) forced clerical sexuality into ever narrower channels; licentious canons and curates reached out from the confessional to procure victims, make more young men like themselves in the seminaries, and replicate their peculiar psychology of overcontrol/undercontrol generation after generation.

Clergy sexual abuse is impossible to understand apart from the meta-abusive supremacist celibate mindset promoted by men who never sin, who may even have acute sexual phobias. An episode of priestly pedophilia, to take this example, is not an isolated aberration; it has ideological implications. It has to do with the selection of victims. It is a form of prejudice against a member of a population construed as "lower." The burden of shame and desire is being laid on someone on whom it *can* be laid in a given social milieu.

The age-old story of male access to women took on a new twist when the church fathers sought systematically to monopolize the sexual consciousness of women; women eventually came to collude in their own domination. Writes Young-Bruehl: "Because ideologies of desire are focused so relentlessly on the bodies of their target groups and articulated with claims of natural inferiority and evil, and because they involve partial identifications and thus disorienting messages of love-and-hate, rejection-and-envy, they are able to undermine the confidence or self-esteem of their victims much more deeply than ethnocentrisms."[34] French sociologist Pierre Bourdieu has settled on the term *symbolic violence* to describe such processes: "The case of gender domination shows better than any other that *symbolic violence accomplishes itself through an act of cognition and of misrecognition that lies beyond—or beneath—the controls of consciousness and will*, in the obscurities of the schemata of habitus."[35] Over time the women of Spain came to regard the supremacist celibate standpoint as "natural," God-given, and to collude in the prejudices against themselves placed in circulation by priests and prelates in a position to do so. The defense of the purity of womanhood is a case in point: Spanish Catholicism made a true fetish of it through the cult of María. Therefore this cult can be seen as a type of symbolic violence whenever it served to underscore the sinful essence of real flesh-and-blood women. If vulnerable females could be a target group for some members of the clergy, it was because their lowly and beastly status had already been constructed by their own Church. This was the stick; the carrot was the idealized view of maternity that women came to accept as their own.

As is well known, women comprise the majority of people who attend mass and devotional ceremonies in Spain and other areas of southern Europe. Why do religious messages that portray their gender in a negative light appeal to them? In part because they have assimilated the symbolic violence done unto them; in part because at some level many women perceive perfectly well that the officiants of the ceremonies have not transcended that all-enveloping link with the maternal order of things. Numerous priestly vocations have been forged in the fires of the intense religious devotion adopted by mothers unlucky in marital love. Hence the irony: the Church is a patriarchal institution that harbors a not-so-latent hatred of the untutored masculinity that many women feel oppressed by in their daily lives. "The Church is dominated by men who do not want to be men," Catholic psychotherapist Drewermann affirms, which is why many inhibited, guilt-ridden, even feminoid priests come across to women as much more refined than ordinary men, cultivated and sensitive, bathed in an ideal of pure love—just the sort of son or father or husband they would have preferred to have.[36]

Most Catholic women, and devout women in general, do not understand that one distortion gives birth to its opposite. Nor do they suspect that the delicate psychic structures of their idealized clergymen predispose them to enter into exploitative relationships with women. In his study of sexually abusive male clergy, Dr. Gordon Benson found "chronic and pervasive feelings of shame which they believed contributed to their sexual misconduct," along with memories of having been abused, emotionally abandoned, or exploited by adults when they were children. All of this predisposed them to adopt a fantasy of "grandiose caretaking" with their female parishioners, while, at the same time, it greatly weakened their ability to control their sexual impulses.[37] The most typical pattern: Emotionally distant fathers plus emotionally incestuous mothers equals potentially exploitative clergy. Many Spanish women who become involved with a priest are surprised to discover the attitude of a rapist behind his soft-spoken seraphic manners. Yet it could hardly be otherwise with men who have been trained to think of human sexuality in black-and-white alternatives: heroic purity or abject surrender to cruel fantasies.

A noted German psychoanalyst who had worked with dozens of clergymen finally refused to see any more because, in his judgment, "it was nothing but an irresponsible waste of time."[38] In many cases Spanish priests correspond to what Dr. Richard Irons has called the "Wounded Warrior" type of sexually exploitative professionals, men still in need of healing from the wounds of an abusive childhood or a controlling mother, men who have merely evolved "from victims to victimizers."[39] Individual clergy can be treated with therapy or punished with jail terms; but how are we to deal with a transpersonal, transnational system that is centuries old and well entrenched? A system that might actually depend for its survival on the same psychosexual immaturity that leads to abuse? Reform may be difficult, particularly when we discover that countries like Spain harbor other old and well entrenched family, judicial, and military systems that are locked in symbiotic embrace with the celibate/sexual power system.

To achieve a more perfect understanding of clergy sexual exploitation in Spain, it is necessary to recognize, as the novelist Clarín did over a hundred years ago, that many women are romantically attracted to priests. Not all of these women can be classified as lost and vulnerable; some actually enjoy giving detailed descriptions of their sex lives as the confessional ritual requires. Unsatisfied women who complain of being ignored by their spouses can arouse the interest of the confessor, quite consciously. In such cases, reports Drewermann, the woman involved is often one who as a girl was burdened with an absurdly high ideal of purity that was inevitably and painfully destroyed when she grew up. "For that reason, it is possible that she feels a kind of malignant and almost tranquilizing satisfaction in confirming that priests too are just men of flesh and blood."[40] One Spanish priest interviewed by sociologist Pepe Rodríguez told of being accosted by an attractive, devout, forty-something female parishioner just months after joining his new parish. "I know that you priests have a rough time of it," she said, "and that it's not easy for you to get along without some help, but I'm a good parishioner and I'm willing to satisfy you with whatever you need." The flustered priest politely refused the woman's advances—but then had to deny repeatedly that he was gay.[41] Recall the ancient clerical cliché of the innocent priest hounded by the perverse woman: "In the battle with temptation, the one who flees achieves victory." Rodríguez affirms that a married woman is perfect for a priest who wishes to break his vow of celibacy: In most cases she is a devout member of the flock, above suspicion; any resulting pregnancy can be attributed to her husband (an old Spanish tradition, as we saw earlier); and, above all, her marital status usually ensures a minimum of affective commitment and effectively reduces the relationship to a purely sexual one.

The psychology of secrecy and seduction is qualitatively different with younger women, inexperienced with both life and sex, more vulnerable by far than women who have been married for fifteen or twenty years. More often than not, says Drewermann, teenage women who seek out a priest to rescue them are either fleeing from or going toward their own fathers, and sometimes both at once, unconsciously. Their desire for the unreachable is fraught with fears and ambiguities that date back to infancy, and a priest should know better than to feel flattered by their "love."[42] Priests who have not known better are behind untold numbers of exploitative episodes, particularly in the rural regions of Spain where the glow of the sacred and the aura of a prestigious institution still cling to the figure of the *párroco*, or parish pastor. A vulnerable young female of peasant or lower-class origins supplies the straw; a lonely, maladjusted celibate brings the spark; then the devil comes along, blows, and ignites the conflagration (to paraphrase an ancient Spanish proverb).

Motherhood and Priesthood

Sixty generations of repression and abuse could not possibly be eliminated overnight, but that is precisely what the impractical leaders of the
Spanish Second Republic (1931–1939) tried to do. There is growing consensus among historians that the Republic dug its own grave through its
vindictive anticlericalism, its fatal underestimation of the inertia of traditional morals, its clumsy efforts to dissolve religious orders and impose
sexual pedagogy in the schools, and its tolerance of vandalism against
churches and convents. Had the politicans truly understood their own
people, they would have known that their radical measures would be opposed by one of the most stubbornly powerful forces in Spain: mothers.

Ethnographers tell us that in numerous regions of Iberia a mother's
relationship with her sons was of the teasing, frustrating type, with practices and sleeping arrangements that simultaneously elicited and repressed the male infant's libido; affective relationships with other female
members of the family (aunts, sisters, cousins) followed a similar pattern,
all within "the framework of maternal hyper-protection that surrounds
children during all of their childhood until the last phases of adolescence."[43] There is widespread consensus among psychoanalysts that
masochism originates with such imbalances in the infant's relationship
with the mother. Beatings and physical abuse are not required: when the
mother rebuffs, ridicules, or punishes, she is, in the words of Dr. Eleanor
Galenson, "setting the stage for masochistic responses through a very
early predefense, similar to identification with the aggressor; in this
view, such children connect the mother with pain, thereby eroticizing
suffering and fostering a desire for a repetition of the early painful experiences."[44] Upon reaching adolescence, male children who have been
forced to "seduce the aggressor" in this way usually have more serious
problems with their core gender identity than do females.

In many parts of Spain, men's liberation from the rigid maternal order
of things is not guaranteed. Anthropologist Isidoro Moreno has hy-
pothesized that when a male child is born into the cofradía of his mother
and conditioned to adore an icon of Mary, he may come to have marked
feminoid personality traits; hence the larger-than-expected number of
effeminate men found in the towns of southern Spain.[45] Here ethno-
graphic evidence jibes with psychology, for these *maricas* are famed for
their passionate devotion to a particular Marian icon (the good mother)
and their readiness to insult rival Marian icons (the bad mother)—just
the sort of splitting/idealization/projection process we would expect in
the context of smothering motherhood. Andalusian machismo represents a desperate attempt to escape the archaic mother's dominions; in
the view of anthropologist David Gilmore, it is "a consolatory ideologi-

cal mystification for the restoration of an endangered masculine ego in this culturally androcentric yet matriarchal society."[46]

No one is more aware of the dark side of Spanish motherhood than Pepe Rodríguez, author of two books on child abuse and religious dysfunction in Spain.[47] While researching clergy sexual abuse he discovered that most of the priests he interviewed derived *both their misbehavior and their vocation* from "the erroneous and harmful relationship" they had experienced with their "castrating" mothers. In case after case, the priests' mothers had been overtly self-sacrificing but essentially self-centered women who brought the boys up in suffocating overprotection and dependence while simultaneously instilling in them a mistrust of other women.[48] Though most young Spaniards are too headstrong to put up with the stifling, sanctimonious atmosphere of the seminary, many others fit in well there because of its resemblance to the homes in which they grew up. Many times a pious mother will project her own fantasized religious "calling" onto her son, inducing him to believe he has a calling of his own. As the priest/psychotherapist Eugen Drewermann points out, religious vocations thrive in homes in which the father is either absent, or weak, or simply in the way, and the mother

takes the reins of the family and the example of her commitment is enough to maintain a certain order and give consistency to the family. . . . In the psychogenesis of the clergy it will have to be recognized that the general norm is the *depressive submission of the child.* Instead of trying to impose herself in a direct way, she will try to cajole the child indirectly, sending out certain signals: by means of her unhappiness and her suffering, and showing her weaknesses, she will end up by making him capitulate.[49]

In the novel *La Regenta,* discussed in Chapter 2, this manipulation by guilt is precisely the tactic employed by Doña Paula to dominate her son—even after he has become the most powerful cleric of Vetusta.

Spanish women do not experience the socially fomented male drive to compulsively disidentify with the mother during adolescence; their own infantile tendency to "seduce the aggressor" is easily subsumed into diverse facets of the Blessed Mother: unconscious imago, object of idolatrous devotion, cultural role model of eternal self-sacrifice. For emotionally unstable women (for example, victims of child abuse), Mary will be there as a kind of supernatural underwriter of warded-off compulsions. The "Unnatural Cruelty" section of Goldberg's *Motif-Index of Medieval Spanish Folk Narratives* contains a number of narratives related to extremely perverse mothering. S12.2.5, for example: "Depressed mother plans to kill baby penetrating head with needle. Virgin Mary intervenes; saves baby; woman enters religious order." From a psychodynamic point of view, it might be argued that the Virgin Mary was as much a part of the problem as of the solution, beneficiary that she was (and is) of the split-off idealization of the archaic mother, as well as guarantor of self-abnegating motherhood as the main source of power and control for Spanish women, and therefore collusive in the development of perverse maternal attitudes of one kind or another.[50] Moreover, for the past five centuries the Spanish tendency has been to transfer loyalty from "regular" icons of Mary to those of the *Mater Dolorosa*—an advocation that quintessentializes the maternal role-model as one of total abnegation, unlimited sacrifice, and implicit rejection of normal ego striving. Ironically, those mothers with the most intense devotion to the Mother of God might tend to feel empowered *only as mothers*, and therefore be unwilling to relinquish the one thing that empowers them—their offspring's utter dependence on them. Under certain extreme circumstances, in other words, the cult of the Blessed Mother may be an accessory in the deformation of the psychological structures of Spanish infants.

This worst-case scenario of primitive aggression is but one side of the coin: the other possibility is neurotic *prevention*, via punitive superego mechanisms that police and enforce the mother's total devotion to her offspring. We saw a similar psychodynamic earlier in the archetypal desert saint—a great criminal barely kept in check by a great soul sharing the same body. We need to expand our definition of perverse mothering to include not only the obviously harmful acts of manipulation but also the behaviors of rigidly dutiful mothers, adopted not so much out of love but out of a need to ward off self-reproach. As Alice Miller explains, "A sense of duty may not be fruitful soil for love but it undoubtedly is for mutual guilt feelings, and the child will forever be bound to the mother by crippling feelings of guilt and gratitude." [51] Such psychological chains predispose him to seek out or accept some sort of guilt-driven dutiful sacrifice in later life—such as a religious vocation. In the context of the Catholic Church, the whole process leads to what Drewermann calls "the psychological perversion of the Christian theology of redemption along sadomasochistic lines":

> To be more precise, the archetypal schemata of sacrifice and reparation, with their corresponding affective ambivalences, have been theologically formulated in such a way that their representatives and ideologues are preferentially men, as in the case of the clergy, whose psychology is marked by an infantile experience of traumatic ambiguities, lived in a climate of cruel ideas of sacrifice and duties of reparation.[52]

This circular paragraph expresses the vicious religious circle that grows out of the early childhood one—both powered not by oedipal conflicts, as many had assumed, but by more basic anxieties. Like skyscrapers

built along a faultline, complex levels of rationalization and theological
speculation are elaborate but precarious attempts to find the reliable
source of security missing from the start.

In broad synthesis, the mother of a future priest can be the one who
was either perversely manipulative or rigidly defensive about her aggressive impulses, or both. In reality we are dealing with one unstable
affective continuum, with undercontrol at one end and overcontrol at
the other. How this works in the real world can be illustrated by reference to the experiences of two Spanish priests.

Case 1: In 1994 the owner of a Barcelona bordello revealed to Rodríguez that one of his habitual clients was a priest of about fifty years of age
who showed up in civilian clothes every two or three months to act out
the same scenario. He would have a female prostitute dress up in a cassock, then kick him and curse him while he rolled around on the floor,
naked, begging forgiveness. When his body was sufficiently bruised, the
priest would crawl into a corner, quietly masturbate, mumble a prayer,
pay up, and depart. He had never attempted normal coitus.[53]

Case 2: Here, a Spanish bishop gives his own account of a terrible experience he suffered one day at work in 1968:

A prolonged grunting, as if from a herd of beasts aroused by abundant prey,
summoned me from my desk and drew me toward the balcony of my study,
which overlooks the plaza of the Cathedral. The beasts were not beasts but a
group of coal heavers, who with words that seemed grunts were flattering an
elegantly naked señorita passing by. The señorita had by her side a señora who
seemed to be her mother, and when they passed by the main door of the temple
they both blessed themselves devoutly. A stinging shame lashed my face and
an anguished feeling of pity and disgust filled my heart. I was unable to determine what afflicted me the most: the triumph of the devil, snorting lasciviously
through the mouths of those wretches, or the defeat of our Jesús del Sagrario in
the Cathedral, mocked by that sign of the cross made upon a shameless breast
by a naked arm.[54]

For purposes of clarification, the señorita was not at all naked, simply
dressed less modestly than the prelate could endure.

Though at first they may seem dissimilar, both cases exemplify fixa-
tion to the trauma. In the psyches of the two clerics, the original relationship between a forbidding mother and a dependent infant has been
transformed into a condensed symbolic union of a generic persecutor
and a generic victim, with the priests identifying first with one then with
the other in rapid alternation. In both cases we find the need to hallow
the hated object and achieve symbolic revenge on it at the same time.
In the sexual perversion of the priest in the first case we find a simple
split-off, manipulative ego control in which surrender to true intimacy
is quite out of the question. The priest could not reach his onanistic cli-

max if he did not identify with both himself as the infinite victim and with the ambiguously gendered prostitute/priest he induces to enact his scenario again and again. Here it is easy to see what Dr. Robert Stoller saw in his perverse patients, that is, "the construction of a script, the principal purpose of which is to undo childhood traumas, conflicts, and frustrations by converting these earlier painful experiences to present (fantasized) triumphs."[55]

In the second case the revenge component of erotic hatred is a kind of sexualized moral victory in which an unjustly humiliated man-of-modesty turns the tables on virility—his own and that of the "grunting beasts" of the working class. "A fundamental prejudice," writes Young-Bruehl, "operates like a rigidly patterned way of falling in love or like a recurrent masturbation fantasy; it is an ideology of social love and hate."[56] In the case of the hysterically prejudiced bishop, the terms he uses for describing his "defeat" have an exaggerated erotic charge that we can only describe as perverse; he projectively identifies with both the devil and the humiliated Christ and in his suffering he savors the women's bodies with a metaphorical frisson that those poor charcoal-hauling workmen could not begin to understand. He abhors what he is drawn to, and vice versa. The bishop has tied himself into a knot, a mission impossible, by attempting to build a superstructure of virtue atop an infrastructure of erotic hatred. In the case of the first priest, two months of overcontrol regularly give way to one night of ecstatic loss of control. As with any perverse script there are specific plot elements that must be in place to elicit either ejaculation or prurient disgust.

The priest's scenario and the bishop's homily both answer to the same continuum of cruelty and subjugation inculcated in infancy and exacerbated by the unrealistic demands of the celibate/sexual system. The difference? In the first case the perversion is relatively private and harmless. In the second case, the bishop is in a position to implant his perverse prejudices into many other minds: the diatribe transcribed above was published in the *Hojas Eucaristizadoras,* a bulletin regularly distributed to the faithful in every church in his diocese.

A recent work by William A. Christian, Jr., affords us a precious glimpse into the power of masochistic scripts in the genesis of new forms of Catholic devotion in Spain, particularly in the pious northern provinces. We can now account for some of the personality characteristics of the priests so entranced by the Marian apparitions that Christian deals with. We are especially well poised to understand why a South American mystic known as Madre Soledad was able to convince so many northern Spanish priests to become as little boys under her tutelage in the 1920s. Daily self-flagellation was only one aspect of Madre Soledad's program for the so-called *Sacerdotes Niños* who flocked to her guidance:

For special penances she prescribed praying with arms outstretched, lying prostrate on the floor, eating only half a dessert and offering the rest to the child Jesus, contemplating the stations of the cross, writing the Lord a letter about one's dominant passion and then burning it, "speaking for three minutes with the Virgin in child talk," offering a bouquet of "posies" to Jesus, or visiting for five minutes the Lord in his playhouse and speaking to him in child talk. . . . But implicit in this program was the priests' personal belief in her spirituality, since in the role of little boys they accepted her as a kind of mother. A prerequisite for joining the association was "to destroy oneself, renouncing in a certain way one's own personality and abandoning oneself totally in the hands of God."[57]

The structural similarity of all this to the cases of perversion we have discussed almost obviates commentary. In the cult of Madre Soledad we encounter masochistic fantasies and sought-out suffering allied with the extinction of normal ego striving, in the context of deliberate infantilization and massive repression of the hatefully erotic nature of the underlying affects being psychodramatized. Christian takes a charitable view of the fantasy boy-slaves of Madre Soledad, conjecturing that "A discipline of puerility may have been particularly attractive for rural Basque and Navarrese clergy as a kind of relief from their inordinate social and political power." Recreation it might have been, but one that corresponded to very special psychological structures. As had happened so often in Spanish church history, the priestly collusion with female mystics was condemned by the Holy Office in 1925. "The unusual submission of male priests to a female had led to unfounded rumors of sexual license."[58] Madre Soledad's playhouse association was dissolved but she continued to see ex-Niños on an informal basis until her death in 1933.

The sublimation of menacing desires through Marianism was perfected by Saint Francis of Assisi (Giovanni Francesco Bernardone, 1182–1226), whose monks specialized in translating the love rhetoric of twelfth-century troubadours into the language of mysticism of later centuries.[59] Many other religious orders rushed to involve themselves in the development of mystico-erotic Marianism because its theology matched their psychology so well. It is important to understand that authoritarian sexuality was spread throughout Spain by fundamentalist priests whose notions of spirituality were closely tied to archaic family schemata. For example, the prime mover behind nineteenth-century devotionalism in Spain was Antonio Claret, archbishop, founder of the Claretian order, best-selling author, trusted adviser to Queen Isabel II, visionary, and ultimately saint. Hearing heavenly voices and witnessing miracles led him to adopt María as a middle name and surrender himself to the ancient siren song of mystico-erotic Marianism:

I, Antonio María Claret, would like to have all the lives of men to employ them in the service of the Mother of God. . . . I wish to die and shed all my blood out of love and reverence for María, Virgin and Mother of God. I desire that Jesus grant me the grace and strength I need in order that all of my members be tormented and cut off one by one out of love and reverence for María, Mother of God and mine also. Let it be done, let it be done.[60]

This prayer/fantasy contains a wish for omnipotence and revenge on virility: Claret would like to have all men at his disposal to make them the Blessed Mother's slaves. His fantasy is also masochistic in the clinical sense of the term, that is, it involves sought-out suffering in patterned dyadic interplay related in some way to castration anxieties. Lest we be misled by the rhetoric of love and reverence, "fantasies of self-mutilation typically reflect unconscious identification with a hateful and hated object."[61] Here once again is perversion's blending of eros and hatred, with defenses strong enough to keep the true underlying affect out of conscious awareness. Antonio Claret might have been actively engulfed by his real mother or a caretaker as a baby boy. A survivor of such treatment, the novelist Leopold von Sacher-Masoch, would surely have recognized Claret as a fellow "suprasensualist"—destined to be forever enthralled by a love that was also "part hate, part fear."[62]

The career of Opus Dei founder José María Escrivá de Balaguer strikingly illustrates how early ontological insecurity mediated by Marian idolatry preadapts for masochistic/sacrificial priesthood. Like numerous other Spanish clergy, he was born in the bosom of a pious middle-class family in northern Spain:

There were six children, the eldest called Carmen, then José María born on 9 January 1902, three other daughters all called María, and the youngest, Santiago. José was not a strong child. When he was only two years old he fell seriously ill. His life was despaired of. His mother Dolores took him to the small shrine of the Virgin Mary at Torreciudad, a local place of pilgrimage housing a statue of Mary possibly dating from the eleventh century. . . . Although the son was thus miraculously restored to health, unhappily for the family the three Marías all died in a period of just over three years between 1910 and 1913. José seems to have believed that he would be the next. He withdrew from the company of his friends and went into a massive depression from which he only slowly emerged—partly at least, it would seem, because of growing confidence that God had him under His particular care: it was at this time Dolores related to him the story of the cure at Torreciudad.[63]

Early childhood anxiety over his very survival bore fruit in the form of a religious vocation and a compulsive neurosis during adolescence. At the seminary, "it was apparently a matter of comment that he washed himself from head to toe every day." But that was not the worst. Catholic scholar and former Jesuit Michael Walsh describes the bathroom in the first residence set up by the young priest for his new organization: "Despite constant washing, its walls were stained with blood from the flagellations Escrivá inflicted upon himself. He used a 'discipline,' a kind of cat-o-nine-tails, to which he had attached bits of metal and pieces of razor blades."[64] As the founder of a powerful "church within the Church" and author of a best-selling manual that recommends such private penitential practices to all, Escrivá far outstripped the success of Saint Antonio María Claret in the nineteenth century; Claret's organization never enjoyed the unwavering support of a forty-year right-wing dictatorship.

According to his main biographer, Father Andrés Vázquez de Prada, Monsignor Escrivá always taught that "the honor of a priest is much more delicate than the honor of a woman."[65] The moral theology of Opus Dei has not changed from its glory days in Francoist Spain; Escrivá de Balaguer is known to have disliked the Second Vatican Council as much as Karol Wojtyla, and his apprehensions about women bordered on the obsessional.[66] Significantly, Opus Dei has maintained the masochistic penitential practices that other religious orders have dropped. The current pope and many high-ranking members of the Vatican curia are closely aligned with the conservative ideology propagated by Escrivá de Balaguer all his life, especially in regard to matters of celibacy and sexuality.

For at least four centuries the seminary has been a crucial component in the celibate/sexual system and its primary means of autoreplication. Numerous ex-priests contend that the power structure of the Roman Catholic hierarchy and clerical culture in general rely upon an adolescent emotional style, fixed and frozen in the seminaries. But what is being placed in a state of suspended animation, some maintain, is a radical existential insecurity that seeks dissociative protection in a rigid persona, a role or a function, rather than in true integration or individuation.

A celibate "vocation" can be a magical solution to years of anxiety and doubts; it presents itself to a fragile teenager as his destiny, an organizing framework for a life that would otherwise be questions without answers. "The institutional church was intuitively perceptive in soliciting candidates for the celibate priesthood at any early age," says Sipe.[67] As currently entrenched in the United States, Spain, and throughout the world, the celibate/sexual power system harbors a quixotic desire to halt the normal course of psychosexual development and solidify it in a phase that makes reality testing difficult. It is a system that rewards submissiveness and obedience rather than critical introspection; emotional needs of seminarians are ignored in order to make their minds fertile terrain for the inculcation of a superiority complex adorned with a divine mission.[68] They are taught to adulate those in authority and aspire to be adulated some day in turn. And during one's seminary years, says dissident Spanish priest Father Diamantino García, sex is lived as the main obsession, the axis around which all temptations, worries, and friendships revolve.[69] By sex he means primarily masturbation, the great stumbling block in the way of every young man's road to saintliness. Another Spanish priest confesses:

My problem began when I was still a seminarian, and it ended up dominating me without me being able to avoid it. Like the rest of my companions in the seminary, I masturbated whenever I needed to satisfy myself sexually, but so great was the aversion to sexuality they taught us and so strong was the pressure to be pure, that soon I began to feel like a sinful rat. I tried to stop masturbating but it was impossible. Prayer and penance soon gave way to mortification of the flesh. I began to use a hair shirt and a whip until my belly and back were raw, but I didn't manage to conquer sexual desire. I ended up putting a spiked bracelet on my penis, but I kept on getting erections despite the pain of the wounds the metal points made. I spent long hours kneeling on little pebbles, pleading with God to stop punishing me. Of all my companions I was the most humble and servile. But nothing could stop my penis and my hand. One day I even put my right hand over a kitchen stove, but all I achieved was a painful burn. When I was ordained a priest nothing changed. I flogged myself daily, a hair shirt was a permanent part of my underwear, and little rocks or uncooked garbanzos inside my shoes reminded me every moment that I was a hardened sinner. I don't know exactly how it happened, nor do I remember when, but one day I realized that the pain was arousing me more. Somehow everything had gotten confused: I no longer punished myself for having satisfied myself sexually—I satisfied myself sexually because I punished myself.[70]

This narrative tends to confirm Drewermann's observation that the real mortal sin is not masturbation but its counterproductive prohibition within the celibate/sexual educational system. Amidst growing feelings of guilt and self-disgust oscillating with violent fantasies, the laws of celibacy "construct upon the ruins of the ego a narcissistic edifice of superego morality whose only goal is to preserve itself through the sacrifice of the real person."[71] Perhaps only another priest could detect the pride that secretly underlies the self-abuse in the above narrative. In discussing a similar case, Drewermann comments that "One is tempted to say to him: Friend, can't you see that you're not so important as to debase yourself like that?" Men who are able to mortify and sacrifice themselves get to play the coveted role of "savior" in the daily psychodramas of their parishioners or counselees.

The tension artificially created in the seminary is almost never resolved; questions of identity or true sexual orientation remain unanswered, dependency anxieties are misinterpreted.[72] Out of the knot of masturbation anxieties emerge masochism, sadism, and every combination of the two; sexually addicted priests, priests with paraphilias, priests who rape, priests who sodomize or arrange to be sodomized by altar boys. Sociologist Pepe Rodríguez calculates that approximately 7 per- cent of Spain's priests have committed a serious act of sexual abuse with a child or adolescent (usually a boy). Applying this percentage to the current population of Spain, Rodríguez estimates that alive today are roughly 262,600 men and 44,800 women who were sexually abused in some way when they were minors. And he concludes that these trans- gressions are not only habitual but logical, in view of the unresolved tensions exacerbated by seminary life.[73]

Anxiety over masturbation is not the starting point for the psycho- genesis of clergy sexual abuse but rather its necessary phase of incuba- tion. In the shame-ridden fantasies that accompany onanism in devout Catholic teenagers, the rigid role-relationship model of early childhood is explicitly sexualized for the first time. Which is to say that suffering becomes eroticized, shame voluptuous, degradation a necessary adjunct to pleasure, and forbidden love the only kind that arouses. Many of the priests who end up on Drewermann's couch tell him that their mastur- batory practices are usually accompanied by sadistic fantasies; the nuns he treats suffer from recurrent dreams of being raped with a mixture of pain and pleasure. When the seminary or convent chaplains urge their young students to avail themselves of the cult of the Virgin Mary to protect their chastity, they are throwing gasoline on the fire. That is a perverse way to defend against "perversion," as we confirmed earlier. A striking similarity obtains between the thoughts that enter would-be celi- bates' minds during masturbation and the language of Marian mysticism spoken in past centuries, with its tingly sadomasochistic metaphors.[74]

Chapter 2
The Anticlerical Imaginary, 1808–1901

Numerous men of the cloth did not turn the other cheek during the Spanish War for Independence against Napoleon (1808–1814). The French may have possessed a worthy laicist agenda, but military invasion is no way to impose it, and certainly not on Spaniards. The coronation of Joseph Bonaparte led to a revolt that ironically gave new prestige to the most reactionary elements of the clergy. "There was apparently not a single province in all of Spain," writes historian Stanley Payne, "that did not produce at least one guerrilla band led by a priest or a monk. Nothing like this had ever happened before in any country occupied by Napoleonic forces."[1] According to Caro Baroja, individual clergymen proved themselves capable of horrible violence. Baltasar Calvo, for example, a former canon of the church of San Isidro in Madrid, went to Valencia and organized a massacre of some 330 French citizens on 5 June 1808 (he was later executed for the crime).[2]

Patriots in the upper ranks of the clergy worked side by side with liberal laymen to draft a new constitution to be promulgated following Napoleon's ouster. But the disasters of war and economic collapse brought out a messianic mind-set in religious personnel as well as in the common people, and the new king had a rude surprise in store for the progressives:

When Fernando VII returned from exile and overturned the new Spanish constitution in 1814, he rejected all reform and exercised a more absolute form of monarchy than his father [Carlos IV] had ever attempted before the invasion. The Inquisition was restored, all changes canceled, and the Jesuits brought back to Spain after nearly half a century. Scores, perhaps hundreds, of liberal clerics fled into exile, and the Holy Office busied itself not so much with morals and religion as with the prosecution of Masonry and the other secret societies that had become the organizational mainstay of liberalism. . . . The full pomp and tone of traditional religiosity were restored, and the crown appointed a total of sixty new bishops, giving the hierarchy of the Church a particularly reactionary quality it had not possessed for about a hundred years.[3]

The seeds of absolutist clerical repression sown by the monarch produced a harvest of radical groups in Spain's cities. In 1820 the conspiratorial activities of anticlerical Masonic lodges, seconded by an uprising of discontented army officers led by Rafael de Riego, forced Fernando to "swallow" the liberal constitution he had betrayed six years earlier. Historians record that the conservative church tried at first to accommodate the liberal state, but the latter wanted too many reforms and coexistence soon faltered. The reexpulsion of the Jesuits was the first declaration of war.

With the Church and the royalists against the ropes, the radicals hastened to disseminate their ideas among the urban masses. Freemasons held noisy meetings in cafés and salons, gave speeches, formed neighborhood militias, wrote and produced plays satirizing the clergy. Cries of "Death to the Jesuits!" were heard on the streets of Madrid. In Barcelona theatergoers flocked to see a melodrama entitled *La Inquisición por adentro* ("Inside the Inquisition") and *El Vampiro*, which was not about vampires but about parasitic clergymen. Another major activity of liberal anticlericals was the publication and distribution of erotic materials. Spain's freemasons were not Shriners. Songs like the famous *Trágala* give us an idea of the violent tenor of the liberal lodges:

Trágala o muere,	Swallow it or die,
Tú, servilón,	You slave,
Tú que no quieres	You who don't want
Constitución. . . .	the Constitution. . . .
Trágala, trágala,	Swallow it, swallow it,
Trágala, trágala,	Swallow it, swallow it,
Trágala, perro,	Swallow it, dog,
Tú, que no quieres	You who don't want
Constitución.	the Constitution.[4]

One "dog" who wished not to swallow the liberal constitution, a parish priest named Matías Vinuesa, was hammered to death by unknown assailants on 4 March 1821. Soon monks and priests were organizing guerrilla bands in their familiar haunts in northern and northeastern Spain. Some, like Father Jerónimo Merino, were veterans of the war against Napoleon's impiety; others, like the Trappist brother Antonio Marañón, were anxious to win their spurs through rural terrorist activities. One hundred Catalan clergymen died in the reactionary campaign financed by the conservative French monarch Louis XVIII.[5] Later reprisals carried out by the liberals in Catalunya, in which dozens of priests were executed, only served to alienate the few clerics still loyal to the constitutional government. In 1823 the increasingly radical regime was overthrown with the help of one hundred thousand French troops and the wily Fernando was back in business.

The new period of traditionalist reaction began with the arrival in Madrid of the militant monk Marañón, alias "El Trapense." Dressed in his religious habit with a crucifix around his neck, a saber, a gun belt with two pistols, and a whip in his right hand, Fray Antonio proudly galloped along, blessing the people kneeling in the streets.[6] When press censorship was lifted many years later, Marañón became the very emblem of reactionary clericalism; widely circulated novels pictured him in the company of his alleged fanatical mistress, Josefina de Comerford.

The second Fernandine reaction (1823–1833) was even worse than the first. Though this time Fernando did not reinstate the Inquisition, he gave free rein to the so-called Juntas de Fe, provincial committees charged with keeping the Catholic faith pure at a local level by persecuting Freemasons, hunting down editions of Voltaire's works, and pursuing other obscurantist objectives. But all was not well with the Church thereby. "There was no indication," historian William Callahan states, "that the condition of the lower clergy had improved as the reign of Fernando VII drew to a close. In 1831 the papal nuncio, Francesco Tiberi, reported to Rome that ignorance and moral irregularities were still common among the secular clergy."[7]

In retrospect, the Jesuits should have packed their bags as soon as Fernando died (1833); but not even these astute elite clerics could have anticipated the outbreak of violence directed against them and other orders during a cholera epidemic in the summer of 1834. It was the very success of the energetic and disciplined Jesuits that got them into trouble. As Sánchez explains,

Clericals and anticlericals alike came to believe that the Jesuits could do everything. If anticlericals believed that the Jesuits could do everything, they also held them responsible for everything. The term "Jesuit" became one of opprobium, and the Jesuit became the most stereotyped of all the clergy. He was portrayed as a man without a will of his own, a robot performing the commands and whims of an all-seeing papacy. Considered almost diabolically superhuman, the Jesuit was seen everywhere, behind every dire event.[8]

The original source of the delusion that Jesuits had poisoned Madrid's water supply was most likely a group of distraught slum residents who had lost children to the epidemic: demagogues took over from there, and off the mob went to the Saint Ignatius Seminary on Duque de Alba Street, brandishing knives and shouting blasphemy. When the young

Father Sauri opened the door and demanded to know what they wanted, someone in the mob shouted "We want your blood, dog!"[9] The furious crowds entered the huge building and hunted down the occupants one by one. Father Sauri was stabbed by men, mutilated by women, and dragged by children to the Plaza de San Millán. Altogether some seventy-five Jesuits and their alleged "co-conspirators" in other religious orders were slaughtered. Historians are not sure if the murders were carried out at the inspiration of La Isabelina or some other semisecret anticlerical society. Liberal journalist Mariano José de Larra said the sordid affair proved that the miserable urban populace of Spain's cities would always be able to impose its rage as helpless governments stood by—prophetic words indeed.[10] Hostility to priests did not mean moral indifference, but the activist readiness to rush to judgment and punish alleged depravity. Persecutory schemata were activated again in Barcelona in 1835. The traditional festival in honor of Sant Jaume had gone badly—the bulls had been ineptly handled and the normal festive *ekstasis* had not been achieved. As the irritated populace streamed tumultuously from the bullring, someone cried, "Let's get the Jesuits!" Numerous religious buildings were burned to the ground that day.

Even more devastating in the long run was the expropriation and resale of Church properties carried out by the liberal minister Juan Mendizábal: "Sales continued at a brisk level until the summer of 1844. By the time they were halted, 62 percent of the secular clergy's property had been sold. Although some Church property remained by the mid-1840's, the massive sales, which had yielded more than 3 billion *reales*, broke the back of the imposing structure of ecclesiastical wealth that had sustained the Church for centuries."[11] What Callahan calls "the domestication of the Church" was to be borne by the lower clergy. They were exclaustrated, assigned a tiny pension paid only sporadically, and generally abandoned to their fates. Hundreds of impoverished monks and friars fled to the Basque provinces, Navarre, Aragon, and rural Catalunya, there to aid and abet the Carlist insurgency that was to hound the liberals until the mid-1870s. Righteous vengeance and justified slayings came to be the modus operandi of the more rabidly proclerical groups. The liberal governor of Burgos was stabbed dozens of times by a Carlist mob in the cathedral cloister itself, apparently with the complicity of several canons. The most feared priest of Spain in 1873 was the Carlist guerrilla leader Manuel de Santa Cruz: "Although assiduous in the daily reading of his breviary, Santa Cruz felt no scruples at having twenty prisoners shot without benefit of confession."

Drawing back from the decades of violence, we perceive a pattern in the relationship between church and state in Spain: neither was ever able to get along without the other. Even the most politically liberal

governments were staffed by social conservatives; they agreed to continue paying a minimum subsistence wage to the secular clergy, and
most clergy looked to the state to uphold law and order and keep the
urban workers in check. By 1861 there were already a hundred thousand
industrial workers in Barcelona, a hotbed of labor unrest and popular
anticlericalism. In what Payne considers myopia of historic proportions,
the liberals and their heirs under different names ignored the many progressive priests who pleaded for better training and working conditions
for the deprived lower clergy, thereby alienating men who might have
become political allies.[12]

At no time in Spanish history was the Church entirely reactionary.
Even during the heyday of the Inquisition, Juan Marichal reminds us,
there were antiinquisitorial dissidents among the high clergy.[13] An excellent study by Fernando Velasco permits us to affirm that many priests of
the nineteenth century were in full recovery from the legacy of religious
dysfunction.[14] But liberal shortsightedness, augmented by chronic financial difficulties, guaranteed that Catholic citizens were to be left vulnerable not only to abuse events of one kind or another but to fundamentalist demagogues who appealed to their reduced cognitive/emotional
repertories. The winds blowing from Rome during two long pontificates
were generally favorable to these fixated ultramontane sectors of the
Spanish church. Gregory XVI (1831–1846) and Pius IX (1846–1878),
both classified as reactionary by Sánchez, helped to preserve an attitude
of intransigence among clericals—and therefore among anticlericals.[15]
Pius IX would convoke the first Vatican Council to ratify the provocative
new doctrine of papal infallibility.

Antonio María Claret was a key figure in the nineteenth-century move
to reclericalize Spain. Like American fundamentalists of the twentieth century, this Catalan prelate and his mission team used sophisticated marketing methods to launch a counterattack on depraved secular
society:

> Between 1848 and 1866 the publishing house Claret established printed
> 2,811,100 books, 1,509,600 pamphlets, and nearly 5,000,000 posters and broad-
> sheets. Claret's adaptation of the mission and his appreciation of the importance
> of religious propaganda within the new society of liberal Spain provided the
> Church with an instrument of popular evangelization that to some extent com-
> pensated for the near disappearance of the proselytizing religious orders. . . .
> Claret's contribution, the *Camino recto y seguro para llegar al cielo* [The straight and
> sure road to get to heaven] was an instant success; it would become the most
> widely published work of its kind in the history of Spanish devotional writing.[16]

The triumphant ecclesiastics of the first Fernandine reaction had simply
prohibited the publication of offensive materials. No longer able to do
that under liberal governments, the Church backed the publishing mis-

sioners and their facile devotionalism. As Payne explains, "The style was emotional and somewhat Romantic, aimed at touching the heart. Doctrinal content was often slighted in favor of repetitive words and affective phrases. Above all, there was strong encouragement to obedience and to constant participation in the sacraments, and in the formal ritual of worship."[17] To complement the rituals of collective hypnosis (processions, novenas, nocturnal adorations), a new form of self-hypnosis was promoted by zealous missioners: the rosary. Monsignor Claret preached that it was the shortest route to "the Heart of the Best of Mothers."[18] It is important not to confuse the heady emotionalism of these practices with subjectivism: the idea was not to get people to think or to reflect, but to turn themselves into loyal instruments of salvation. Rationality was equated with sinful pride.[19]

Given the chance, anticlericals would put their own messages into circulation—some positive and liberating, designed to override old scripts; others negative and projective, mere pretexts for the emergence of primitive rage-forged schemata. Rational argument and its dysfunctional shadow are usually found together in what might be termed Spain's anticlerical industry. By this I mean the mass production and consumption of plays, pamphlets, novels, and newspapers that portrayed the Church and its personnel in a negative light. The anticlerical industry (and its perennial tactical ally, pornography) had an abortive start in the brief interlude (1820–1823) between the first and second Fernandine reactions. The unenlightened despot's death and the return of noted liberals from exile ushered in both disentailment and Spanish Romanticism—two parallel movements obsessed with getting cloistered nuns out of the cloister. From 1834 onward, affirms Caro, there was not a single Spanish novelist or playwright who failed to feature an unsatisfied nun as the main character of a work, in order to promote or justify the liberal exclaustration program—even though the vast majority of nuns chose to remain in their convents when allowed to do so.[20]

A recurring theme of these works is that true heterosexual love must be assigned pride of place over a life of convent celibacy. This in itself might be considered a relatively positive idea, but it does not appear in isolation. In famous Romantic works like *El trovador* or *Don Juan Tenorio*, the seduction of the nun or novice necessitates and even justifies the murder of some man with power over her will, usually a father or possessive brother. Such Oedipal themes are commonly elaborated via allusions to sinister aspects of Church history—the Inquisition, the autos-da-fé, the secret prisons, mysterious acts of sacrilege, the ability of clerics to mesmerize young women, and so forth. These motifs show up in both higher and lower cultural spheres and were later used to rationalize the real murder of real priests (the ultimate *fathers*).

The first boom in anticlerical publishing came in the mid-1840s, co-inciding with rapid growth in the publishing industry in general. This spurt was closely associated with the translation into Spanish of popular French novels whose anticlericalism was not merely patent but violent. Don Benito Hortelano, a liberal Spanish publisher, wrote in his mem-oirs about the tremendous popular demand for exposé novels about the secret iniquities of the Jesuits; eager consumers included Queen Isabel II, and in some cases the demand was enthusiastically supplied by ex-members of rival orders like the Dominicans. Caro notes with irony that a good many non-Christian authors found ammunition in the puri-tanical Pascal's vitriolic attack on the Jesuits two hundred years earlier.[21] Haliczer gives pride of place to the French historian Jules Michelet and his anticlerical novel *Le Prêtre, la femme et la famille* (1845), which fasci-nated major Spanish authors with its "theme of the moral seduction of women in the confessional and the impact that it could have on the family and society."[22]

In the final quarter of the nineteenth century, young Spanish pro-gressives armed themselves with an entire arsenal of new philosophies (*cientifismo, hegelianismo, krausismo, regeneracionismo, socialismo,* and *anar-quismo*), all seeking to renew the ideological project of Spanish liberal-ism that had been symbolically cut short by the suicide of Mariano José de Larra in 1837.[23] A considerable number of professors, lawyers, scien-tists, engineers, economists, and naturalists inspired by Darwin were seeking a philosophically based laicism "in which mothers, women, and daughters were to be excluded," says Caro.[24] (Note the association of lib-eral anticlericalism with male gender anxieties.) Most adepts of the new ideologies considered the Church to be a major obstacle to the mod-ernization of Spain. Following the failure of the First Republic in 1873, the Spanish state settled into a relatively stable but corrupt parliamen-tary monarchy known as the Restauración. By 1876 a formidable laicist intelligentsia had taken root in Spain's universities, forming the critical counterpoint to every succeeding government. The Restauración was much too conservative for politicized academics, just as it was far too liberal for the clerical faction.

Both intellectual and vulgar forms of anticlericalism found an outlet in *El Motín,* founded in 1881 by a Sevillian journalist named José Nakens, and in *Las Dominicales del Libre Pensamiento,* founded in 1883 by Fernando Lozano. These two popular and long-lived periodicals, and others of briefer existence, entertained readers with obscene jokes about priests and monks, up-to-date reports of crimes and immoralities committed by clergymen, articles in which the popes were revealed as hypocrites and the Church as a gigantic business concern, and essays in which Jesus was portrayed as a revolutionary friend of the workers. The systematic anticlericalism of the journalists was reinforced by a spate of best-selling novels that fed the popular appetite for hatred and prurience. The title of one such work is exemplary: *THE SECRETS OF CONFESSION. Revelations, mysteries, crimes and monstruosities; sacrileges, aberrations and absurdities; misery, social or religious problems, and human extravagances; immoralities of conservative and ultramontane morality, and other excesses or sins heard from penitents during long experience in the confessional by Constancio Miralta, presbyter.* Published in 1886, this work is a purported "tell-all" book by a parish priest of La Mancha who lost his job after a love affair; Caro considers it illustrative of the most vulgar variety of anticlerical imagination: it even ends with a fanciful description of an orgy in a convent.[25]

Intransigent anticlericals were answered by intransigent clericals like Father Félix Sardá y Salvany, a Catalan priest whose highly successful pamphlet *Is Liberalism a Sin?* embodied the dim view of Spain's Restoration State taken by conservative Catholics. Another best-seller was *Pequeñeces* by Father Luis Coloma, a Jesuit who combined avant-garde literary techniques with retrograde messages about divine punishment (suffered upon two children) and sexuality (embodied by the free-living, free-loving women of Madrid). Father Coloma also insisted that "the good work performed by religious schools is nullified by the immoral behavior and attitudes which the child finds at home."[26] The clerical faction, which included not only priests but renowned historians like Marcelino Menéndez y Pelayo and renowned novelists like José María de Pereda, believed the solution to Spain's problems lay in improved hierarchy and a return to the sacromilitary asceticism of the past. The key fears and prejudices of the Spanish Right had already appeared in fully developed form by 1872, as revealed by a fictional but psychologically coherent account of a rich woman's dream, or rather nightmare, as to what Spain would be like if the working class really took over.[27] Analyzing the dream-story from the standpoint of Spain's political unconscious, Manuel Pérez Ledesma uncovers the following beliefs: that a revolutionary Madrid would be like revolutionary Paris, with its churches destroyed or turned into factories; that ugly, ill-mannered workers would greedily control national sovereignty and bank reserves; that all hallmarks of bourgeois prestige (houses, servants, carrriages) would be lost; and finally that their children would be packed off to prisonlike boarding schools for purposes of reeducation—eerily similar to those actually established under the Restauración for rebellious working-class youths. Here Pérez Ledesma detects a fear that the proletariat was spoiling to give the bourgeoisie a taste of their own medicine.

The prevailing composite stereotype of the immoral/ alcoholic/subversive/church-torching worker provoked labor organizations into a spirited counterdiscourse. "Despite its situation, despite its lack of education, the working class is more moral and honorable than the exploiting class," Barcelona's *Centro Obrero* argued, going on from there to a point by point refutation of the stereotypes.[28] Novels that testified "to the moral degradation of the ruling classes" were a staple of proletarian culture for decades; workers able to read were encouraged at every turn to revile the "noxious bourgeosie, the useless aristocracy, the absurd clergy."[29]

In all of the above we see the link between habitus and the particular forms that social hatred takes. The social space occupied by the clericals gave a hysterical tinge to their prejudices, while the social space occupied by the anticlericals selected for the obsessional mode. The hysterical ideology of desire wants to keep its lowly target group in its place; the obsessional mode would be happy to flush away its enemies, constructed as socially superior, feared and envied for their diabolical cleverness, hated as insidious social pollutants. It is only among a minority of clericals, a group that might be called anti-anticlericals, that obsessional-type prejudices and paranoid ideas become salient—but here again social space is a determining factor. The more radical clericals are gripped by the notion that their superiors in the hierarchy have in some way sold out to the enemy. Conspiracy theories and eschatalogical urgency reflect a beleaguered self-concept and a marginalized position in the field of power. If "normal" clericalism was profoundly conservative and hierarchical (looking down on a threatening underclass), radical or fundamentalist clericalism defines itself by ferreting out the devil-inspired plots of the insiders and the machinations of the truly powerful.[30] Obsessional prejudices find fertile terrain in the minds of the politically disadvantaged, but, as Young-Bruehl notes, they also appeal to "alienated or disillusioned intellectual or professional people whose obsessionality has been functional for their education and advancement but who then find themselves without a sense of place."[31]

The radical writers discussed earlier fit this description. Conspiracy theories allied with literary talent were rampant in late nineteenth-century Spain, as best seen in the career of Vicente Blasco Ibáñez, who was far more tendentious than Catholic anticlericals like Benito Pérez Galdós. According to Hispanist Brian Dendle, Blasco shared the anarchists' equation of early Christianity with their own iconoclastic idealism. With *La araña negra* (1892), Blasco attempts to equal the success of Eugène Sue's *Le Juif errant*, often stooping to plagiarism to paint his portrait of the Jesuits as "an immensely powerful organization, plotting world domination, using murder, lies, calumny, banditry, and rape for their aims, and looting Spain for the benefit of Rome." In another novel Blasco portrays one Jesuit killing another with the Eucharist; the victim vomits out the Host shouting "mierda." Voilà the anticlerical imagination at its most vulgar. Blasco's massive projections are buttressed with retorts to Father Coloma's defense of religious schools. Coloma had affirmed that Jesuit teachers cared more about the welfare of students than their own parents; Blasco replies that the child is better off at home than "in the hands of sexually-perverted sadists." The custody battle was joined. The novel ends on what was intended to be a hopeful note but which we now read with anguished hindsight: a young revolutionary named Agramunt dreams of a new kind of Inquisition designed to burn everything standing in the way of a better future.[32]

The ongoing battle for custody of young Spanish minds, especially female ones, heated up as the turn of the century drew closer, even as a new kind of erotic anticlericalism began to captivate many male minds. Working-class movements had grown and clashes with authoritarian police forces became more and more frequent, thereby radicalizing an important sector of the intelligentsia. A case in point is Luis Bonafoux, the French-born, Spanish-educated Puerto Rican of great interest to us as an exemplar of the "missing link" between cultured anticlericalism and the kind that would be practiced later by organized gangs of church burners, image desecrators, and priest killers.

Bonafoux was editor-in-chief of *La Campaña* and *Heraldo de París*, two Spanish-language newspapers that to avoid censorship were published in Paris and distributed throughout Spain and Latin America. The brand of hatred circulated thereby scarcely distinguished between political and religious villains. "In order to reform the Phillipines," writes Bonafoux, "it is necessary to reform the friar: because the friar is to the perverted politics of Madrid what a crow is to a cadaver."[33] For many progressives the Catholic Church became a convenient scapegoat for Spain's disastrous loss of overseas territories to the United States in 1898. Both the anticlerical and the anarchist imaginations were obsessed with sexual liberation. This was not the refined aesthetic eroticism of the *modernista* Valle-Inclán, Inman Fox explains, but an "almost pornographic" one designed to affront the bourgeoisie; writers were enjoined by Bonafoux to include frank descriptions of the sex act in their collaborations. At the same time, the clergy was routinely identified with debauched sexuality. "In no human being can the pleasures of love be greater than in the priest," writes José Nakens.[34]

Anticlerical words became anarchist deeds. In 1896 someone tossed a bomb at Barcelona's most solemn Catholic procession, Corpus Christi, killing six people and seriously wounding another forty-five. Bonafoux later came to believe that a French anarchist named Jean Girault was the real—and incompetent—perpetrator (the bishop had escaped unscathed). The Spanish military threw itself into an orgy of repression against all anarchist organizations, including the peaceful ones. "So hideous were the brutalities," writes George Esenwein, "that the expression 'the revival of the Spanish Inquisition' became a popular phrase. From all the available evidence produced at the time, such an indictment was not misplaced."[35] In the dungeons of Montjuïc prison, a certain Lieutenant Portas kept falsely accused anarchists in completely darkened cells for lengthy periods of time, interrupting the monotony only to scorch their testicles. News of the torture sparked a number of anticlerical riots during the summer of 1899, the first in more than a generation. When eighty thousand workers went on strike in Barcelona in February 1901, the Spanish army routed them with machine guns; many were arrested and taken onto a prison ship for more torturing sessions similar to those of Montjuïc.

The consequences of such treatment were to shape the course of Spanish history. The penal code in any society is the chief internal check against violent revenge; it is supposed to *prevent* the escalation of social conflict. Mere logic obliges us to recognize that when the penal code becomes an *instrument* of revenge, brutalization, and humiliation, the society will lose its grip on social conflict. Experts point out that traumatized people sometimes seek refuge in "tightly knit organizations that encourage their followers to adopt a paranoid stance, in which outsiders are singled out as scapegoats who are responsible for their current plight."[36] In Spain, harsh repression only served to radicalize moderate intellectuals and further unhinge the already radical ones. The target group of scapegoating obsessional prejudice would be the clergy: journalists mistreated in jail by the government became ever more irresponsible in their anticlerical diatribes. Rodrigo Soriano wrote that "Being a priest or a monk is all that is required in order to rape or kill almost with impunity. . . . The country is divided into two castes: those with cassocks, on one hand, and those without, at their feet."[37] Bonafoux published articles on how to make dynamite or why Leon Czolgosz (President McKinley's assassin) was really a heroic martyr. In the meantime, the young José Martínez Ruiz (the future "Azorín" and stellar member of the so-called Generation of 1898) kept himself busy disseminating anarchist sentiments, translating or echoing the thoughts of Peter Kropotkin or Sebastien Faure, the French ex-Jesuit and free-love propagandist. Fox reports that Martínez Ruiz frequently satirized the carnal desires of the clergy, attacked religious education, and declared marriage to be an outmoded and immoral institution that kept women as chattel and killed the spark of sincere erotic love.[38] Christ was really an anarchist, thought Azorín, because he took a stand against powerful hypocrites and preached universal love. During the first decade of the twentieth century, Esenwein notes, Madrid's *La Anarquía* and Barcelona's *La Tramontana* "never tired of blaspheming religion and caricaturing the clergy."[39]

Doña Perfecta: The Harm That Good Women Do

This book connects authoritarian sexuality with the cult of Mary, engulfment styles of motherhood found in Iberia, and the difficulties many priests experience with their core gender identity. The anticlerical counterdiscourse involved a struggle to *disidentify* not only from the mother but also from the mother's religious beliefs. A clear pattern emerges out of the biographies and autobiographies of Spain's nineteenth- and twentieth-century anticlerical writers. The male child typically started his life under the influence of his mother, grandmothers, aunts, and female caretakers in general, absorbing their "fussy, sentimental, almost superstitious beliefs," as Caro puts it.[40] Many boys were allowed and even encouraged to dress up as priests and pretend to say mass. But with the onset of puberty and peer-bonding with male cousins or friends, the erstwhile little angel learned to mock feminine piety, and indeed to reject anything that might seem "sissy." Only in old age with the proximity of death would a man's man consider returning to regular religious practices.

Sometimes peer pressure to cement a gender identity triggered out-and-out rebellion against parents, teachers, and authority figures in general. "A great number of men belonging to the Spanish bourgeoisie born between 1840 and 1860 were anticlerical, rabidly anticlerical; and, contrary to what some wish to think, they were at the same time men of extraordinary talent and ability," writes Caro, who finds it significant that many anticlericals had been sent to reputable religious schools, only to "react furiously" against their educators.[41] Perhaps in some cases the rage had its roots in some shame-inducing, hushed-up episode of physical punishment or molestation. At the very least it would seem that the vehemence of many an anticlerical was an indirect measure of the strength and staying power of negative religious messages and the repressive regimes—familial, ecclesiastical, and national—that permitted these messages to proliferate.

Spanish women writers of the nineteenth century were, generally speaking, disinclined to make such attacks. This does not mean that they were incapable of spotting symptoms of religious dysfunction. The devoutly Catholic Cecilia Böhl de Faber, for example, writing under the pseudonym Fernán Caballero, peopled her novels with characters like Doña Inés de Córdoba, in whom aristocratic virtues coexist with blind intolerance and rigidity; when the countess impedes the marriage of her son to the protagonist, Elia, this heretofore passionate young woman finds solace in a sudden relgous conversion and gets herself to a nunnery, quite willingly.[42] Such endings will simply not be found in mainstream (male) anticlerical writers, unable as they were to find any redeeming qualities in lifelong celibacy. In the latter years of the century two other important women novelists, Emilia Pardo Bazán and Concha Espina, avoided the clerical/anticlerical debate and focused instead on the virtues of individual Catholics.[43]

The model male anticlerical (but still Catholic) writer of the nineteenth and early twentieth centuries was also the most important Spanish novelist since Cervantes. Benito Pérez Galdós (1843–1920) may have absorbed some elements of Fernán Caballero's realist style, but he belongs both to a gender identity formation and to a political persuasion that had set out to deconstruct Spanish ultra-Catholicism (even as it was being busily reconstructed by Monsignor Claret and other mystics). His first novel, *La fontana de oro* (1868) "portrays a priest's attempt at rape and decides that religiosity is the result of sexual repression, if not mental illness." At age thirty-three Galdós published what was to become the classic work of liberal anticlericalism: *Doña Perfecta* (1876). We can read this novel today as the first major exposé of the rigid priestly and motherly personalities that sustained religious abuse in Spain.

As in most anticlerical novels or plays, the plot of *Doña Perfecta* is a dysfunctional family drama. Readers are meant to identify with José (Pepe) Rey, age thirty-four, the ideal liberal martyr: a well-educated, patriotic, and scientifically oriented man whose tragic "flaw" is his inability to lie or refrain from criticizing what needs to be criticized about Orbajosa, the archetypal provincial Spanish town. Pepe makes his first big mistake when, under the relentless goading of the wily priest Don Inocencio, he launches into a devastating critique of the bad taste on display at the local cathedral, particularly the garish baroque clothing that adorns icons of the Virgin Mary and the Child Jesus. This faux pas is what the priest has been waiting for:

"Very well, Señor Don José," exclaimed the canon, laughingly and with a triumphant expression, "this image that seems so ridiculous to your pantheistic philosophy is Our Lady of Succor, patroness and intercessor of Orbajosa, whose inhabitants venerate her so much that they are capable of dragging through the streets anyone who speaks ill of her. . . . You shall know also that your aunt Doña Perfecta is lady-in-waiting to the Holiest Virgin of Succor, and that the dress that seemed so grotesque to you is, well, that dress so grotesque to your impious eyes was made in this very house, and that the trousers of the Child Jesus are the product of the marvelous needle and unblemished piety of your cousin, Rosarito."[44]

In one economical scene Galdós has communicated the intimate connection between earthly and supernatural women, the desire of the
young engineer to distance himself from sentimental maternal superstition, and the readiness of the townspeople to protect their Protector
with violence if necessary.

A principal theme of the novel is the harm that good women do
when they have internalized an omnipotent sense of a mother's rights
and duties. Galdós hastens to say that the maternal instinct is basically a
good thing that allows for a certain amount of exaggeration, but "Nevertheless, a most striking phenomenon often occurs in life; when this exaltation of maternal affection does not coincide with absolute purity of
heart and perfect honesty, it can go astray and become a lamentable
frenzy that can contribute, like any other unbridled passion, to great
errors and catastrophes." The unwholesome consequences of dysfunctional or perverse mothering styles are studied through the characters
of Doña Perfecta Polentinos, widow, and her friend and former maid
María Remedios, the priest's niece and live-in housekeeper.[45] Their first
victim will be Perfecta's daughter Rosarito, enamored of Pepe. Late in
the novel Perfecta confides to María Remedios that "Rather than see her
married to my nephew, I prefer any other evil to befall her, including
death." María Remedios has a less drastic solution in mind; when the
priest presumes that Rosarito has already given in to the libidinous urges
of her cousin Pepe, María Remedios shouts that the girl is still "pure as
an angel" and that her infatuation with Pepe can easily be cured "with a
couple of swipes on the chops or six good whacks."

The link between a rule-bound religiosity and personality distortion
does not have to be "read into" *Doña Perfecta*. I cede the floor to Galdós
himself (or rather his omniscient narrator) regarding Perfecta:

Her bilious constitution, combined with excessive dealings with devout persons
and things that exalted her imagination in a sterile way, had aged her prematurely, and even though she was young she did not look it. It could be said that
with her habits and her way of life she had fashioned an outer crust, a stony
cover, callous, like a snail in its little portable house. . . . We do not know what a
loving Doña Perfecta would have been like. In abhorring she had the inflamed
vehemence of a guardian angel of discord among men. Such is the effect produced in a rigid character [*carácter duro*] and lacking in natural kindness by religious exaltation when, instead of following conscience and the truth revealed in
principles as simple as they are beautiful, it bases itself upon narrow formulas
that only answer to ecclesiastical interests.

A liberal Spanish priest of our day has identified "perfectionist rigidity"
as one form that celibacy can take in man or woman.[46] And as psychiatrist David Shapiro points out, a rigid and defensive personality

tends to do one thing and one thing only in a crisis situation: stiffen further.[47] Thus Galdós is psychologically astute when he portrays Perfecta's increasing rigidity and messianic paranoia in the latter chapters of the novel.

Indeed, there is much to learn in *Doña Perfecta* about the masochistic personality types associated with Spanish ultra-Catholicism. Here we find what Shapiro found in his patients: not resignation or acquiescence but a dignified refusal to forget past humiliations, and indeed nurse or exaggerate them in order to achieve at least a "moral victory" in the end.[48] This determination to never forgive or forget is just what we find in the clergymen who surround Doña Perfecta. By 1876 the liberal Spanish state had managed to disentail Church property and place limits on the number of religious communities; the early 1870s had seen the final outbreaks of clergy-inspired violence in the Carlist hinterlands of Aragon and Catalunya. Thus there were many priests who sincerely felt themselves to have been victimized and humiliated by the liberal Spanish state—even in the conservative pseudoparliamentary facade it congealed into following the failure of the First Republic (1873). In *Doña Perfecta*, accordingly, we find a portrait of the dean of Orbajosa's cathedral, an old man with an eating disorder whose world had been turned upside down years earlier by Mendizábal's liberal reforms: "He spoke only of religious matters and from the beginning manifested a most thorough disdain for Pepe Rey." But the priest who really has a chip on his shoulder is Don Inocencio, a member of the secular clergy, confessor and presbyter of the cathedral as well as the local high school Latin and rhetoric teacher. He is constantly offended by newcomers from Madrid who find fault with Orbajosa's socioeconomic backwardness. His defensive pride is matched by his sense of inferiority to Pepe Rey's modern scientific learning (as displayed in the young engineer's eloquent rehash of eighteenth-century rationalist critiques of superstition). The priest responds with exaggerated self-deprecation, unflinchingly ackowledging his vulnerability to humiliation by heaping praise on the intellectual gifts of the young university graduate.

This reaction is simply an outflanking maneuver of the kind described by Shapiro, "a picture not of the individual who surrenders but of the one who concedes territory on his own terms precisely in order to avoid surrender."[49] The Israeli psychiatrist Rena Moses-Hrushovski regards trauma-induced shame as a key factor in the psychogenesis of what he calls "deployed persons." "After years of suffering and of having been humiliated victims, all that is left for them now is to demonstrate how they have been wronged and to protest against it."[50] Such personality traits were prevalent among the churchmen of Spain. By the 1870s, writes Callahan, "Ecclesiastical energies were not directed to reforming the Church from within but to blaming an array of external forces for attempting to 'de-Catholicize' Spain—the liberal State for having sold Church property, politicians for disregarding the Church's theocratic admonitions, and intellectuals for advocating cultural innovation."[51] Thus the picture Galdós paints is both psychologically and historically accurate: the priests and monks most victimized by the central government took refuge in regionalism as a bulwark and defensive position. Local pride was not some innocent variation on American-style boosterism; in nineteenth-century Spain it was inseparable from religious dysfunction, clerical paranoia, Carlism, agrarian backwardness, and civil insurrection. "Orbajosa, dear aunt, has little more than garlic fields and bandits—that's the only word for those who in the name of some political or religious idea rise up to seek adventures every four or five years."

The landholding plutocracy that arose under disentailment soon realized that to maintain its power in Madrid it needed to control towns and villages throughout the countryside (where the lands were located). The much-feared Guardia Civil was created in 1844 to protect the new owners' property rights and repress malcontents.[52] *Doña Perfecta* opens with a scene of renegade peasants summarily executed by Civil Guards. Later on the central government sends a detachment of troops to Orbajosa to discourage a Carlist-type uprising; the soldiers are commanded by friends of Pepe Rey. In response, Perfecta has stiffened and constructed a perfectly Manichaean and millenarian view of the situation.[53] The manner in which Don Inocencio incites the brutish local lads to rebellion while paying lip service to peace would certainly have struck a strong chord of recognition (and repulsion) in the novel's first liberal readers. But what might strike an even stronger chord in readers of today is Don Inocencio's accurate prediction of future massacres of priests: "I know very well that terrible days await us, and that those of us who wear a priest's habit have our lives hanging by a thread; for Spain, let there be no doubt, will witness scenes like those of the French Revolution, in which thousands of the most pious priests perished in a single day."

Following Pepe's insult of the town's sacred mother figure, Perfecta had forbidden her daughter to marry him and indeed locked her in her room, an "Inquisition-style confinement" for her own good. When he is finally able to communicate with his loved one, Pepe successfully breaks the spell cast upon her; that is, he leads her to comprehend that her nervous illness is the result of "the horrible violence" that is being done to her by her proclerical mother. "Pepe, you're right," Rosarito finally says. "I am not sick, I am only intimidated, or better yet, fascinated." For Pepe, Rosarito is "an angel of God" hypnotized and controlled by her mother: "The spectacle of this injustice, this unheard-of violence, is what turns my rectitude into barbarism, my reason into force, my honesty into violence similar to that of murderers and thieves." Elsewhere we are told that Pepe feels "that mood in which the most prudent man feels violent flames inside himself, a blind and brutal force inclined to strangle, strike, break skulls, and crush bones." Despite his righteous rage, he never adopts the scorched earth tactics of the mothers, Perfecta and María Remedios, and in the end he will fall victim to their machinations.[54]

La Regenta: The Psychology of Priestly Desire

Doña Perfecta portrays a society still up for grabs, still liable—like Rosarito in the end—to go off the brink into madness (civil war). But the Alphonsine Restauración had proved itself by the next decade—by proving itself the loyal subordinate of capitalism. Railroad and mining interests had fallen under foreign control; national power was wielded by the Andalusian agrarian bourgeoisie, supported by the mercantile and financial communities, tolerated by the military, and administered from Madrid by a legion of loyal bureaucrats. The Church hierarchy had been persuaded by conservative liberals to abandon the Carlist pipe dream, and the country had stabilized into mostly cooperative, mostly peaceful, mostly corrupt social relations.

Spain was already "the kingdom of the favor," as one political scientist terms it, by which he means the pervasive Spanish system of personalistic patronage known as caciquismo.[55] A cacique was essentially a doer of favors, and a collector of them on voting day, at local and provincial levels. In the 1880s the system entered its golden age, with "Liberal" and "Conservative" parties in collusion, taking turns at power (the so-called peaceful rotation). As historian Robert Kern argues, the new leaders of the Restauración resembled the enlightened despots of the eighteenth century in believing that economic modernization could be effected without social change; thus they continued to cherish "the values of hierarchy, patronage, and familialism in a period in which achievement, not privilege, activated the positivistic liberal movements elsewhere in Europe."[56] Spain's conservative liberals realized that the Church was their best bulwark against increasingly restless trade unionists, journalists, and university professors. The bourgeoisie—including numerous families whose ancestors had rushed to snap up disentailed church properties at bargain-basement prices—now eagerly participated in a neo-Catholic resurgence in all spheres of life.

The movement was strongest in provincial Spain, the world portrayed so accurately by novelist Leopoldo Alas, a.k.a. Clarín (1852–1901), the most penetrating observer of clergy behavior and misbehavior of his times. His masterpiece, the two volumes of *La Regenta* (1884–1885), is *check* set in "Vetusta" (the fictional name of Oviedo, capital of the province of Asturias in northern Spain). Clarín is never as tendentious as Galdós; perceptive critics have hailed *La Regenta* for its surprising, Cervantes-like "ideological neutrality" and sociological acumen.[57] A more distanced perspective enables Clarín to engage in a thorough examination of the role of religious dysfunction in the lives of Spaniards, and in so doing he gives us the first psychology of celibate sexuality worthy of the name.

The first characters we encounter in *La Regenta* are altarboys and victims of abuse. One, a substitute bell-ringer nicknamed Bismarck, "lived accustomed to receiving slaps and kicks without knowing why."[58] Bismarck's concept of authority, of being someone important in the world, is nothing other than the power to slap and kick at will. Even more disturbing is the fledgling deviant personality of his companion:

Celedonio was twelve or thirteen years old and he already knew how to adjust his facial muscles to liturgical requirements. He had large, dirty-brown eyes, and when the little rogue considered himself in ecclesiastical functions he moved them with affectation, from down to up, from up to down, imitating the many priests and *beatas* that he knew and associated with. But unknowingly he gave them a lubricious and cynical look, like a corner prostitute who announces her sad commerce with her eyes. . . . In the acolyte yet without holy orders one could predict a future and proximate perversion of the natural instincts, already provoked by the aberrations of a distorted education.

Clarín would have had no trouble understanding Alice Miller's concept of poisonous pedagogy.

The formidable power of the higher clergy is admirably embodied by Don Fermín de Pas—theologian, eloquent preacher, holder of the most coveted offices in the cathedral hierarchy, and right-hand man of the bishop himself. In Clarín's novel he is often referred to as "El Magistral" or "el señor Provisor." Well in advance of Foucault, Don Fermín has realized that power flows from knowledge secretly obtained in the confessional:

The Magistral knew a kind of subterranean Vetusta: it was the hidden city of consciences. He knew the inside of all the important houses and all the souls that were useful to him. Astute as no other citizen of Vetusta, religious or secular, little by little he had managed to attract to his confessional the chief believers of that pious city. . . . Connecting the confessions one with another, gradually he had drawn up the spiritual map of noble Vetusta. Like meteorological observatories that announce cyclones, the Magistral could have predicted many stormy events in Vetusta, family dramas, scandals, and love affairs of all kinds. He knew that when a devout woman confesses her sins, if not careful she will inadvertently reveal the foibles of her entire family. . . . Many times, in the houses where he was received as a trustworthy friend, he would listen in silence to family arguments, with discreetly downcast eyes; while his demeanor implied neutrality or lack of understanding, he was perhaps the only one truly in the know, the only one who had the key to that tangled knot of unhappiness.

Here we find a remarkable foreshadowing of our modern family-systems experts, though Don Fermín has no intention of sharing his insights with the parties involved nor freeing them from the religious ties that bind.

Like his predecessors among the high clergy of the Golden Age, the Magistral is charged with disciplining members of the lower clergy who use their confessionals for base purposes of sexual solicitation. Clarín's sociological acumen shines in the scene in which Don Fermín aims the heavy artillery of his erudition at the oafish parish priest of an isolated mountain village, accused of using his confessional to foist himself upon the local virgins:

I know everything, my good man, and I am sorry to say that your case is practically hopeless. The Tridentine Council considers the crimes you have committed to be similar to heresy. I do not know if you are aware that the *Universi Domini* of 1622, established by His Holiness Gregory XV, calls you and others like you execrable traitors. The punishment reserved for the crime of soliciting *ad turpia* your female penitents is most severe.

The Jesuit-educated Fermín soon tires of quoting ecclesiastical precedents to the sexually abusive rural clergyman and throws him out, knowing all the while that he will find some way to mitigate the severity of the punishment mandated by canon law. The irony of the scene derives from Fermín's growing but still unacknowledged attraction to Ana Ozores ("La Regenta"), his own fetching female penitent. Another irony: she initially goes to Don Fermín to seek the sophisticated spiritual guidance lacking in her former confessor, the aging Father Cayetano Ripamilán, much favored by the city's aristocrats because of his laxity and the leeway he affords them with their sexual peccadilloes.

A different kind of knowledge constitutes power for Don Alvaro Mesía, the elegantly corrupt *cacique*, French-style materialist, and man-about-town specializing in adultery. "Like a bad clergyman who abuses his confessional, don Alvaro knew the comic or disgusting weaknesses of many husbands." Many of the women he seduces tell him of their encounters with sex-starved priests. Thus he is convinced that "in a clergyman the woman seeks the secret pleasure and spiritual voluptuosity of temptation, while the clergyman abuses, without exception, the opportunities offered him by the institution." When Mesía sets his sights on an affair with Ana Ozores, his biggest fear is that Don Fermín de Pas might have already used "the subtle and corrosive labor of the confessional" to beat him to the punch.

In the priest's tense relationship with his mother we have "one of the most powerful accounts of family discomfort to be found in Spanish literature," according to literary critic Alison Sinclair.[59] Like the mothers in *Doña Perfecta*, Doña Paula's hold over her offspring is like a return on a lifelong investment of suffering and hard labor. Long before her son was born she had personally confirmed the imperfect nature of the vow of celibacy: a young priest considered chaste and saintly tried to rape her one night. She successfully resisted and from that moment onward she was able to blackmail the poor man — "A moment of weakness in his loneliness cost the priest, without being satisfied, many years of slavery." Later she finds employment as head housekeeper to another parish priest who eventually becomes bishop of Vetusta and her son's patron. With her new ecclesiastical employer there will be no sin of impurity, for the good Don Fortunato's heart "was kindled in a fire of love for Holiest María." The lesson is clear: behind every great Spanish clergyman lies a powerful terrestrial or supernatural mother. Well aware of woman's power to transform mild-mannered clergymen into satyrs, Doña Paula discreetly arranges for comely rural maids to serve in her son's household as a "precaution." One of them, Teresina, relieves the priest's libido with unspecified acts when he feels most tempted by his penitent, Ana Ozores, who is a married woman as well as a sincere and innocent Catholic.

Don Fermín's ecclesiastical career had followed an archetypal pattern: an invisible father, a distant but hyperprotective mother sacrificing all and demanding nothing less in return; seminary training under the Jesuits; the embracement of an ambitious function instead of a true self; the defense of papal infallibility and other authoriatarian dogmas; a demanding and punitive superego. But that was before the summer of his friendship with a woman. Now,

he wanted nothing more than to sink his soul into that unnamed passion that made him forget the whole world, his clerical ambition, his mother's sordid deals of which he was executor, the calumnies, the intrigues of his enemies, the shameful memories, everything, everything, except that bond between two souls, that intimacy with Ana Ozores. How many years had they lived as neighbors without knowing each other, without suspecting what fate had in store for them! Yes, fate, the Magistral thought, for he did not want to say "Providence" to himself; no more theology, no more mental knots that had made his adolescence and early manhood a sterile desert populated only by phantasms, crazy apprehensions, apocalyptic figures. No more of that ever. Nor that which had followed it: the blindness of the senses, the brutality of low passions, satisfied surreptitiously to the point of glut; this was shameful, more than anything else because of the secrecy, the hypocrisy, the darkness it had come enveloped in.

In this remarkable passage we can see the priest letting go of the old malapaptive defenses, the legacy of tortured hermit saints and the paranoid/schizoid position underlying them, while liberating new mental territory for ego growth. Fermín deliberately inhibits certain associations or venues of thought (theology, Providence) and courageously faces shameful aspects of his education—precisely in order to transcend shame. He is no longer in denial about the negative consequences of the celibate/sexual system and the guilt-ridden addictive processes it puts in motion—degraded and degrading forms of sex lived out in dissociation or disavowal. Naturally his close relationship with Ana began under the auspices of his ministry—as her confessor, spiritual director, and friend. That is usually how men in the priesthood meet women. Ana could not guess that beneath the elegant manners and imposing intellect of the priest lay an inhibited adolescent, still chained to the maternal imago, and that her presence in his life would trigger a belated and much needed developmental process.

Clarín gives us a portrait of the emotional evolution of a priest that current psychotherapeutic practice confirms exactly. Drewermann could easily be referring to Don Fermín when he speaks of the typical priest falling in love:

So a warm breeze starts to melt the icy depths of his priestly existence, and his ontological insecurity starts to progressively dissipate. If this evolution continues a sufficient length of time, it can happen that, in the end, a new personality emerges that no longer needs to justify its existence by priesthood—or membership in a religious order, as the case may be—but that lives the profession according to the dictates of the ego, that is, as a *person*, and not merely as a *function*.[60]

By definition this new identity or personality is not exploitative, but reparative; exploitative events are part and parcel of the defense mechanisms that many clergymen are recovering from. Spanish priest Javier Garrido says that between thirty and forty years of age many of his colleagues experience a keen desire to live what they have not lived and love a concrete human being instead of everyone in general (Fermín is age thirty-five when the novel begins). The ensuing identity crisis can lead to the abandonment of the vocation, but more commonly to a "double life" that combines priesthood with secret sexual escapades.[61]

Don Fermín's favorite task is the direction of the girls' catechism classes held in a local church. He is especially glad one day to see the fruits of his catechumenical labors in the person of an attractive fifteen-year-old girl—"the pearl in his museum of *beatas*"—who saucily recites "a philippic against modern materialists, only slightly moderated by the euphemisms of jesuitical rhetoric. . . . It was woman's blind obedience speaking; the very symbol of sentimental fanaticism, the initiation of the *eternal feminine* in eternal idolatry." As William Christian points out, the Spanish priests who promoted sodalities like the Daughters of Mary "knew they could count on adolescent girls for piety and enthusiasm."[62] It is precisely the ambitious Fermín's power to "fascinate" young women that angers the liberals of Vetusta, few as they are, and their allies in the working-class neighborhood. They all watch in dismay as the lovely Ana Ozores does the bidding of her confessor and marches barefoot in the Holy Week procession—right alongside the abusive local schoolmaster purging his guilt with a rough-hewn cross.

According to Father Leo Booth, many religious addicts ingenuously hand over their finances, relationships, and decisions big or trivial to a clergyman.[63] The Magistral prides himself on his ability to position himself as the one true master for several wealthy, ultra-Catholic families of Vetusta, directing not only their charity but the very lives of their daughters. The Carraspique family perfectly embodies the portraits of religious addiction presented by Father Booth. Don Francisco de Asís Carraspique and his wife are obsessed with their souls' salvation, spellbound by Don Fermín's "pious pessimism," generous and unquestioning contributors to the Alms for Rome Program, the Hermanitas de los Pobres, the Santa Obra del Catecismo, the Novena de la Concepción, the expenses of a Jesuit preacher working the sermon circuit, and indeed any other good cause suggested to them by Don Fermín, the family spiritual director. Two of the four Carraspique daughters have already decided "of their own free will" to become nuns. The family doctor complains that no choice can be free if a girl is only exposed to one alternative during her upbringing: At age ten she is sent to a convent school, where she remains until age fifteen; the next three or four years are supposedly meant to enhance her experience of the real world, but in practice the girl's daily routines are shaped by one devotional ritual or another. Would-be boyfriends are sent away, priests are the only men allowed into the house—defined by the doctor as "a mystical barracks"—and when the girl finally "chooses" to remain celibate forever, the Church has scored an easy and patently unjust victory over secular society. Young Rosita Carraspique has already taken her vows, changed her name to Sor Teresa, and entered the local Salesian convent that the doctor describes as "a toilet"—a decrepit old building built on top of the drainage area for the sewers of the entire neighborhood, with no sunlight or fresh air to alleviate the humidity and odors. Though aware of the problem, and of Rosita's delicate health, Fermín de Pas had delayed closing the convent to avoid bad publicity for the Church. When Sor Teresa sickens and dies in her cell, Vetusta's liberals voice their outrage in an obituary published in their newspaper:

We will only say that, according to the most accredited experts, the loss we lament was not unrelated to the lack of proper hygiene in the miserable building occupied by the Salesians. However, in addition, it occurs to us to ask: "Is it really hygienic that *certain rodents* be permitted to penetrate the bosom of our homes in order to undermine, little by little, with deleterious pseudoreligious influence, the peace of our families and the tranquility of our minds?"

Public opinion quickly blames Fermín de Pas for the death of poor Sor Teresa. Among the most frequently heard comments: "He is a spiritual vampire, who sucks the blood of our daughters" and "This is a blood tribute that we pay to fanaticism." *La Regenta* succinctly lays bare a major underlying fantasy connection between a specific kind of religious abuse and the righteous rage of anticlerical journalists.

Clergy sexual abuse will have its own metaphor: perversion equals viscosity. We are meant to feel the final repugnant sensations and spiritual devastation through the character of Ana Ozores, although it takes the innocent, hysteroid woman some four hundred pages to realize that the priest is in love with her: "Yes, in love like a man, not with the ideal, seraphic, mystical love that she had imagined. He was jealous, he was dying of jealousy. The Magistral was not her big brother of the soul, he was a man who underneath his cassock concealed passions, love, jealousy, anger. . . . Ana shuddered as if touched by a cold and viscous body." And in that moment she recalls her deceased father and his circle of liberal friends, and remembers all the things that as a child she had heard them say about the clergy—"The clergy corrupted consciences, the priest was like everyone else, ecclesiatical celibacy was a sham." Now she fully understood what they meant.

In Spain anticlerical lore lies dormant until some cleric does something to elicit it. Ana's subsequent reaction is remarkably similar to that of recent American Catholics victimized by their pastors: her spiritual development comes to an abrupt halt. Later, after she has been seduced and abandoned by Alvaro (who also kills her husband in an honor duel), she desperately attempts to return to the confessional, only to be rejected most uncharitably by the spurned Fermín de Pas. When the priest takes a murderer's step toward her, she faints from terror and he flees. Then the sexually ambiguous young Celedonio finds her alone in the darkened cathedral: "Celedonio felt a miserable desire, a perversion of the perversion of his lust; and so to enjoy a strange new pleasure, or at least taste it to see if he liked it, he inclined his disgusting face over that of the Regenta and kissed her lips." So in the end there she is: helpless and inert on the cold marble floor of the cathedral, degraded by representatives of the one true religion. When Ana awakens she has the vague impression that a toad has been sitting on her face.

In the case of Fermín, the maturational process that seemed to be going so well was finally sabotaged, from within and without. In the final

chapters he regresses into his habitual defensive style, the same one ob-
servable in so many flesh-and-blood priests in whom the unconscious
conflicts have solidified into rigid schemata that are resistant to new
working models or greater levels of consciousness.[64] By no longer permit-
ting his readers to be privy to Fermín's thoughts, Clarín ingeniously con-
veys the priest's reduced self-awareness, his isolation, his ego-depleting
retreat into the brittle shell of a function: el Magistral. Thus the novel
ends as tragically for Fermín as it does for Ana herself, though at least
the priest will continue to enjoy the protection and complicity of the
Church. Ana discovers too late that a spiritual director and confessor
cannot guide you beyond his own level of psychological development.

La Regenta was assailed by the sectors of Spanish society most in denial regarding ecclesiastical mind control and the pitfalls of celibate
sexuality. Literary historians relate that Clarín was greatly upset by this
hostility and resolved to avoid antagonizing religious intransigents for
the rest of his career.[65]

Electra: Galdós and the Anarchists

Neither La Regenta nor exposé novels of lesser caliber impeded a revival
of authoritarian sexuality in the late nineteenth century, spearheaded by
Jesuits and flanked by other orders involved in primary and secondary
education. The consequences would be endless. As Payne found, "Thousands of former students among the middle classes reacted against the
form of education they had received, once they reached their maturity.
Whether or not it was the result of this kind of personal experience,
revulsion against a perceived pedagogical backwardness later became
central to the thinking of the intellectual leaders of the new anticlericalism."[66] Constancia de la Mora, for example, the granddaughter of a
famous conservative Catholic politician, "included in her autobiography
a brief but passionate denunciation of stifling years endured at the colegio of the Slaves of the Sacred Heart in Madrid."[67] At the same time,
however, there were numerous former students, especially alumni of the
pontifical universities, who maintained close ties to their beloved alma
maters and helped to preserve a Catholic mentality among the middle
and upper classes in Spain. During the latter years of the nineteenth century and the first decades of the twentieth, the grateful former students
outnumbered but did not always outmaneuver the disaffected ones.[68]

Most of Spain's liberals were not anarchists, but they often emulated
the anarchist combination of erotics and anticlericalism and spoke out
against the continuing influence of the clerical faction. Exacerbating
the problem were hundreds of French monks and friars who settled

in Spain after the French government's radical exclaustration laws—suppression of religious orders went much further in France than in Spain at this time. In 1900 a conservative Spanish government approved the proposed marriage of Princess María de las Mercedes to the ultra-Catholic and ultramontane Don Carlos de Borbón. Liberals were outraged, and their fury mounted after a public scolding by Father Montaña, confessor to the queen mother and moral guardian of the future King Alfonso XIII. The priest was dismissed but the whole government came tumbling down in January 1901, with concomitant suspension of the Spanish parliament. Fox reports that the Spanish liberal press began a campaign against the collusion of clericalism and monarchy, publishing articles with edifying headlines like "The Jesuit Is the Enemy" and "I Hate Jesuits."[69]

Adding fuel to the fire was a celebrated court case that pitted the Society of Jesus against parental rights. A Jesuit priest named Father Cermeño had secretly convinced a young woman named Adelaida Ubao to become a nun without the her mother's consent. The mother, a wealthy socialite, retained the legal services of Nicolás Salmerón, famous liberal and president of the short-lived First Republic twenty-five years earlier. The lines of this nationally prominent custody battle could not have been drawn more clearly. The mother and her distinguished attorney were temporarily stymied by the stubborn resistance of the Jesuits and of the young novitiate Adelaida. The case, scheduled to be heard by the Spanish equivalent of the Supreme Court in 1901, was a liberal cause célèbre and Fox believes that it was the main inspiration behind the most notorious anticlerical play ever produced—penned by the premier Spanish anticlerical himself, Benito Pérez Galdós. This play, entitled *Electra*, allows us to probe the unconscious factors at play in progressive Spain's war against authoritarian sexuality.

In the manner of *Doña Perfecta* (which Galdós made into a play in 1896, much to the chagrin of the Church), *Electra* presents a family drama centering around access to the mind and body of an eighteen-year-old girl. The clerical element is symbolized by Don Salvador Pantoja, a "reverend friend" dressed in black who exercises a powerful influence over the charitable aristocrats on whose estate most of the action transpires. We are made to understand that Electra might be the result of a sin of impurity committed years before by Pantoja, who is now obsessed with preserving the girl's virtue whether she wants it or not. The comely teenager resents Pantoja's interest and protection—she says she feels "horribly weighed down by the consciences of other people."[70] (This line always got a strong ovation during public performances of the play.) Pantoja works closely with the mother superior of a local convent, Sor

Bárbara de la Cruz, to save Electra from bad company, for example, the liberal Marqués de Ronda who urges Don Urbano (the girl's uncle and legal guardian) to resist the excessive piety of his wife, Evarista. Once again we encounter the theme of the affluent female religious addict with maximum authority in the domestic sphere, but who is still putty in the hands of narrow clerical interests.

On the brighter side, Electra is able to consolidate her inner aspirations of freedom through friendship with the liberal hero of the play, Máximo, a young scientist who is gradually falling in love with her. Here we have a schematic replay of Pepe Rey's struggle to liberate the daughter of Doña Perfecta, but fortunately times have changed and Electra is less "fascinated" than her Galdosian predecessor and far more aware of the harm that good people do.

ELECTRA: They want to nullify me, enslave me, reduce me to something . . . angelical. I don't understand it.
MÁXIMO (vehemently): Don't let them, for God's sake. Electra, defend yourself.
ELECTRA: What do you suggest in order to escape them?
MÁXIMO (without hesitation): Independence!

Pantoja's obsession with sexual chastity combines with his mania for control as the de facto custody battle heats up. "I must have her under my dominion, in a saintly and paternal way," says Pantoja to Evarista. "Let her recognize that she is obliged to suffer for those who gave her life, and by purifying herself she will help those of us who were bad to obtain forgiveness." Pantoja is at his most "jesuitical" when he tells a white lie to Electra to make her think that her beloved Máximo might really be her brother. Terror that her love might be incestuous propels Electra into a state of extreme dissociation (much like the one suffered by Rosarito, Doña Perfecta's daughter), and the teenager is immediately rushed to . . . a convent.

Máximo, as the latter-day reincarnation of Pepe Rey, feels righteous rage growing within him (to which Pantoja responds with the classic martyrological stubbornness we first saw in the priest of Orbajosa). "You are driving us all mad!" Máximo shouts at the sinister Pantoja. "Who but you would have had the diabolical power to spoil my character, dragging me into these terrible fits of cholera?" And later, "If you are trying to make a murderer out of me, you will succeed," and shortly thereafter he simply states "Hay que matarle"—"He has to be killed." And then again, shortly thereafter, "That man, that monster, he has to be killed." The Marqués de Ronda sounds a note of caution:

MARQUÉS: Not so fast, son. We should imitate him, be as astute, insidious, persevering.

MÁXIMO: No, let us be like me, sincere, direct, valiant. Let us go undisguised against the enemy. Let's destroy him if we can, or suffer ourselves to be destroyed by him . . . but once and for all, in a single action, in a single charge, with a single blow. Him or us.

When the Marqués recommends clearheaded and efficient means, Máximo can only respond: "Yes, the most efficient ones of all: set fire to this convent and set fire to Madrid."

More provocative and potentially deadly lines could hardly be imagined. We have reached a turning point in our study of religious abuse and anticlericalism in Spain, for now the respected gray eminence of Spanish letters is pandering to the most puerile sentiments of the public with what for us is a transparent Oedipal rescue fantasy. To Pantoja's stated ambition to save Electra from evil adults we have Máximo's corresponding drive to save her from the hypnotic influence of the Church—all in concrete and Manichaean terms as unevolved and simplistic as the anticlerical dramas of the Romantics six decades earlier. Let's kill the repressive father-figure who is hypnotizing and blocking access to the beautiful innocent teenaged girl.

Literary critics agree that "in order to achieve and maintain a popularity as great as his, Galdós remained very attentive to the tastes of the reading public, not to serve them but to make use of them and try to dignify them."[71] This cannot be said of *Electra*. Far beyond the requirements of plot or stagecraft, Galdós had reduced a very complex problem to the most elementary schemata possible—family ones, naturally, or dysfunctional family ones, with rigidity disguised in self-congratulatory liberal poses. One problem with intellectuals is their tendency to forget how literal-minded people can be. So when some fine young man standing on a stage in Madrid exclaims in good Castilian that the Church must be destroyed or that priests must be killed, there will be consequences unforeseen by the playwrights. Did his financial problems motivate the elderly Galdós to write what young parlor anarchists wanted to hear?[72] Fox reproduces the article in which a young firebrand journalist, Ramiro de Maeztu, recounts the emotions of the dress rehearsal of the play. Maeztu unhesitatingly refers to the character Pantoja as *el jesuita* or *el neo* (short for *neocatólico*) and recounts that whenever the bad guy appears on stage "our compressed hatred explodes."[73] There was delirious cheering every time the actor playing Máximo shouted his "Hay que matarle" line. Maeztu unwittingly paints a chilling portrait of Madrid's radical set as they identify not with the sensible liberal Marqués but with the hotheaded Máximo.

The first performance of *Electra* set the theme and the ambience for hundreds of subsequent performances. It was a colossal public success and an opportunity for radicals to shout "Down with the Jesuits!" or sing antimonarchical ditties during the performance. When the liberals returned to power in March 1901, Sagasta formed what was popularly known as his Electra cabinet. Small but vocal anticlerical demonstrations accompanied the play to the provinces, and in Bilbao, Seville, Barcelona, and Cádiz there were serious disturbances, followed by troop movements and declarations of martial law. The unhinged panegyrics of liberal newspapers guaranteed that the mediocre play would become a best-selling book as well.

One small note of sanity would still be heard from a recovering parlor anarchist, the young Martínez Ruiz, who must have been insufficiently schooled in basic principles of scapegoating. Azorín wrote that the huge success of *Electra* profoundly discouraged him because it made manifest the immaturity and frivolity of his country's liberals.

Yes, it is a great shame. Galdós must be laughing inside at this poor ignorant Spain, so vulgar, so fanatical, where in order to make art reach the heart of the people you have to prostitute it and make it a lackey of religious and political programs. And it is a sure thing that if four or six phrases had been omitted from the drama, it would never have won the fevered acclamations of the public and the insubstantial flattery of the press.[74]

In a heated reply Maeztu accuses Martínez Ruiz of collaborating with the church to discredit both Galdós and radical writers, and insinuates that his rival might even be helping the Jesuits in the Adelaida Ubao case, the very same custody battle that inspired *Electra*. At the Spanish Supreme Court hearing held one week after the melodrama's premiere, the family attorney Salmerón introduced two old letters written by the teenaged Adelaida Ubao to the Jesuit Father Cermeño,

in which she told of her love for a young man and her doubts about her religious vocation. Salmerón described the actions of the Jesuit as "moral kidnapping." During and after the hearing there were popular demonstrations in practically every neighborhood of Madrid. The judges deliberated for several days, during which the people of Madrid continued to participate in the street protests. Finally, the decision was announced in favor of Salmerón and the family, by a vote of five to two, and the young woman was returned to her family.[75]

Later Maeztu took credit for this outcome, writing that his applause and enthusiasm were meant not only to praise Galdós but also "to liberate the deceived señorita Ubao from the convent along with thousands of other unfortunate ones who purge in perpetual cloister their credulity or their physiological squalor."[76]

After three years of further psychological growing pains, Martínez Ruiz published his "Todos frailes" article in Madrid's progressive *Alma Española* (1904). Commissioned to write an anticlerical diatribe, Azorín confesses that he no longer has the passion to do so, adding that in reality we are all a little like the friars—sad, resigned, spiritually empty. This is the closest thing we can find to an adoption of Melanie Klein's "depressive position" among Spain's intelligentsia, and, depressingly, the example was not followed. Fox finds it amusing that one conservative Catholic newspaper declared Galdós to be "today's most dangerous liberal," but, in historical retrospective, we are compelled to concur with that evaluation. Though proclaimed by the radical youth of his time as a hero, Galdós had done his country a grave disservice, lending his pen and prestige to polarizing messages that were taken quite literally by the wrong people. The messages reached not only parlor anarchists but also the dispossesed, nonphilosophical variety, the ones most likely to organize their worldview along millenarian lines: men victimized by the penal code or slapped around by the army's anal-sadists; humiliated men with a thirst for vengeance. Delgado argues that historians' traditional distinction between "cultured" and "popular" anticlericalism" is impertinent, an illusion and a false problem, since what even the most philosophical anticlericals wrote became a rationalization for people who wanted to pulverize icons and martyrize priests.[77]

The message did not travel quite so directly from respected authors to organized cells of arsonists and murderers. Some credit, if that is the word, must be given to unscrupulous demagogues like the Catalan politician Alejandro Lerroux. Lerroux had first won over the working classes of Barcelona with his articles and ardent speeches denouncing the torture at Montjuïc and similar affairs, going on from there to recommend the sexual liberation of the convents. He reached out to disaffected petit-bourgeois professionals, resentful students, and fellow journalists to form his own *Partido Radical,* then perfected his propaganda techniques with a team of semiprofessional orators. A strategic alliance with the real anarchists was the next step. As Joan Ullman relates, by the turn of the century a significant number of anarchists had despaired of terrorism as an effective tactic; the new strategy called for the infiltration and subsequent manipulation of labor unions, and educational activities designed to prepare a future generation for revolution.[78] Many of these anarchists and ex-anarchists joined forces with *lerrouxismo* as the only middle-class movement that sympathized with their utopian dreams. Proletarian women known as *damas rojas* collaborated with somewhat better-heeled women known as *damas radicales* to propagate advanced social ideas.

Lerroux's crack demagogues came to be known as *comecuras,* or "priest-eaters." One of them recommended putting Jesuits in cages on the streets before strangling them; Lerroux himself urged the workers to "exterminate without pity." [79] The corrupt cacique of Catalan republicanism is most notorious for his rabble-rousing speech of 1906 in which he called upon Spanish youth to raze churches and impregnate nuns.

Young barbarians of today: Sack the decadent and miserable civilization of this luckless land; destroy its temples, finish off its gods, lift up the veils of the novitiates and elevate them to the category of mothers [a pun] in order to make the race more virile. Don't stop at tombs or altars. There is nothing sacred in this world. The people are the slaves of the Church. The Church must be destroyed. Fight, kill, die! [80]

The Church could not effectively counter such diatribes nor achieve rapprochement with the increasingly restive workers and their radical allies. As Payne explains, priests "often found it physically and emotionally awkward even to approach workers, and their manner was often detested by the latter for its apparent condescension. Catholic schools and social centers were frequently scorned for snobbery, class bias, and lack of concern for workers' problems." [81] At least these accusations are plausible; in the actual recorded incidents of sudden riotous attacks against the clergy or local churches, the mob's rationale was absurdly fantastic: the Jesuits had poisoned the wells, the nuns had hidden treasure in their cellars, the Franciscans had stockpiled an arsenal, and so forth. Sometimes the motive for the frenzy could not be articulated at all. Mobs burned eighty religious buildings of one type or another during Barcelona's Semana Trágica (Tragic Week)—a strange outcome for what started as draft riots. During an assault on an orphanage maintained by the Paulist order, the following conversation was overheard between a nun and a rioter:

"But what do you want?"
"We want a republic!"
"And what's that?"
"How should I know!"
"But what's going to happen to the poor children we take care of here?"
"That's not my problem!" [82]

The rioters did not rape the sisters, but they did dig up and display more than fifty mummified corpses of nuns who had been buried in the convents.[83]

The last effective leader of the Conservative party, Eduardo Dato, fell to bullets in 1921; anarchosyndicalists assassinated the Cardinal Archbishop of Zaragoza in 1922. By 1923, writes historian Eduardo González Calleja, the crumbling Restauración had incubated every one of the violent subversive strategies that would hatch out during the Second Republic.[84] "Lerroux could not extinguish the revolutionary fervor he had unleashed," concludes Ullman,[85] and the same should be said for numerous writers, academics, and political leaders playing with dynamite during the first decades of the twentieth century. Blasco Ibáñez, for example, had spent his youth denouncing a "clerical conspiracy against moral progress in Spain." By the 1920s this best-selling author had a new habitus, hence a more moderate political stance, and finally stopped demonizing the Church; but the obsessional messages he had helped to propagate were to have fatal consequences in Spain. They were also useful, incidentally, to the Ku Klux Klan in the United States.[86] Under no circumstances should the intellectuals who deliberately sought to inflame passions be let off the hook, ethically speaking. Anticlericalism was a legitimate cause whenever it attempted to liberate people from negative religious messages or clergy abuse of one kind or another; it was illegitimate and counterproductive when it served to foster terror.

Chapter 3
Spanish Sexual Politics, 1901–1939

In Spain the struggle to recover from authoritarian sexuality cannot be separated from the political struggle waged by the modernizing urban middle classes, undersized as they were, against more conservative or traditionalist social groups. The crisis caused by a disastrous war with the United States (1898) and the subsequent loss of Spanish colonial possessions contributed to the emergence of new attitudes toward sexuality in Spain. I do not make this assertion frivolously; when one strand of hegemonic discourse begins to unravel, others often follow.

National identity conflicts led Spaniards in many directions. One of them was the new erotic awareness that informed the politicized essays and novels of the so-called Generation of 1898 and gave new impetus to the entire counterhegemonic discourse that had been brewing during the final quarter of the nineteenth century. Like all forms of discourse, the fin-de-siècle erotic discourse in Spain sought to build an emotional and ideological consensus around a set of values defined in opposition to another set of values.[1] In its definitive form (as embodied in the journal *Alma Española*, 1903–1904), Spanish reformist or regenerationist thought is petit bourgeois, republicano (antimonarchist), decidedly and often ferociously anticlerical, less repressed although still quite moralistic, and dedicated to improving the condition of Spanish women.[2]

In this uniquely Spanish synthesis of anticlerical social reform movements we can situate the tremendous spurt in the production and consumption of erotic novels, images, and songs in the period 1900 through 1936. In reality we are dealing with a politico-erotico-literary-business project first perfected by Felipe Trigo (1864–1916). Trigo and the writers who emulated him set out to defy sexual authoritarianism and oppressive gender roles. They spurned not only the discreet approach to matters erotic adopted by Galdós or Pardo Bazán but also the bohemian *modernismo* of Ramón de Valle-Inclán. The new breed of Spanish writer maintained that naturalistic or decadent treatments of sexuality did not adequately convey the mystical power of the orgasm (all of this in advance of the theories of Wilhelm Reich), so they made sexual desire the hub around which all narrative action had to revolve, including stylistic elements, language, stories, and values. The whole process was to be guided by a paradoxical notion of physical love as a quasi-spiritual ideal. They reached out to the mass reading public and proposed that the "sexual question" was really the central one for Spaniards. Happiness lay in the satisfaction of desire, not in its repression by religion; the commandment to love thy neighbor was to be taken literally. The route to a better future for Spain could be read like a map in the progressive erotic novels they were writing—and selling like hotcakes.[3]

A hard-working military doctor, Trigo had achieved celebrity status as the only survivor of an ambush on Mindanao Island perpetrated by Philippine nationalists in 1896; upon returning to Spain he was interviewed by every important periodical in the country. To the chagrin of his conservative commanding officers, the outspoken young doctor publicly attributed the growing disaster in Spain's overseas possessions to the influence of powerful religious orders like the Jesuits.[4] The whole experience inflamed his desire for national regeneration and whet his appetite for further fame. As a general practitioner in his native Extremadura during the following years, Trigo became increasingly convinced of the connection between many of his patients' symptoms and repressive sexual norms. Following his examination of one young rural woman, the doctor angrily declared:

Damn this job that obliges me to contemplate such miserable things! That girl will sicken and die before her fiancé gets a raise! . . . I might well have said to her mother: "Imbecile, your daughter is not lacking in life, she has too much of it, it's burning her, suffocating her since she was fifteen years old, driving her crazy with desire for love, coming back alone to her solitary, hateful virgin bed, while her boyfriend, the one who ignites her, goes off to finish the night on top of some prostitute!" But so you see, I give her iron drops and I charge her ten *duros*, because if I gave them the real prescription, to the mothers, for these poor virgins—and martyrs—, I'd have been condemned long ago as a shameless fool, and no one would come to my practice. Oh, what a farce life is![5]

In his *Entre naranjos* (1900), Vicente Blasco Ibáñez had portrayed a dying peasant girl who undertakes a fatal pilgrimage to the Virgen del Lluch rather than go to doctors who would force her into "shameful exhibitions of her sick organs."[6] The following year Trigo published his first novel, *Las ingenuas* (1901), subtitled "*novela de señoritas.*" It is a sociological, psychological, and gynecological examination of the Spanish female, as well as a spirited defense of adultery and a call for the abolition of conventional family values in general. Trigo ascribes most of the physical ailments of young female Spaniards to a defective clerical educational system, the Church-reinforced cult of virginity, and a backward concept of modesty that impeded proper feminine hygiene.

Trigo consciously wrote his novels for the young women of the modernizing middle classes who he hoped might one day be in a position to bring about a new order of things in Spain. Wholesome hygienic sex was not the only thing the doctor ordered. Trigo's prescription for Spanish women also recommended talking about sex openly in public, an activity that verged on scandal in early twentieth-century Spain, especially in the provinces.[7] The complete treatment, finally, required a moral emancipation—not an emancipation from morals, but an emancipation procured by the higher morality of sublime erotic love, far from the madding taboos their parents sought to impose.

Popular novels of the latter nineteenth century had dealt with erotic love as a theme, but not until Trigo's generation does the most progressive sector of the Spanish bourgeoisie seem ready to openly abandon religious connotations or referents and replace them with a new morality more in tune with their own lifestyle, a morality both worldly and idealistic. The old-fashioned amoral aristocratic libertine (like Don Juan or the lapsed Catholic Marqués de Bradomín, Valle-Inclán's great creation) is condemned, as is any form of lewd passion or perversion. A pure and virtuous desire is what the young need. Pleasure is greater when it is justified, when it forms part of an emancipatory social agenda. The sex act must be sublime; the orgasm has to have a higher moral meaning.

In all this the critic García Lara finds a troubling pusillanimity. He doubts that the new eroticism had really severed its ties to the older morality; he perceives in Trigo's fractured prose the presence of defense mechanisms designed to ward off intrusive personal anxieties of a sexual nature.[8] Even if this were true, Trigo represented an improvement over the sexophobic and pessimistic ideas to be found in more prestigious writers like Pío Baroja or Azorín. As García Lara himself points out, Trigo's literary practice was just the opposite of the Generation of 1898. The doctor's second novel, *La sed de amar* (1903) coincided in the market with Azorín's *La voluntad* and Baroja's *Camino de perfección*, both of which portray sex as a negative, will-sapping force. One clever critic referred to Baroja, Azorín, and Unamuno as "the three misogynists."[9] Compared to them, Trigo was both a feminist and an optimist. For him the royal road to national perfection was sexual emancipation. Ironically, American undergraduates are still saddled with the three misogynists in their Spanish literature classes, but it was Trigo and similar authors who were really being read by immense numbers of Spaniards who in so doing believed they were installing themselves at the intersection of "the sexual question" and "the social question" of their epoch, far from timid academic confines.

check

Lily Litvak finds Trigo's stance "extremely revolutionary for its time," since he believed that woman's social liberation had to be based on her erotic freedom and, by implication, her freedom from the moral theology of the Roman Catholic Church.[10] The Fathers stood squarely in the way of the kind of woman Spain needed. Many young women believed what they had heard during their years in convent schools, for instance, that a passionate kiss was enough to get them pregnant. Their ignorance in sexual matters was "absolute." Poorer women were actually more knowledgeable, partly because of the lack of privacy in working-class living quarters. For Trigo the middle-class Spanish women were all *ingenuas* (naive), the title of his 1901 novel. For them, he said, "it's all the same to obey the confessor or the pope and get married to Christ or their boyfriends." Trigo had to struggle not only with the clergy but with numerous medical doctors whose teachings about sex were influenced by the Church. For example, sins of the flesh were thought to be the major cause of cancer.

In *Jarrapellejos* (1914), his finest work, Trigo portrays provincial Spain as a land of corrupt politicians, clerical pandering and philandering, poverty, social injustice, and incompetent physicians. Trigo skillfully plays one ill off another to arrive at a global condemnation of Spanish sexual despotism and its hysterical milieu. The novel is especially sharp when revealing the tragicomic aspects of standards of female modesty entrenched in provincial Spain and personified by Pura, the daughter of the local parish priest of La Joya, Don Roque and his not-so-secret lover Doña María del Carmen (the mayor's wife). Throughout the first chapters of the novel Pura is under the inadequate care of Dr. Barriga, much sought after by the women of the middle class because he does not oblige them to disrobe during examinations. This tactic has led him to believe that Pura suffers from severe water retention. Scandal ensues when the less tactful but more competent Dr. Carrasco throws modesty to the winds, gives Pura a complete gynecological examination (as her girlfriends flee the room), and finds her eight months pregnant. The mother's plan to keep Pura pure by forcing her to wear ugly discolored underwear had failed. The priest Don Roque slaps Pura's mother and shouts, "Good-bye! Good-bye, María del Carmen. You have not known how to watch out for the innocence of my daughter!"[11] In the meantime, we discover a principal forge of future rebels and terrorists in the novel's descriptions of horrible rural poverty and neglected children in Extremadura.[12] The conservative Catholic doctors satirized by Trigo ushered in a new era of authoritarian gynecology in Spain following Franco's victory, as I discuss in Chapter 4.

The very name Felipe Trigo symbolized liberation for the body politic and intolerable license for the celibate mind. The golden age of the erotic novel runs from approximately 1910 through 1925. Were we to limit our attention to the mass-market erotic novel alone, we might come away thinking that popular culture eroticism was solidly anchored in moral earnestness. As García Lara is quick to point out, the erotic novel was just one among many avenues explored by the Spanish urban middle classes in their interest in and desire to resolve their society's "sexual question."[13] Hence the advantage of looking at other vehicles of the discourse: in popular urban theatrical comedies and songs, we find forces of a more physical, sensual, and above all playful nature — less edifying than the erotically moral novels, perhaps, but liberating and therapeutic in their own way.

The final years of the nineteenth century were characterized by a blurring of the borders among the different genres of Spain's lyric theater and the appearance of new formats like music hall and *varietés*. Out of this creative chaos will come the *cuplé*, which can best be defined as the type of song sung by a *cupletista*, a sexy female singer. To study the evolution of this music is to grasp one of the essential keys of Spanish culture from 1900 to 1936, according to French Hispanist Serge Salaün.[14] Salaün is struck by the fact that, in contrast to his native France, where *vedettes* at the turn of the century could be either male or female, Spain was characterized by a rather rigid division of labor: only women sang, danced, and exhibited themselves in the new shows (men were behind the scenes composing, arranging, and managing), and this situation was to remain relatively stable until well after the Spanish Civil War. During the period 1900–1936, thousands of young women tried their luck at some type of public singing — zarzuela, *género chico, género ínfimo, varietés*, music-hall, *salón, cafés cantantes*, cabarets, and so on. Naturally there are differences between these genres but they are not germane to the present discussion. Salaün says that the general tendency was to perform songs in smaller and smaller locales, thereby creating a physically closer and psychologically more intense fantasy relation with the female singers. Thus the demand for them greatly increased during the first decades of the twentieth century.

A good deal of disguised prostitution went on in these venues of popular music as well. The term *señoritas de alterne* was coined to describe single women who alternated singing and dancing on the stage with behind-the-scenes sexual services to the customers. French girls were in great demand for this work throughout Europe, especially in

Spain and Portugal; hoodwinked by employment announcements in newspapers and led on by their dreams of fame, they often woke up to find themselves in a very different situation. Salaün underlines that this was not the norm but a tendency, the dark side of show business during this period. Spain's neutrality during World War I enabled its major cities to become Europe's centers of sexual high jinks for several years. In the 1920s many cabarets and music halls continued to be thinly disguised clearinghouses for prostitution. In addition, affluent provincial hedonists organized excursions to famous bordellos in Spain's large and middle-sized cities. As the noted Spanish writer Juan Eslava points out, the higher prices paid for sex acts in northern urban areas (Madrid, Barcelona, Bilbao, Zaragoza, and so on) led numerous poor women from Andalusia to migrate there, changing their looks to aspire to a more select clientele, losing weight, bathing more frequently, cutting their hair to the latest flapper fashion.[15] In other words, prostitution was a modernizing force for significant numbers of rural women. In keeping with such progress, there was a spectacular increase in venereal disease in the late 1920s and early 1930s; the government responded with shock campaigns to increase public awareness of safe-sex methods and the dangers of promiscuity.

The vast majority of the young Spanish women who filled the saloons and cabarets were of humble origin with little or no education. Some had been orphaned at an early age, others (like La Fornarina) had been forced into prostitution; many were illiterate. Gossip had it that during the filming of *Carmen*, the star cupletista Raquel Meller tried to contact Prosper Mérimée to discuss certain modifications she wanted to make in the script. The great exception to the rule was La Goya, who spoke four languages, wrote, painted, played the piano, and was immediately dubbed *la tonadillera intelectual*—"the intellectual singer." Ironically it was the untutored Meller who became the first great international star produced by Spain in the twentieth century and the first star anywhere to market perfumes and clothing under her own name. For every woman who reached that degree of fame, hundreds remained in the trenches. Salaün notes that the generally low cultural level of the singers made them much more dependent on the men who ran Spanish show business. It also made them easy prey, he affirms, for the most conformist and even reactionary ideas: Salaün labels the women "jingoists" and "ultra-Catholics." Apparently the vast majority of singers and dancers abandoned the stage as soon as they were able to contract an honorable bourgeois matrimony—often with a businessman or even an occasional aristocrat who had become enamored of them during their public years.

It turns out that the majority of women singers, even the most famous, did not have good singing voices. Unlike Italian operas with their bel canto virtuosity, Spanish zarzuelas had been characterized by an easily memorizable melodic line, duos and trios rathers than solo parts, the great importance of the chorus, and, above all, the overwhelming presence of mezzos and baritones that abound in Spain. All things considered, Spain's lyric theater traditions were relatively undemanding, and the new fin-de-siècle genres were less demanding still. Salaün is quick to point out, however, that the Spanish zarzuela tradition more than makes up for any shortcomings with its strong emphasis on diction, expected to be as agile and intelligible as possible. The cupletistas used costumes, saucy gestures, and as much emotive talent as possible to augment their good pronunciation.

The French Hispanist's richest insights have to do with the first great epoch of the cuplé, from approximately 1900 through 1910, when it was identified almost exclusively with *sicalipsis*, a neologism first seen on a theatrical bill in Barcelona that had clumsily misspelled *apocalipsis* in an effort to sell tickets. The word (and variants like *sicalíptico* or *sicalipsismo*) spread quickly through the world of Spanish show business and journalism and came to mean anything naughty, erotic, or pornographic in connection with any size musical production or publication.[16] The trend had actually begun in the waning years of the nineteenth century, when zarzuela producers used scantily clad chorus girls to attract a masculine public and boost revenues. In an 1891 production, *El monaguillo* (The Altar Boy), Luisa Campo "provoked an erotic frenzy" by singing her song seated on a burro with her calf showing. Between 1897 and 1901 (precisely the years of Spain's international prostration), major theaters of Madrid and Barcelona began to include humorous and erotic numbers on an ever growing basis. The phenomenon quickly achieved a stable and lucrative format with the cupletistas who, in league with theater or nightclub owners and composers, competed furiously to see how far *sicalipsis* could be taken. The public rushed to see attractive women wearing ever skimpier costumes singing ever naughtier songs.

Masculine tastes of the times were unanimously in favor of singers and actresses who today might be classified as overweight. Spanish journalists never used the word *gorda* ("fat") but instead dozens of pleasant-sounding metaphors to describe the ample and voluptuous dimensions of the cupletistas. Conchita Catalá, for example, possessed "an impressive exuberance, accentuated in the posterior region," and La Guadita boasted "abundant and sculptural bulges as hard as cement," while Rosita Rodoreda "awakened mad appetites with her massive and overflowing flesh."[17] Salaün himself is comfortable with these women in an ideological sense. For him they incarnated a more lighthearted, jocular, and genuinely popular kind of eroticism, a feminine image much closer to the women that men of the times actually courted and married: "They evoke attainable roundnesses and a happy, charming corpulence. Perhaps this is the most promising epoch of Spanish song, its authentic character, and the one most likely to massively foment a new sociability of the body in Spain, with all the limitations one might think of but nevertheless more laicized, more extroverted, and freer."[18]

But all good things must come to an end, it would seem. A different type of cuplé emerged between 1911 and 1925, at the hands of stars like Raquel Meller and La Goya. The tragic themes of the second-generation songs were accompanied by, and may even have helped bring about, a radical change in the prevailing female body type. This phase is characterized by the decreasing volume and increasing prestige of the cupletistas, sought after by the cream of Spanish authors, journalists, painters, composers, diplomats, politicians, aristocrats, and wealthy bullfighters.

The painter Julio Romero de Torres (1874–1930) must be mentioned in this context, for his sensual portraits of the thin and thinly clad women of Córdoba became the industry standard for Spain. Though decried by the bishops, he cannot in my view be associated with a *new* erotic discourse so much as an aggiornamento of the old one, with its sexual fatalism and its idealization of virginity: the same ingenuous provincial females criticized by Trigo were rendered in loving tones by Romero de Torres. Trigo's sister, also a medical doctor, posed for Romero de Torres's painting *Judit*, part of his series of biblical femmes fatales.[19] The artist produced numerous paintings of beautiful young nuns with come-hither expressions and *cupletistas* with saintly, mystical expressions. He was particularly close to the flamenco world, whose emotive art forms were closely tied to the lifestyle of racialist Andalusian playboys. Romero de Torres played a major role in the marketing of the image of the sultry Spanish woman in twentieth-century Spain, before and after the civil war. His death in the spring of 1930 was followed by a multitude of public acts of homage; his name and legend were circulated in numerous songs, flamenco shows, and musicals during the Second Republic, including Fernández Ardavín's *The Flames of the Convent* (1935), a reference not to the burning of a nunnery but to the fires of female passion burning inside. So great was the dead painter's prestige that in 1932 a gang of underclass arsonists risked their lives to rescue one of his paintings from a stately mansion they had just set on fire.[20]

Erotic discourse advanced steadily on many fronts. That a woman had a right to an orgasm was increasingly recognized by Spanish men, and the result was a burgeoning market for products designed to enhance or prolong male vigor. Beauty contests came to Spain in 1929 and proliferated thereafter, promoted by risqué magazines like *Vida Galante* and *Pentalfa*; erotic novels and defenses of free love routinely reached best-sellerdom.[21] In November 1932, Madrid's Editorial Fénix began to publish a sex education library designed for the general public and written by Angel Martín de Lucenay, a self-proclaimed "Diplomado en Sexología." In some sixty volumes of approximately one hundred pages each, Spaniards could finally learn everything they wanted to know about sex but had been too intimidated to ask. This amazing series was sold at local newsstands throughout the 1930s and can fairly be seen as the publishing culmination of the new erotic discourse in Spain, with its relentless demystification of monogamy, its description of birth control and amorous techniques, its treatment of sexual dysfunctions, and its stimulating vignettes of the exotic customs of primitive groups the world over. Only doctors had previously been privy to so much information in the Spanish-speaking world.[22]

Enlightened or at least intellectual forms of anticlericalism can be distinguished from vulgar ones. By the same token, a medical or philosophical erotic discourse can be contrasted with an illiterate one. In the first years of the Second Republic, sexy musical comedies and striptease spectacles were all the rage. Many took the advent of the latter as a measure of the maturity and modernity Spaniards had achieved. There was a tremendous market for female flesh, says Eslava, and many were the household maids or seamstresses who dreamed of occupying the erotic dreams of Spanish men (as represented on stage and screen) and getting rich in the process. In reviewing Madrid's first show with topless chorus girls, one journalist approvingly took note of "five girls who have had the authentically modern desire to hang their brassieres on the shelf of useless articles. . . . We cannot deny to those ten breasts that show themselves so generously, youthful and jiggling, all the importance they have as an unequivocal sign of progress."[23]

Seeking to nip budding feminist objections, another writer had stated that he saw no incompatability whatsoever between women's rights and "the opulence of their flesh. In fact, I believe that their flesh is precisely one of their rights."[24] Shortly after the topless breakthrough in Madrid some dancers in Seville went even further, appearing on stage with their nudity covered with only the fringes of a shawl. The climax of the spectacle, impatiently awaited by the male customers, was the *meneo*, wherein the girls exited the stage one by one "spasmodically wiggling their rearends to the beat of a drum," as the men in the audience shouted encouragement.[25] Clever theater producers quickly adapted their shows to the tenor of the times, as exemplified by the 1934 production of *Las comunistas*. In this zarzuela, an enterprising young woman seeks to establish the "libertarian communism of love" in a small town in Aragon; one of the musical numbers calls for the actress to do a languid striptease while clutching a banana and singing a Cuban rumba: "¡Dáme, negro, la banana! ¡Anda, negro, dámela!" (Give me, negro, the banana! Come on, negro, give it to me!). "An indisputable masterpiece," Salaün notes sardonically.[26] The eroticism of the thirties was increasingly graphic and visual: a beautiful girl, usually adorned with only a Phrygian cap, was the very symbol of the Second Republic on the posters of 1931 and thereafter. Spain's first feature-length pornographic movie, *Carne de fieras*, was in production by 1936—only to be interrupted during editing by General Franco's revolt.[27]

With regard to the commercialization of the new erotic discourse, we can say that supply had met demand. In my view, the spectacular growth of an entrepreneurial class whose prosperity derived from the violation of Catholic sexual norms was the twentieth-century equivalent of the absentee landowning class spawned by nineteenth-century disentailment: two forms of wealth created at the expense of the Church. Erotic novelists, singers, artists, and models all contributed in their own way to the undermining of the moral authority of the priests. That said, it would seem reasonable to conjecture that Church-sanctioned sexual repression was a secret incitement that virtually guaranteed a huge market hungry for satisfaction and new erotic materials. But such are the logical contradictions of authoritarian sexuality and the psychocultural forces it sets in motion.

The Sacred Family Order Under Siege

The waves of eroticism splashing over Spanish culture during the first decades of the twentieth century were bracing in themselves, but they were also the continuation of politics by other means for many liberal-minded citizens. Sexual attitudes and gender roles had become a battleground where modernizing Spaniards struggled against the inertia of tradition and the formidable educational and financial power of the Church.

The great revival in Catholic teaching during the first decades of the twentieth century streamlined the implantation of ancient sexual pessimism in young minds. Repressive pedagogy was reinforced by new lay sodalities dedicated to the Virgin. "All these Marian congregations laid heavy emphasis on personal piety and chastity," writes Frances Lannon. "Similar attitudes of defensive piety and suffocating prurience were inculcated in dozens of similar sodalities."[28] Special activities were organized to keep the young people from meeting peers who attended laicized mixed schools, and great efforts were expended to keep them away from theaters, cinemas, swimming pools, and beaches.

One of the most successful sodalities was the Alianza en Jesús por María, founded in 1925 by the Basque priest Antonio Amundarain. By 1931 there were chapters all over Spain, with a significant percentage of the girls going on to become nuns. As William Christian notes, "With this order Amundarain worked to preserve women from corrupt modern society, especially its sexual side. And he tried to ensure that these women at least would not make modern society more corrupt. Some women have told me that in those years in the confessional he concentrated heavily on the sins of impurity. And in this sense the Alianza was an extreme expression of a reigning preoccupation."[29] Young women under the control of conservative priests were made to atone for the sins of young women not under their control. In the 1930s the sexophobic Amundarain would play a key role in the propagation of the Ezkioga visions of the Virgin—described by Christian as "a kind of dialogue between divinities and the anticlerical left."

Though greatly alarmed by the first epoch of Spanish history in which pornography was mass-distributed, prelates and priests of the 1920s were living in what for them was the sunshine of the Primo de Rivera dictatorship. The general was Catholic to a fault: his plan to make Jesuit university degrees the equivalent of state ones led to student revolts (at the public universities) that contributed to the downfall of his regime. The Church hierarchy was to pay dearly for its support of the relatively benign dictatorship, writes Payne:

> Even though so major a Catholic organ as *El Debate* had gone into opposition in 1928, the identity of Catholicism with a rightist authoritarian regime made the Church a prime target of the republican reaction that developed. After the experience of the seven-year dictatorship, the most liberal members of the middle classes were more convinced than ever that Catholicism was the bulwark of authoritarianism and reaction and hence the main obstacle to progress and enlightenment. In somewhat parallel fashion, urban workers and the southern rural proletariat saw the Church as the cultural and moral support of the possessing classes, the principal dike against revolution. Thus when the monarchy collapsed in April 1931, the Church would find itself even more exposed and vulnerable than at the start of the liberal regime.[30]

A hundred years earlier the bishops had been forced to contend with proletarian mobs and the expropriative impulse of the laicist liberal bourgeoisie. Under the Concordato of 1851—still in effect in 1931—the Church accepted disentailment but retained the right to acquire properties. Catholicism was reaffirmed as the only legal religion of Spain and the guiding moral principle of education. The Spanish state had agreed to pay not only for the upkeep of churches but for the salaries of the priests as well; the Vatican was determined to hold any and every Spanish government to this pledge. Following the ill-fated war with the United States, thousands of Spanish missionaries returned from Cuba and the Philippines; new religious centers were constructed, and the Spanish Church became wholeheartedly capitalist. One Catalan businessman claimed that it controlled one third of the nation's capital resources. Historian Hugh Thomas cites a 1921 catechism that poses the question "What kind of sin is it to vote for a liberal candidate?" and answers "A mortal sin." But to the question "Is it a sin for a Catholic to read a liberal newspaper?" the right answer is "He may read the stock market quotations."[31]

Thomas is quick to add that early-twentieth-century Spanish Catholicism was charitable to a fault and that orders like the Jesuits and the Augustines administered excellent schools and universities. At the same time, notes Payne, half a million families or some three million individuals of northern Spain belonged to the well-run cooperatives and credit associations of the Confederación Nacional Católica Agraria, a Catholic farmers organization set up to improve life without disturbing the rural status quo (small landholdings mixed in with larger estates). Membership in the Confederation was "frequently structured around the local priest."[32] No such organization existed in the south, where the Church had long ago thrown in its lot with the richest landholders and thousands of hungry, landless laborers were being won over by anarchist group-fantasies.

The oligarchic clientelism of the Restauración could not and did not give way overnight to democracy or mass political mobilization. By the end of the 1920s Spanish republicanism in a transitional stage, represented by some 450 "clubs" with more than 100,000 members: intellectuals, teachers, medical doctors like Felipe Trigo, craftsmen, journalists, office workers, and Freemasons (Spain's were considered the most anticlerical in Europe). The legitimate aspirations of these political activists, as well as their self-defeating passions and prejudices, were perfectly embodied by Manuel Azaña Díaz, a belletrist, orator, founder of his own party (Acción Republicana), and key figure in the Second Republic, which finally replaced the discredited Alphonsine monarchy. Azaña's personal grudge against the Church dated from his days as a schoolboy in the monastery of El Escorial.[33] In keeping with the legacy of *Electra*, many of Azaña's hyperbolic anticlerical utterances were phrased in terms of a national custody battle: the good parent had to keep the bad parent from brainwashing the child. As he put it in his most famous speech, "This constant pressure of the religious orders upon young consciences is exactly the secret of the political situation Spain finds itself in and which is our responsibility as republicans—not as republicans but simply as Spaniards—to prevent at all costs. Let no one come to me saying this is against freedom, because it is a question of public health."[34]

Feminist historian Danièle Bussy Genevois argues that the goal of the republicans was not social revolution; the architects of the Second Republic only wished to "bring an end to the excesses of the theocratic state" while avoiding the excesses of the new Soviet state and remaining respectful toward the institutions of marriage and family.[35] Too many people thought otherwise at the time, of course, with good cause. In order to fulfill their Oedipal rescue fantasy, Azaña and his allies needed to permanently alter Spanish family schemata by arranging for a quick divorce between church and state, with special attention to the forced de-Christianization of reproduction, family law, education, and marriage customs, and the promotion of a new divorce law. The parallels with the opening stages of the French Revolution are striking. Historian Lynn Hunt says that in Paris "differences over family policy divided a broadly defined political left, which proposed sweeping changes in family laws, from a broadly defined right, which resisted those changes."[36] In Spain, even more than in France, the projected divorce of church and state was not to go uncontested. It would lead to the worst civil war of modern times.

On the day of the official proclamation of the Republic (14 April 1931), the presence of large numbers of women in the spontaneous street celebrations seemed entirely fitting: many of the new leaders were personally and professionally concerned with alleviating the pains of menstruation and childbirth with new treatments imported from abroad.[37] But such praiseworthy ideals were obscured in less than a month by the smoke pouring out of some one hundred religious institutions—including grade schools—set on fire by small bands of extremists throughout Spain. Azaña excused his government's timidity and vacillation during the crisis by saying that all of the convents of Madrid were not worth the life of one republican.[38] More insightful republicans, like José Ortega y Gasset, Ramón Pérez de Ayala, and Gregorio Marañón, immediately described the destruction as "stupid" and "repulsive," a warning sign of the threat fanaticism posed to the new state: "To burn convents and churches does not show true republican zeal nor a progressive spirit, but rather a primitive or criminal fetishism that leads people both to adore material objects and to destroy them."[39] Even Alejandro Lerroux denounced the church burnings as a crime of demagogy. This was not a case of the pot calling the kettle black: the wily Catalan politician had greatly moderated his old anticlerical views.

The arson continued sporadically month after month because the arsonists knew they were going to get away with it—even when caught red-handed as Antonio Fernández Soto was in Madrid or Rafael García was in Seville. Worse still, in July 1931 the leftist secretary of labor Largo Caballero advised insurance agencies not to write any policies protecting religious institutions from fire or theft.[40] In the opinion of Ortega's successor Julián Marías, the new government's "strange respect for the despicable" was the first big step in the spiral that would lead to civil war;

it was at this point that large segments of Spanish society would begin to regard other large segments as irreconcilable.[41] The error was compounded when the ruling republicanos opted to play the blame game, outlawing not merely the monarchist newspaper *ABC* but also *El Debate*, the organ of Madrid's liberal Catholic intellectuals who were committed to both democracy and the welfare of the urban proletariat. In other words, groups that should have formed part of the democratic experiment were not only excluded but turned into scapegoats.

More farsighted revolutionaries, like Lenin or the Spanish socialist Pablo Iglesias, had argued that the real enemy was not the Church but capitalism; fomenting violent actions against religious institutions was "a typical bourgeois deformation" and an attempt to distract the working masses from the real issues.[42] As an anarchist sympathizer, anthropologist Manuel Delgado rejects this view, finding instead a "hidden logic" of rational modernization even in the actions of brutal anticlerical mobs. They embodied, he says, Spain's tardy embrace of the healthy purifying impulses of protestantism and urban renewal.[43] Delgado's call to erase the conventional distinction between intellectual and popular forms of anticlericalism was not meant to expose the pandering of the intellectuals but to legitimate the church-burning mobs, assimilate them to higher cultural spheres, and assign them a role in the march of civilization itself: "From the end of the eighteenth century onwards, iconoclastic violence in Spain increasingly answered to a need that a significant portion of non-powerful classes made their own: to modify and urgently redefine the totality of the existing cultural order in the direction of incorporating themselves to the principles of Modernity."[44] I find this difficult to swallow.

The inexpert Azaña and his fellows had not truly taken the measure of their "enemy." It was not simply that in 1931 the Spanish church boasted one thousand male and four thousand female religious communities, with sixty thousand nuns, twenty thousand monks, and thirty-five thousand priests.[45] Then and now, the majority of Spaniards were not actively practicing Catholics; most men went into church only for baptisms, marriages, and funerals—this much was admitted by the Church. But it was an imprudent provocation for Azaña to proclaim on 13 October 1931 that "España ha dejado de ser católica"—Spain has ceased to be Catholic. That night he smugly confided to his diary that the speech had gone very well indeed, "like a dream," adding that "Lerroux heaped praise upon me." This was both ominous vanity and wishful thinking. As Spanish sociologist Gustavo Bueno puts it, Azaña and his fellows were not nearly as Machiavellian as the times required.[46] Instead they were courageously clumsy enough to alienate the substantial part of Spain that *was* still Catholic. By creating an atmosphere that nurtured hatred and fantasies of violent revenge, Azaña and other liberals needlessly radicalized their adversaries and sowed the seeds of their own destruction.

The new government of the Second Republic was not myopic and maladroit in everything. It quickly promulgated a large number of emancipatory decrees and laws based on progressive ideas dating as far back as 1789. This vast catching-up process aspired to open up new psychological spaces for women and put Spain in the vanguard of parliamentary democracies of the time; the initial republican period acted on the same ideals of love and feminism defended by Felipe Trigo and many others since the turn of the century. The proponents of the new erotic discourse had finally come to power—and they did not intend to let the Church forget it.

Where the liberal bourgeois government gave an inch, Marxist and anarchist organizations took a mile. Throughout 1931 the covers of mass-circulation magazines like *La Traca* depicted priests and nuns being driven from Spain or thrown out of windows. In subsequent years their pages would feature numerous cartoons of clergymen engaged in lewd behavior. As Lynn Hunt observes, political pornography provides important clues to "the psychosymbolics of the revolutionary imagination."[47] The graphic imputations of clergy sexual misconduct widely distributed in Spain during the 1930s have their antecedents in hundreds of obscene images circulated during the French Revolution that depict the aristocrats, Marie-Antoinette in particular, in all manner of sexually aberrant poses. "The pre-1789 pamphlets tell dirty stories in secret; after 1789 the rhetoric of the pamphlets begins self-consciously to solicit a wider audience. The public no longer 'hears' courtier rumors through the print medium; it now 'sees' degeneracy in action."

The psychogenesis of anticlerical pornography is as follows: The Spanish clergy were forged by, and helped to forge, a culture that was self-consciously moralistic but quite lacking in moral "breathing room." Far too many Spanish priests and nuns (the pseudoparents) had specialized in avoiding self-disgust by locating and harshly criticizing "disgusting" elements in school children—girls riding bicycles, for instance.[48] Some children or adolescents learned to ward off this degraded self-concept through a reversal of the original role-relationship model. In the words of obscenity expert Robert Stoller: "Victim is to become victor by dumping the dark, moist, smelly, hidden, mysterious, swollen interior's contents onto society's sin-sniffers."[49] Historical periods of social conflict strongly resuscitate the degraded self/harsh critic problematic, with political pornography as one "solution" to the problem. It was a facile ego boost for many Spaniards to projectively shame and soil the image of their erstwhile social (familial) superiors. Rendered schematically:

Motivating desire	To ward off a degraded self-concept with its anxiety and sense of worthlessness.
Authoritarian projection	"You are a dirty little boy (or girl). Shameless, shameless, shameless."
Pornographic projection	"But now I am big and you are powerless to stop me as I fling the caca back at you."
Ideal adaptive solution	Replace archaic role-relationship model with nuanced, self-owned inner critic.[50]

In 1933 *La Traca* sponsored a contest for its readers, asking for their response to the question, "What would you do with people who wear cassocks?"

The majority of the answers—of which "geld them" was almost unanimous— were along the lines of "The same thing you do with grapes: you hang the good ones, and you crush the bad ones underfoot until they have not one drop of blood remaining" and "Put them on the power cables, douse them with gasoline, set them on fire and afterward make sausages out of them to feed the animals with." Or, "Castrate them. Grind them up. Boil them. Shred them [*hacerlos zurrapas*]. Throw them into the manure pit."[51]

In the early part of the decade new publishing houses rushed to produce and distribute anticlerical and antireligious tracts. The Library of the Godless Ones, for example, edited such edifying titles as *Jesus Christ, a Bad Person* and *The Apostles and Their Concubines*.[52] Some one million copies of anticlerical newspapers were sold in Madrid daily, while conservative papers had a daily press run of about two hundred thousand. That such a crude defamation campaign was successful tells us something about the psychological state of the Spanish mass public as well as the fantasies and/or greed of the men who pandered to it. Not that American anarchists or freethinkers were more balanced. In *Spain, a Land Blighted by Religion*, Joseph Lewis (author of *The Tyranny of God* and *The Bible Unmasked*) takes his readers through famous cities of Spain to explain why every single thing wrong with them is the fault of the Catholic Church. A small sample of his credulity: "During the period of the Inquisition, nearly three hundred years, it has been reliably estimated that more than one million victims were tortured and killed."[53]

A similar problem of fanatical ignorance prevailed in the Second Republic's Cortes Constituyentes, set up to produce a new laicist constitution for Spain. In the view of a leading Spanish political scientist, the anticlericalism of such men "must have had very complex and profound roots, that might be found in personal experiences in small cities and towns in daily contact with the clergy and their educational institutions."[54] They may have been reacting to a legacy of abuse, but they were certainly not recovering from it: mentally, most of the delegates were stuck with the same simplistic hatreds that even Lerroux had abandoned. Unlike governments that seek to incorporate adversaries and soothe feelings after elections, the militant republicans went after the different groups they opposed with a vengeance: their dream was an antipluralistic society, a dream that much to their chagrin would only come true under Franco. Even before the new constitution was promulgated, the impatient municipal leftists of Madrid and Barcelona passed spiteful ordinances against local religious institutions and groups. When the constitution was passed, the Jesuits had to start packing once again, for the fourth time in a century. The order was banned early in 1932 and its extensive properties confiscated; Spain's private educational system was thrown into chaos.[55] Then a divorce law was passed, then all the crucifixes were forcibly removed from the public schools, and then the cemeteries were confiscated and brought under government control—supposedly due to popular demand for nonreligious funerals. Statistics show the particular absurdity of this last measure. As late as 1934, in Madrid, there were 17,033 Catholic funerals held, versus 231 civil ones.[56]

In 1932 the government banned Holy Week processions in many parts of the country, supposedly to keep extremist violence in check. A better way of challenging traditional family schemata—and playing into the hands of the far right—could hardly have been found. In 1933 the governing boards of Seville's confraternities suspended the processions as a pressure tactic.[57] Harsh and arbitrary exercise of authority was a major Holy Week theme itself, of course, and one that Andalusians had centuries of bitter personal experience with; for them the issue was not the ideology of power but who had it. Hence the success of the 1934 saeta first heard on the streets of Seville:

Han dicho en el banco azul
que por ser republicana
España ya no es cristiana.
¡Aquí quien manda eres Tú,
Madre de Dios Soberana![58]

They have said in parliament
that because she is republican
Spain is no longer Christian.
Here the one in charge is You,
Sovereign Mother of God!

People whose identities were anchored in loyalty to supernatural parental protectors naturally resented any attempt by mere terrestrials to limit the sacred authorities' sphere of action. Such attempts only served to make people cling to their maternal and paternal icons more fervently than ever.

What William Christian calls "a dialogue between divinities and the anticlerical left" began in northern Spain with apparitions of the Virgin Mary. In the early 1930s tens of thousands of believers flocked to Ezkioga and other locales hoping to catch a glimpse of her. Christian carefully chronicles the trance states that enabled the seers—many of them children—to communicate with the Virgin and seek answers to pressing questions of a local or national nature. "As a rule," he writes, "seers progressed from lesser to greater states of dissociation."[59] Could the susceptibility to such states have originated in some form of culturally patterned parental ambivalence or corporal punishment? Christian does not pursue this line of inquiry, but he does make a valuable suggestion: "It could be that the visions derived from elements in the seers' memories. The phenomenon of déjà vu is perception experienced as memory because of a short-circuit in the brain. The Ezkioga visions may have been the converse: memories that the force of fear or desire recombined and seers experienced as perception."[60] It so happens that the perceptual organization of traumatic experience constructs memory networks prone to confuse past and present in this way, according to posttraumatic syndrome experts.[61] Philip Greven cites examples of people who experienced a dissociative state after only one beating, though "most people who experience corporal punishments have repeated encounters with pain, each of which is imprinted on the memory and stored for future reference, providing a kind of psychic warehouse of assaults, fears, and pains from which future experiences, actions, fantasies, and thoughts will draw, shaping the character and life of those who have suffered these forms of abuse early in life."[62]

Christian devotes an entire chapter to the grandiose apocalyptic themes that emerged in the visions of his seers, with special attention to their prophecies of an impending chastisement.[63] The "psychic warehouse" of the Spanish seers included other items that strongly suggest a traumatic genesis, or at the very least a punitive one. On 17 July 1931 "a man saw the Virgin threaten him with her hand." The visiting Irish writer Walter Starkie was much struck by one visionary child's facial expression—"She looked as if she had already borne the brunt of a whole life's sorrow." Fifteen-year-old Ramona Olazábal cut her hands with a razor blade near a crowd of twenty thousand people, many of whom took it as a miracle (as she intended) and rushed to dab up the blood with their handkerchiefs. At least two young men were "stunned" and "spooked" into their first vision states by the Virgin approaching in a threatening manner; "the press did not report some of the more trau-

matic visions of women because they considered the women hysterical."
The seers' facial expressions were not always beatific — "In Ormaiztegi a
priest's sister said, 'What faces! They had fear on their faces. If they were
seeing the Virgin would they look that way? I cannot conceive it.'"

It is intriguing to learn that José Antonio Laburu, perhaps the most
brilliant and famous Jesuit lecturer of his time, personally investigated
the sightings of Mary and subsequently took the lead in debunking
them, in part because of the stunted spiritual growth of the visionaries
and their public:

Although the Jesuit referred favorably to the public display of faith at Ezkioga,
he warned that people could not deduce from this piety that the visions were
supernatural. He distinguished "a true faith, solidly reasoned and cemented, a
faith instructed and conscious," from "faith of pure emotionality or family tradition held by sentimental and mawkish persons who confuse secondary and
unimportant things with what is essential and basic in dogma." After reviewing
diocesan policy in regard to Ezkioga, he emphasized that the diocese had made
no formal inquiry because there was no trace of the supernatural to investi-
gate. Finally he showed his films of the seers and compared them with a film of
patients in insane asylums.[64]

Does the inability to transcend simplistic family schemata in a religious context constitute evidence of prior trauma? In some cases it
does. Religious psychotherapists tell us that the ideal course of human
development calls for the uninterrupted growth of ever more inclusive
schemata that gently carry a person from infantile narcissistic omnipotence to mature object relations.[65] Abuse trauma stands in the way of
such growth. Moreover, a vast corpus of research into the history of
childhood shows that some degree of childhood trauma has been almost inevitable, given our fundamental vulnerability to even mild or
unintentional forms of abuse.[66] Trauma paradoxically facilitates the development of certain schemata that *block* the emergence of higher-order
ones that might deal with the trauma more effectively. Organized into
scripts, archaic schemata can stubbornly resist competing paradigms.
Hence we could speak of a "posttraumatic Spanish Catholicism," a type
of faith still laboring under the burden of past traumas, a religiosity
both authoritarian and credulous.

Many thousands of people ignored Laburu's scientific attack on the
visionaries and continued to believe in them. Faith took root in the kin-
based clerical culture of the north and in the "permanent, hidden, con-
ventual mystical network" filled with women familiar with visions and
seers.[67] Sightings of Mary proliferated quickly: Christian traces the rash
of "mini-Ezkiogas" in rural communities all over Spain. Themes of sacrifice, suffering, and impending chastisement resonated throughout the

country during the decade of the 1930s—and with the outbreak of a "holy war" against Spanish atheism many prophecies appeared to have been fulfilled.[68]

The government could have handled the Catholic Church much more prudently; by concentrating on the creation of new schools, for example, instead of sabotaging the good religious ones already in existence.[69] It was in the context of counterproductive attacks against the Church that the fledgling Opus Dei began to make real progress. Founded in 1928 by a zealous and conservative young priest, Father José María Escrivá de Balaguer, this idiosyncratic combination of a lay sodality and a religious order would grow to be an immensely powerful and secretive society, a true "church within a Church."[70] This unwitting legacy of Spanish anticlericalism still affects Catholics around the world.

* * *

Although numerous Spanish women found employment in their country's burgeoning erotic industry, the majority had rather more sophisticated notions of their needs and rights. Thanks to dozens of (mostly women) scholars of several different nationalities,[71] we now know a great deal about Spanish women's political organizations during the thirties and the periodicals that showcased the diverse social class viewpoints among them. One of the largest and most respected republican organizations was the Asociación Nacional de Mujeres Españolas (ANME), founded in 1918 and dedicated to women's suffrage, world peace, and education and skills-training for its members. In the world of journalism, mainstream moderate republicanism was represented by *Mujer* and *Cultura Integral y Femenina.* Readers on the left bought *Nosotras,* the communist *¡Compañera!* or the anarchist *Mujeres Libres,* while the most important publications for women on the right were the middle-class *Aspiraciones* and the upper-class *Ellas.*[72] Dissimilar as they were in their social positions and their notions of proper gender roles, politicized women of the time were destined to make a common and fateful discovery: violence. Communist and anarchist women were the first to break with moderation, rapidly acquainting themselves with demonstrations, strikes, street fighting, and the inside of jails. Here the role model was Dolores Ibárruri, alias "Pasionaria," a miner's wife, once a devout Catholic and now a devout Marxist, known for her stirring albeit fanatical oratory and black legend: a conservative chronicle testified that she had flung herself upon a friar in broad daylight and severed his jugular with her teeth.[73] She was too sexually liberated for at least one of her fellow communists, who later complained that "Pasionaria forgot that she had two sons of the same age as her lover and forgot that her husband, Julián Ruiz, had fought on the northern front; she forgot decorum and modesty; she forgot her years and her gray hairs to shack up with Antón, caring nothing about the indignation of those who knew of her illicit relationship."[74] Street-fighting women of the thirties could also look back with pride to an earlier generation of proletarian sisters: During Barcelona's "Tragic Week" of July 1909, vociferous fishwives and prostitutes were in the forefront of the mobs that sacked convents and burned churches. Their names are a matter of historical record.[75]

What one feminist scholar finds most fascinating is the psychological transformation of women on the right, who turned from defensive to offensive tactics following passage of Azaña's anticlerical laws.[76] Normally delicate Christian women became aggressive militants almost overnight and adopted a variety of strategies, seeking to open parallel schools for their children, helping outlawed Jesuits to escape detection, parading in mourning clothes when anticlerical laws were passed. Boycotts of "red" business establishments and other forms of anticommunist agitation constituted the next stage, organized and promoted from the pages of *Aspiraciones*. A campaign for the restoration of the death penalty followed, then a call to lynch anyone who attacked a Civil Guard, and finally, in 1934, an unhinged plea for a "Spanish Hitler" who would know how to deal with the "Jewish octopus," the "Marxist vulture," and the "filthy workingman." Women in 1930s Spain had a variety of opinions regarding what they needed, remarks Bussy Genevois with considerable understatement.[77] The elite *Ellas*, in the meantime, advised its readers to avoid wearing kneesocks—the trademark of their despised sisters of the atheistic left.

A majority of Spanish women had tired of the political fray by the middle of the decade. Disillusionment and bitterness had begun to take hold in the largest women's organization, the mainstream ANME; though supporters of the Republic, these women were deeply troubled by the anticlerical measures adopted by the government as well as the pornography boom in Spain. For them the demystification of monogamy had gone far enough, and they began to drift toward the right. Here is the next twist in the plot: historians believe that Spanish women's right to vote, hailed as a triumph by the liberal government of 1931, was actually used by huge numbers of them to vote *against* the liberals in the elections of 1933.[78] In the months following the rightward swerve in these elections, the conservative women's magazines were systematically coopted by the bishops. Cardinal Gomá, whose prestige had doubled since the passage of the anticlerical laws, and the prolific Jesuit Father Laburu began to sign editorials in *Ellas* with one overarching aim: the restoration of Woman to her throne (that is, the home). That meant the exaltation of maternity, the acceptance of hierarchy and the concept of the pater familias, the fight against alcoholism and gambling, and the reimposition of chastity.

Stung by the electoral triumph of family-values conservatives, frustrated leftists organized an abortive coup in Asturias the following year —just as the monarchist Gil Robles ("the politician on the Right with the greatest strategic vision") expected they would.[79] Even women who supported democracy were terrified by the miners ("savage beasts"), and, most significantly, disgusted with the miners' wives, mothers, and sisters for failing to control their men.[80] Before they were crushed by troops under the command of a young Francisco Franco, the Asturian revolutionaries managed to burn fifty-eight churches and murder thirty-four priests and nuns.[81] Historian Paul Preston gives an illuminating account of Franco's "deep-seated attachment to Catholicism inherited from his mother . . . inextricably tangled with his military-hierarchical view of society," as was his "racialist contempt" for left-wing workers.[82]

Young-Bruehl notes that apologists of the hysterical/ hierarchical mind-set situate the family, or groups structured like it, at the center of the social universe.[83] Christian does not use the concept of hysterical ideology of desire, but he does paint a fascinating picture of the very milieu that, in Young-Bruehl's view, fosters that ideology:

The women who had visions at Ezkioga worked in the houses of persons who could patronize the visions. . . . The same spiritual adventure joined servant, mistress, and sometimes master in a new way. In Tolosa a sister of a servant held visions and there would appear on her tongue a white wafer, seemingly out of nowhere, all in the house of believing masters. A Portugalete family held regular vision sessions with two servants, a man and a woman, as seers. Anna Pou had visions in the house of her masters near Vic in the winter of 1933. In Barcelona some of the same people who went to Ezkioga were followers of the washerwoman Enriqueta Tomás, whose messages appeared written on her arms. For all of them the story of Gemma Galgani [an Italian seer] must have had a special resonance. She too was a kind of servant, experiencing visions and re-enactments of the Passion in a house where she helped with the laundry and ironing. The visions inevitably affected the relations of seeing servants and believing masters. In his lecture denouncing the visions Laburu used the fact that Carmen Medina [an Andalusian aristocrat] and the girl from Ataun ate together as evidence against the visions. A servant seer prominent in Spain in the 1980s went from serving meals to her masters to being served meals by them. Servants are trained cultural mediators. In order to serve they have to learn the idiom of their masters and be sensitive to their needs and inclinations. . . . Masters sometimes treated servants as ignorant and innocent boys and girls, which made the servants' visions more believable for their masters.[84]

Note the intertwining of prejudice and credulity. There is also a striking similarity between the attitudes of Spanish upper-class believers and the tropes of Western primitivism.[85] The willingness to serve one's servant

seer does not signify a healthy embrace of egalitarianism. Affluent vision
"connoisseurs" like Carmen Medina collected and exhibited their favorite seers even as they longed for civil war with rebellious factory workers.

There was by no means ideological unanimity among the Spanish
bourgeoisie; not all of them, for example, believed workers to be crimi-
nally depraved subversives. The number of those who did, however,
grew quickly during the 1930s. In the end the affluent came to fear
the workers as much as the bishops feared anticlerical sexual liberation.
This unholy alliance of fear and prejudice led to a crude bargain: If the
middle and upper classes were willing to adopt sexual repression as one
of their official identity signs, the Church would throw its weight behind
sociopolitical repression of the proletariat and leftist politicians. A theological justification of rebellion against the Republic was already in place
by the end of 1933, penned and published by a priest in Salamanca.[86] It
was in the same year that Wilhelm Reich wrote the following:

When the entire social organization is plunged into a state of political upheaval,
the conflict between sexuality and compulsive morality will of necessity reach
an acute peak. Some will view this state of affairs as moral degeneration, while
others will see it as a sexual revolution. . . . Viewed objectively, it is only the
system of sexual dictatorship that breaks down, a system designed to preserve
compulsive moralistic values in the individual in the interest of authoritarian
marriage and family.[87]

Authoritarian sexuality is predicated on a fear of punishment first inculcated by the Desert Fathers. It bewildered Spain's fathers to see godless magazines, shows, novels, and songs spreading a new erotic gospel
with *impunity*. But most of the members of the plutocracy, the landowning and financial elite, and prosperous businessmen were not nearly as
alarmed about sex as the prelates were. Many Spanish capitalists jokingly
identified themselves as religious "only from the waist up." Conversely,
many if not most of the women who made money by exhibiting their tal-
ents were socially and politically conservative; there were no feminists or
suffragettes among the scantily clad cabaret singers, a mystified Salaün
laments.[88] Perhaps that is because they specialized in what Reich called
"the pleasure born of the contradiction between morality and instinct —
the pleasure of a dictatorial society, *debased, sordid, pathological pleasure.*"[89]
I think Reich would have repudiated the equation of perversion with
"subversion" made by many modern literary critics. Acting on forbidden
desires does not change their underlying schematic scaffolding; hypocritical, split-off, or perverse sexuality was perfectly compatible with
political conservatism, exaltation of the military and the fatherland, and
belief in visionaries.

"The Plan Was to Kill You All"

Republican liberals and moderates embraced their comrades on the far
left and on 16 February 1936 their Frente Popular came to power, setting off another round of frenzied church burnings. On 14 May the convent of the Salesian nuns was sacked and burned; numerous sisters were
beaten after it was "learned" they had distributed poisoned candy to
children. This episode tells us much about the mental state of the mob
of Madrid. The leaders of the new Popular Front government did not
"lose control" of public order; they never had it in the first place. The
revolution was already well under way in early spring: From 16 February
through 16 April 1936 there were 11 general strikes, 169 riots, 58 attacks
on political party headquarters, 106 churches burned, and 39 firefights
between rival factions leaving 76 dead and 346 wounded.[90] It is correct
to say that the *immediate* cause of the Spanish Civil War was the Second
Republic's inability to control retaliatory homicide in the streets.

It would be absurd to deny the objective social and political differences between the "two Spains," but violence is the great equalizer, at
both unconscious and ideational levels, especially when propelled by
the perverse logic of a blood feud. Spanish philosopher Julián Marías
speaks of the hypnotic effect exercised by extremist groups in 1930s
Spain, with their constant and mind-numbing reiteration of simplistic
sophisms: the soft political center could not hold when all around it
people were falling prey to polarization and somnambulism.[91] "Group-
fantasy is not 'like' a dissociated trance-state," writes psychohistorian
Howard Stein. "It *is* a trance in origin, structure, and function."[92] It is
not difficult to imagine where a general *susceptibility* to social dissociation might have come from—limited schema repertories, abusive family
systems, rural and urban deprivation, mock-violent folk customs, vindictive ideologies—all linked in some way to the psychological legacy of
authoritarian sexuality, all with the latent potential for catastrophe. Two
other theorists of social delirium, Gilles Deleuze and Félix Guattari, affirm that "an unconscious investment of a fascist or reactionary type can
exist alongside a conscious revolutionary investment."[93]

On 17 July 1936, the day before Franco's uprising, *La Traca* published another one of its surveys. To the question, "What would you do
with people who wear cassocks?" readers had come up with clever answers like "I would hang the friars with the guts of the priests."[94] In
response to the Nationalist rebellion, radicals took over the radio stations to rally support for the Republic and broadcast messages like "the
Church has to be destroyed" over and over again. *El paseo* was the euphe-
mism coined for the standard operating procedures for finding priests
and monks hidden in private homes, taking them out, torturing and

shooting them; women often participated in these executions. The murders were authorized by the directors of many different groups, known collectively as the Antifascist Militias. As one of these directors later explained to a priest, "el plan era asesinaros a todos"—the plan was to kill you all. On 26 July, when it was learned that the nightly body count of murdered priests had gone down to only eighteen, the anarchosyndicalist *Solidaridad Obrera* warned militants that a mere 2 percent of priests and nuns had been "suppressed," that the "religious hydra was far from dead" and "these people have to be extirpated." By the following week the nightly body count was back up to fifty. Andrés Nin, head of the same Partido Obrero de Unificación Marxista that tried to kill George Orwell, proudly punned at the end of the month that "the working class has resolved the problem of the Church simply by not leaving even one standing." An editorial in an August issue of *Solidaridad Obrera* explained that "The Religious Orders have to be dissolved. The bishops and cardinals have to be shot. And church assets have to be expropriated." And again, with millenarian overtones: "We have lit the torch and set purifying fire to the momuments that for centuries projected their shadows over every corner of Spain, the churches, and we have spread throughout the countryside, purifying it of the religious plague." One anarchist newsletter observed that "The temples have been fodder for the flames, and the people have dealt with the ecclesiastical bodies that were unable to escape." Although Franco's Nationalists made more constant and conscious use of religious symbols to advance their "crusade," numerous symbols seized upon by the revolutionaries were patently sacral in nature. There were "saints" on the left as well as on the right.[95]

"The anticlerical fury of 1936 has a special meaning and significance," writes historian José Sánchez. "It was the greatest clerical bloodletting in the entire history of the Christian Church. No other fury in modern times approaches the Spanish conflict in the total number of clerics killed, or the percentage of victims of the total, or in the short time span involved."[96] By all accounts no nuns were raped during the period of "purification," but at least 283 were murdered. The first reliable body count was arrived at by Antonio Montero Moreno, who put the total number of clerics killed at 6,832.[97] Further research by Vicente Cárcel Ortí puts the number at well over 7,000.[98] To this must be added the lives of thousands of prominent Catholic laypersons (especially members of Acción Católica) as well as the relatives of murdered priests and monks. In many localities entire families were wiped out.

Cárcel Ortí confirms Montero's finding that Valencia (home of *La Traca*) was indeed the "epicenter of hatred": "Almost all of the individual murders and some of the collective ones were preceded by physical and psychological tortures, mutilations, beatings, insults, and so forth. . . .

In more than one case the furious barbarism [*ensañamiento*] continued after death."[99] Many priests, like Fathers José Fenollosa and Enrique Gimeno, were found with their skulls pulverized. The chaplain of an order of nuns who helped the elderly homeless had his tongue, an eye, and an ear cut off before he was executed. The parish priest of Santa María del Mar was tied to a tree, doused with gasoline, and set on fire. Several priests, like Vicente Peretó and José Martí Bataller, were taken to bullrings where they suffered numerous knife wounds, including castration. One rural pastor was jabbed with sharp axes and picks (like a bull in the ring) before he was shot to death. Unknown assailants took one elderly priest to a remote gorge, stripped him naked, cut off his genitals and forced them into his mouth before shooting him. Another was killed slowly with twenty-two pistol shots beginning with the extremities. Another clergyman's brains were literally beaten out of him with a club. One had his head hammered and his throat sliced with a sickle. Another had his eyes gouged out with the crucifix of his rosary. Another was tied to a streetcar and crushed to death; his relatives were told to recover the remains with a spatula. The elderly parish priest of Navarrés was dragged from his sickbed through the town streets. Another was obliged to drink urine before execution. One was used as a human pin cushion before being hanged from a tree in a festive atmosphere. The *beatas* of one small town (Cheste) were forced to watch their priest being flayed alive in the town square; he was kept alive as long as possible for greater amusement.[100] Militiamen of the Círculo Industrial of Alcoy preferred to hack their clerical prisoners to death and sack the body parts. Nine teaching nuns were murdered in Cullera, as were another dozen in Picadero de Paterna. Seventeen nuns over sixty years old (the oldest being eighty-six) were burned to death in Mislata.

In the words of French writer Paul Claudel, an eyewitness to many of the atrocities:

Taine speaks in his book of spontaneous anarchy. Here [in Spain] we have directed anarchy. Without an agreed-upon operational order and methodical organization, it is in fact impossible to explain why all of the churches without exception could have been set on fire [in the Republican zone], all religious objects carefully sought out and destroyed, and the overwhelming majority of the prelates, religious men, and religous women murdered with unheard-of refined cruelty, hunted down everywhere like wild beasts.[101]

Historians can ponder a document found in Bilbao, dated October 1936, signed and sealed by the anarchosyndicalist CNT: "The bearer of this safeconduct pass cannot be ordered to assume any other duty since he is currently employed in the destruction of churches." The stevedores of Barcelona took special pride in the number of priests they had killed.

Murder victims included many members of Catholic lay religious organizations like Jóvenes Cristianos. There were numerous group executions of priests and seminarians, with victims as old as ninety or as young as seventeen. The record was set with a mass execution in the cemetery of Lérida—seventy-four priests and an unknown number of nuns. In March 1987 Pope John Paul II beatified three nuns of the Descalced Carmelite order who were hunted down and slaughtered in Guadalajara on 24 July 1936.[102]

Let us step back from the bloodletting to see if we can connect its remote causes to its proximate ones. Scholars associated with the Fundamentalism Project (American Academy of Arts and Sciences) have recently focused on how small groups of true believers in different nations and historical epochs manage to captivate large parts of the body politic; research reveals that the hard-core support of the movements studied "has time and again proved to be statistically insignificant."[103] It turns out that in almost every known movement we can find leaders formulating dramatic eschatologies of an impending cosmic upheaval—even in cultures that have no prior tradition of sacred apocalyptic texts. In Spain the same apocalyptic notions that motivated some men to murder led others to write poems. The civil war provoked an unprecedented output of ballads, songs, and poems composed by non-professionals, giving voice to their millenarian dreams.[104] To the chagrin of Marxist critic Serge Salaün, prolific anarchist poets almost always used the traditional Spanish octosyllabic folk ballad meter rather than one of greater "theoretical maturity."[105] This suggests that they were beholden to a whole series of folk paradigms, and not in a good sense.

Delusions of persecution were apparently common. In the first days of the war, as Sánchez reminds us, many people really believed that the priests were actively going after them—sometimes with poison bullets, sometimes with lethal injections (a charge leveled at the order that ran Barcelona's San Pablo Hospital). Madrid's newspapers featured delusional titles like "Chauffeur Attacked by a Group of Friars" and "Large Group of Friars Kills Six Militiamen."[106] A kind of "social trance" overtakes individuals and groups who are investing historical events with unresolved unconscious tasks with their origins in trauma and deprivation. The trance spreads when there is an insufficient number of mechanisms at the psyche's disposal to test the reality of the claims made by the most fanatical members of the group.

Political pornography had represented an earlier stage in the formation of the terrorists' group-fantasies; it gave them a consensual outlet for all manner of projections and anal-sadistic impulses—though they seem almost benign when compared with the lethal delusional stages that incubated themselves in the prisons following the abortive

Asturian coup attempt. Not all of the authorized church-burners and priest-murderers were created equal. Although many had a long history of affiliation with one revolutionary organization or another, many others were very recent affiliates of anarchosyndicalist organizations like the so-called Del Rosal Column that killed the bishop of Cuenca and numerous other clergy. Many of these new members had been in jail for crimes committed well before Franco's uprising. They were not political prisoners but *delincuentes comunes*, or common criminals. As Salvador de Madariaga explained, "In the first days a frenzy of freedom had opened the doors of the jails that, already emptied of political prisoners months before by Azaña's order, could only vomit out common prisoners to the torrent in the street."[107] It is conceivable that some of these men, members of the dispossessed rural or urban proletariat, were eager to mutilate and murder priests in the "folkloric" ways noted earlier, but modus operandi is not motive.

Therefore the question remains: How can political prisoners and common criminals be transformed into terrorists and mass murderers almost overnight? A certain type of recruiting pitch would seem essential. Criminologist Jack Katz discovered that murder is almost invariably linked to traditional moral concerns and a traditional panoply of paradigm scenarios that he calls "moral emotions: humiliation, righteousness, arrogance, ridicule, cynicism, defilement, and vengeance. In each, the attraction that proves to be most fundamentally compelling is that of overcoming a personal challenge to moral—not to material—existence."[108] The anticlerical young heroes of Galdós succumbed to homicidal moral outrage when their access to the beloved was blocked by pious intransigents. This type of righteous rage is, as C. Fred Alford points out, "the morality of revenge rather than of reparation, based upon the most primitive aspects of the superego."[109] As we go from individuals to groups, the primitive structures are not diluted, but become more powerful:

The problem with groups, to put it as simply as possible, is that they discourage those emotional developments that lead to the ability to experience depressive, reparative guilt. By giving paranoid-schizoid anxiety an objective focus, groups legitimate and reinforce paranoid-schizoid defenses, such as splitting and idealization. The individuals in the group are made to feel less anxious, but at the cost of emotional development. It is as if the analyst said to the paranoid-schizoid patient, "You really are being persecuted. Let me help you by naming your persecutors and telling you who your true friends are, friends who are also being attacked by these persecutors. Together you and your friends can fight the persecutors, and praise each other's righteousness, which will help you realize that the source of aggression and evil is out there, in the real world. And you thought it was all in your head!"[110]

As investigators of cult mind control have discovered, the success of such messages is in most cases "traceable to specific experiences, manipulative techniques, mental and emotional stresses, or extreme and prolonged changes in the individual's surrounding information environment. . . . The final threshold is crossed when words turn into actions, when group leaders no longer simply preach doom and holy warfare but begin to acquire arms," thereby enabling them to become "the point men in floating terror cells."[111]

In revolutionary Spain there was no identifiable correlation between the morality of a priest and his martyrdom. Many sexually abusive priests were spared, many known to be truly celibate were killed—all according to the peculiar political psychology of each different locality. Sánchez affirms that "nineteenth-century pious Jesuitism" was the target of the militiamen; it was a cultural ethic that the priests had attempted to impose on everyone. "As far as national differences go, what is more likely is that Spanish priests were no more oppressive and obscurantist than priests elsewhere; it was just that they were more militant about it. In no other country had the clergy as much political, social, and economic power as they did in Spain in the first half of the nineteenth century; and nowhere else did they have the degree of social and educational power up to 1936."[112] But all was not well with the Spanish Church thereby. In 1907 the papal nuncio Antonio Vico had found Spain's seminaries to be sorely lacking "in ecclesiastical spirit as well as discipline, morality, and education."[113] Following the Great War, Pope Benedict XV backed an ambitious plan for improving the lot of Spain's clergy, never implemented because too many bishops feared losing power to the Jesuits. In 1933 the new papal nuncio, Federico Tedeschini, sent three members of the Spanish high clergy on a fact-finding tour of every single seminary in Spain. The results of their mission were not made available to Pope Pius XI until 1936, when the Spanish Church was literally fighting for its life. In the words of Tedeschini, "I daresay that the fundamental cause of the current Spanish revolution resides in the ignorance of the clergy and the people. The seminaries have been barracks or reform schools, full of immoralities and intolerable license."[114] In other words, the "right" conditions for the manufacture of abusive clergy had existed for several centuries. Note that the source for the deplorable situation of Spanish seminary training was a high-ranking churchman, not some hotheaded anarchist.

As we have seen, clerical intransigence was more a reaction to than a cause of anticlerical intransigence; yet we have also seen the power of unconscious revenge schemas in the actions of anticlericals reacting to but not recovering from a legacy of humiliation at the hands of their

Catholic educators. Yet the men who finally did the dirty work were far removed from Church institutions and personnel. and much closer to organizations like the Federación Anarquista Ibérica (FAI), formed in 1927 to keep the CNT from becoming too moderate (they succeeded in this goal).[115] The so-called faístas were not the only people with a fascist unconscious lurking beneath their manifestly revolutionary propaganda—members of every political organization on the left took part in the mayhem. But not all of it was propaganda, either; at least some of it was the seductive phenomenological immediacy of violence, arson, and murder. All over the world, men of poor neighborhoods find it intimately rewarding to band together into intimidating "street elites."[116]

The rapid massacre of priests and nuns was clearly an unexpected side-effect of the Nationalist uprising in July 1936; ultra-Catholic as most of them were, the military conspirators could not control or predict every reaction of the Spanish body politic they presumed to be rescuing. The violent purge of priests, in other words, was a chaotic, fast-breeding, self-propelling "death spiral," a term employed by Conway and Siegelman to describe "a fatal pattern of response that may arise in the life of cults, sects and social organizations of every kind."[117] The two antagonistic Spains themselves were like twin spiral systems interacting and intertwining with frightening speed; once terror was unleashed it spread uncontrollably. As Julián Marías has remarked, most Spaniards did not want a civil war—they simply "wanted *what turned out to be* a civil war." The years of the Second Republic were "dominated by a lack of imagination, the inability to foresee or anticipate consequences."[118] Cultural institutions had helped to make people gullible instead of discerning, highly manipulable instead of autonomous. Add to this the incredibly stubborn prejudices of politicians, union leaders, journalists, bankers, landowners, archbishops, intellectuals. It would be easier to assign responsibility if we could locate at least one group that had a real understanding of the logic of the whole social field, hence of its own position and game. None did. A global view is the melancholy privilege reserved to our generation. I do not wish to simplify the complex chain of events that led to the massacre, but in schematic form it might look something like this: Traumatized body politic → polarized institutions → collective vulnerability → individual abuse trauma → impaired maturation → affect dysregulation → thought distortion → (re)exposure to paranoid ideology → recent radical change in information environment → anxiety → manipulation by group-fantasy leader → rewarding violence → traumatized body politic.

To recruit a gang to murder clergy, first find men with "simple" minds —plentiful in a society made simplistic by institutional polarization— and further simplify them with a delusional narcissistic ideology that is

renforced and enhanced by the act of killing (hence the desire to prolong it with torture and mutilation). With all due respect to Monsignor
Tedeschini, the only responsibility I can assign to the Spanish church
is a general and indirect one, to be shared with other purblind Spanish
collectives whose preference for simple answers to complex questions
left the entire culture vulnerable to terrorism and social trance.

A Woman Can Be the Enemy

To the initial improvisatory phase of the war belongs one of its main
mythic symbols: the *miliciana* (militiawoman or female volunteer soldier). The myth had its basis in the genuine heroism of real women.
Rosario Sánchez lost a hand on the battlefield at age seventeen; Lina
Odena fought on the Andalusian front and committed suicide to avoid
capture by Franco's legionnaires. Countless posters of beautiful young
women dressed in blue coveralls and aiming rifles functioned as powerful tools of recruitment—not for women but for men. As Mary Nash
points out, provocative images of women filling a traditionally masculine
role almost obliged workingmen to sign up and vindicate their virility. It
was "an instrumentalization of the feminine figure for war objectives."[119]

The miliciana played a huge *negative* role in the elaboration of Francoist mythology. She is a stock villain in novels like Gonzalo Torrente
Ballester's *Javier Mariño*, in which a heavyset woman named Irene is the
archetypal "pioneer communist who wore on her face a primitive animal
smile, a smile of health and satisfied instincts."[120] For one Francoist writer
unafraid of sweeping generalizations, the milicianas were all stunted,
with "ugly and deformed legs" and "prognathous teeth incapable of
friendly dialogues." "Without the treasure of a spiritual life, lacking the
refuge of religion, their femininity was suddenly extinguished."[121]

The typical profile of the miliciana (in reality) was that of a young
woman without children or domestic ties who had been active in political, union, or feminist activities before the war and had subsequently
enlisted right along with her male friends or husband. Although some
milicianas did see combat duty, the majority were assigned to noncom-
bat roles as nurses, cooks, cleaning women, and sometimes administra-
tors. Writing in 1937, an anarchist/sexologist named Félix Martí Ibáñez
claimed that many of the young women were motivated by romantic or
novelistic dreams but fainted when they saw their first mutilated corpse
and subsequently sought consolation in bed with the first militiaman
they met. Although he had been an energetic proponent of radical
sexual reforms and a promoter of abortion, Martí wanted women as far
away from the front as possible. In his view, sexual relations were sap-
ping the strength and energy of the soldiers and thereby endangering

the outcome of the war. It was the patriotic duty of women to facilitate sexual discipline; no longer should they make themselves so available and thereby "put in the steel of his muscles the softness of erotic fatigue."[122] In other words: *make war, not love.* Strange advice from a sexologist!

In Eslava's interpretation, many milicianas were "perhaps a little simpleminded, but sincerely convinced that raising their legs contributed mightily to the morale of the combatants and the crushing of fascism."[123] It is a fact that a number of labor unions converted into regiments overnight sometimes rewarded their members by giving them tickets that entitled them to a night with one of the female syndicalists.[124] One female veteran of the war recounts how as a highly idealistic seventeen-year-old miliciana she was recriminated by a young soldier she had rebuffed.[125] Perhaps more to the frustrated soldier's liking would have been the milicianas who allegedly embraced promiscuity with the same enthusiasm as smoking in public or handling rifles, or one of the prostitutes who adopted the guise of militiawomen in order to stay close to the troops and ply their flesh trade.

Mary Nash does find examples of young women who joined up out of a sense of adventure or even a "vacation spirit," but many more were highly politicized women who wanted to play the most active role possible in the struggle against fascism. They were a nearly endless source of surprises for their masculine comrades. And while some milicianas did commence love relationships with men on the front lines, many others have reported that they were far too busy surviving or fighting off cold and hunger to think about sex. Some milicianas were constantly propositioned by their masculine counterparts; others were never bothered. And while admitting that there were a small number of prostitutes and former prostitutes among the milicianas, Nash affirms that under duress they carried out their military or auxiliary tasks with valor and distinction.[126]

The downfall of the miliciana was as rapid as her mythification during the first months of the war. In one of the very few areas of accord ever reached by the rivalrous factions of the embattled Second Republic, the milicianas were withdrawn from the front lines and returned to the home front. What Nash finds most disconcerting about this was the acquiescence of the feminine and feminist organizations of the time, who not only did not defend the milicianas but spoke vaguely of military tasks being unsuited by nature for women. The miliciana's existence was intimately tied to the egalitarian military model that had arisen spontaneously in the summer of 1936; when it gave way to a much more conventional, hierarchical army model, she could not last. But what really sealed the fate of the miliciana, unjustly or not, was the spectacular rise in the incidence of venereal disease among the Republic's troops. Nash argues that the venereal disease problem can best be attributed to the soldiers' intense activities in red light districts during their leaves, but the highly visible female soldiers made tempting scapegoats.

Governmental authorities worked hard to control a health problem that was also a military problem: syphilis and gonorrhea were causing as many casualties as Nationalist bullets.[127] Many prostitutes were apprehended and sent off to redemption centers called *liberatorios de la prostitución*, which Eslava compares to the special convents for fallen women run by the Church in olden days.[128] "Venereal diseases are Nature's fascism," as one poster put it, while another warned the militiaman that "A woman can be the enemy. Protect yourself from her with lavatives, condoms, preventives, or better—with abstention." According to Inmaculada Julián, posters attempting to reason with men were the exception: the majority went for the jugular and portrayed prostitutes as evil in themselves, as dangerous as the other kind of femme fatale—the spy.[129] Some of the more effective posters resurrected hoary medieval images of beautiful women embracing men with skeletal arms. This too was a way of turning back the clock. Small wonder that disciplined communists played an increasingly influential role in the Second Republic since they were encouraged to spy on each other and report any sexual misconduct. One aging member of the Spanish Communist Party with whom I spoke in the late seventies had done just that; he was still proud of having ferreted out sexually undisciplined comrades, some of whom were sent to the front as punishment.

As it happens, prostitutes were not the only women to find their services in greater demand under the new wartime conditions. Singers, dancers, and actresses enjoyed boom times as well. After the established stars, wealthy and politically reactionary, had fled the Republic in July 1936, the door was opened for newcomers to debut on the stage and for former underlings and understudies to rise to much higher show business ranks than they had enjoyed before the war. The minimum wage for the showgirl's most enthusiastic clients (militiamen) was ten pesetas a day, considered quite generous at the time; but a *vedette de variedades* could make as much as 175 pesetas per performance in 1938 (though many gave benefit performances without remuneration).[130] Popular demand for shows and spectacles was so great that even girls aged four to six were recruited for one fundraiser organized by anarchosyndicalists. At a more mature level, directors like María Teresa León or Irene Falcón had a chance to develop projects with a degree of control that was unheard of in the prewar days when men dominated Spanish show business; the women were particularly eager to try out new consciousness-raising or propagandistic theatrical genres.

The Organización de Mujeres Antifascistas Españolas was by far the largest and most important association of women supporting the embattled Second Republic. It contained women of all social classes and several ideologies (even Catholic women and some nuns in the Basque regions), united in their desire to halt the violent spread of Spanish-style fascism. Carmen González affirms that they were tremendously active in organizing kindergartens and lunchrooms, handling refugees, visiting hospitals, factories, and the fronts, providing assistance to working mothers, and in numerous other activities designed to improve women's standing in the harsh circumstances then operative.[131] Their position on the proper role of women in the war, as expressed in their mass-circulation magazine *Mujeres*, was not radical and can be summarized thus: Since woman's principal mission in life is that of procreation, she is in a sense the owner of the lives she creates and therefore must vigorously defend all life. A mother should be antifascist for the very reason that she is a mother, in other words, life-affirming but willing nonetheless to send her sons into battle to die for the salvation of the Mother Country. Woman-as-wife should send her man to the front with pride and even with joy, because "it is better to be the widow of a hero than the wife of a coward."[132] As Sainz Bretón and her colleagues show, the propaganda campaigns carried out by *Mujeres Antifascistas* were entirely in keeping with the tenor of the times; in other words, they were simplistic, Manichaean, strident, tendentious, and designed to appeal to old-fashioned sentiment rather than logic. After the war was lost, many members of this group fled or went underground to become the Unión de Mujeres Españolas, working in clandestine cells throughout Franco's Spain to help guerrilla fighters or denounce the execution and torture of political prisoners. Dolores Ibárruri ("Pasionaria") and other Spanish activist women would play a key role in keeping Franco's Spain excluded from the United Nations following World War II.

Scholars consider a different association, Mujeres Libres, to be the prime example of "proletarian feminism" (as opposed to the bourgeois or petit-bourgeois varieties).[133] Formed by leading women anarchists in April 1936, Mujeres Libres came to have some 147 chapters and 20,000 members in the areas controlled by the Republic. Taking their cue from Bakunin rather than Proudhon, they called for absolute equality in rights and duties and total sexual freedom. In theory the anarchosyndicalist CNT-FAI was opposed to any form of hierarchy or authority, but many male militants were unwilling to extend their politics to the area of gender relations; even more vexing, laments Martha Ackelsberg, were the rivalries that soon sprang up between Mujeres Libres and other anarchofeminist organizations.[134] Their common enemy turned out to be not Franco so much as the Spanish Communist Party, whose position on women's emancipation was the same as its position on emancipation in general: it could wait until the war was won.[135]

Still other organizations sought to channel the vitality of younger women into numerous activities traditionally monopolized by men. One of the most successful was the Unión de Muchachas that supplied the needy Republic with female truck drivers, bus drivers, streetcar drivers, electricians, and shopworkers, while simultaneously organizing all manner of courses, from basic literacy to university level offerings. Even as the bombs fell on Madrid, the female students kept attending their classes, sure of victory and the role they would play in the new Spanish society they were helping to forge.[136] Little did they suspect that a victorious Franco would declare all degrees earned during the war on the Republican side null and void.

Women living in the areas controlled by Franco also had to replace men in the factories, organize cooperative kindergartens and lunchrooms, participate in fund-raising campaigns, sponsor public lectures, and work in the hospitals. But the ideology constructed to give meaning to all these activities was quite different: in the New Spain being forged with help from Hitler and Mussolini, women were to adapt their minds and bodies to a special breed of men who were being told to think like Franco, feel like Franco, talk like Franco, and be like Franco, that is, *mitad monje, mitad soldado*—half monk, half soldier. In reality, Franco's troops were warlike but hardly monklike: bordellos abounded in the areas controlled by the Nationalists and the Church simply looked the other way.

The warrior-monk identity is as old as authoritarian sexuality in Spain. It was highly functional throughout eight centuries of skirmishes with the Moors; it was given a new lease on life by Ignatius of Loyola (founder of the quasi-military Jesuit order during the Golden Age); it was reintroduced by José Antonio and embellished by Spain's fascist intelligentsia. Unlike the atheistic and promiscuous "Reds," the Nationalist men were instructed to aspire to an asceticism that was both religious and martial, a messianic mystique of virility and purification by bloodshed not unlike the one discovered by Klaus Theweleit in young German *Freikorps*. Julio Rodríguez Puértolas points out that the novels written during and after the war by Franco partisans portray the Republic as a chaotic quagmire where hordes of implacable, obscene, hyenalike women savored the smell of burning churches and rotting corpses. The miliciana assumes a powerfully negative role for the novelists, as does the aristocratic-woman-turned-leftist out of sheer delight in sexual perversion.[137] Albert Machthild finds Spanish Falangist authors actually sympathizing with the "Red" militiamen forced to service the degenerate fantasies of their women; ideological barriers dissolve into "a common anxiety and horrified rejection that unites men in order to condemn (to death if possible) the woman-monster."[138] The depraved woman is just a more sophisticated version of the sexually threatening and ugly proletarian woman, who grabs her rifle and heads for the front hoping that peacetime aesthetic criteria will be waived to enable her to fulfill her lust (according to another Nationalist novelist). Scenes of cruelty mixed with eroticism occur with great frequency in the warrior-monk novels, more than enough to confirm once again that authoritarian sexuality is an ideology of discipline *and* desire. The books also feature heroines acceptable to the writers, of course, decent wives and mothers victimized by atheistic/Marxist politicians, or idealistic and asexual nurse-types, who still must be kept in their places.

What about the flesh-and-blood women who were called upon to adapt themselves to the official fantasies? As it happens, a grandiose subordinate mission was in the offing for them, based on a mystique of the home and maternity. Appropriately, it was the women of the ultra-Catholic and bellicose Carlist faction that had gone the farthest in the codification of this role. When the Carlist women were united by decree with the Falangist women of the Sección Femenina, they were rechristened Sección Femenina Tradicionalista but continued to be known informally as "Las Margaritas."[139] These women were pious and self-sacrificing, but they had no use for supposedly feminine traits like delicacy or weakness. Only strong women with convictions had a right to be queen of the home and angel of love; only strong women could fulfill the most noble mission in life—motherhood; only strong women could make contributions in the crucial areas of education (schools were seen as an extension of the trenches), charity (the Margaritas were Good Samaritans to a fault), piety (especially public displays of it), and propaganda (as simplistic and Manichaean as the enemy's). Other goals defended by the Margaritas included the defense of Spanish traditions and the "purification of public customs."

Florencia Carrionero and her colleagues make an important point: when people on the Nationalist side were talking about women, they were talking about morality; when they were talking about morality, they were talking about the family; hence they were talking about society, hence about Spain. Hence, Woman equals Spain. Therefore debates about hemlines or female sports were not trivial. Woman was wife and mother, nucleus of the family; as the fundamental national unit, the family had to be defended from egalitarian feminism, divorce, and pornography. Wartime conditions made the traditional woman active outside of the home—not to change her role but to make her a *collective* mother or spouse, sacrificing herself for an extended family whose members were busy fighting the Republic's laicism. A marriage that could be dissolved was an aberrant institution of exploitation, intimidation, and terror for all Spanish women.

A conference organized early in 1938 in Salamanca by the Juventud Femenina de Acción Católica featured numerous speeches that compared the reconquest of Spain by Nationalist troops to the reconquest of the home by their womenfolk. For the neotraditional women of the New Spain, writes Giuliana Di Febo, the home had already become a mythicized microcosmos from which all feminine functions were to draw their energy.[140] In the new scheme of things the most valued part of a woman's body became her hands, constantly occupied with whatever labors or tasks the family or nation needed. It was therefore appropriate in a surrealist sort of way that the mummified hand of Saint Teresa of Avila, miraculously discovered a year earlier, would come to be the special protector of the Caudillo and the patron of the all-encompassing Sección Femenina de la Falange, as well as mythic symbol of the "racial essences" of Spain. As Di Febo points out, the biographies of both Saint Teresa and Isabel de Castilla were tinkered with by regime ideologues to make them into models of "Christian feminism." Perhaps the least valued part of Spanish woman's body was her mouth. Glowing references to the hivelike silence and hushed labors of traditional women abound in Francoist propaganda.

*   *   *

The brutal repression following the war was unquestionably the darkest phase of the Franco regime. By the end of 1939, there were by official count some 270,719 men imprisoned, most of them charged with (of all things) *rebellion*. Many thousands had already been executed, and still more thousands had been assigned to forced labor in so-called workers' batallions.[141] To aid the regime in its ongoing struggle with a "Jewish-Masonic-Communist Conspiracy," the ancient cult of Santiago the Moor-Slayer was revived. This identification of the Spanish martial spirit and Spanish religiosity is both historically accurate and radically one-sided. The Santiago myth was the perfect example of a metanarrative forged through the violent imposition of meaning ("cultural unity") on subject peoples.[142]

To the victors belonged the right to criminalize behaviors that the vanquished had deemed heroic during the war. In the case of one large group of female political prisoners, their wartime conduct was redefined as mentally ill. An in-depth examination of their "sickness" was carried out by eminent psychiatrists Juan Antonio Vallejo-Nájera and Eduardo Martínez and published in 1939 in a Spanish medical journal.[143] The study is as chilling as it is fascinating. It was carried out with fifty "Marxist delinquent women" imprisoned in Málaga; four had been given twelve-year sentences, another three were serving twenty-year sentences, ten had been given life terms, and no fewer than thirty-three had been given the death penalty (commuted to life imprisonment through *the magnanimity of the Caudillo*). All of the women had taken some kind of active role in either military encounters or, more commonly, in the anarchic violence that characterized the first months of the war and that reached an unusual degree of ferocity in southern Spain. Some had revealed the hiding places (and hence facilitated the lynchings) of well-known *franquistas*. Some had been milicianas, serving on the front dressed in blue coveralls and carrying firearms; some had harangued the mobs; and some were guilty of what the psychiatrists termed *necrofagia*, by which they meant the perpetration of unseemly acts with corpses.

Such acts had actually taken place in many localities, according to numerous eyewitnesses. David Gilmore refers to one incident of atrocity perpetrated by impoverished villagers in Extremadura: "After hacking the police to death and gouging out their eyes, they lit a bonfire and the women danced around the burning bodies." [144] When Eduardo Bayo was murdered in 1936 and dragged through the streets of Málaga, a group of women screamed "Fascista, fascista!" while one of them "opened her legs, hiked up her skirts, and bathed his bloody face with urine." [145] When large numbers of right-wingers were executed and left lying by the roadside, women from working-class neighborhoods went to urinate or defecate on the cadavers by moonlight. On another occasion, a "certain miliciana with moist armpits and powerful hips" kept a wounded man from getting medical attention; she just stood there "drinking in his agony with the same joyful cruelty that neighborhood children employ with blind birds, disemboweled cats, and bloody puppies." According to the memoirs of Remigio Moreno and Father Tomás López, women of all social classes joined in the sadistic fun. Journalists described how women would put cigarettes in the mouths of assassinated enemies and then stamp them out; others cut off the ears of the dead and hung them on their lapels; others uncovered the genitalia of murdered nuns—those who had not been forced to disrobe and parade through the streets before their deaths. Children were present at all these events.

The two psychiatrists note numerous points of coincidence between the psychology of women and that of children and animals; hence periods of social ferment quickly break down their already weak instinctual controls to bring out the worst in women, from latent sexual appetites to political passion to outrageous cruelty: Spanish female delinquents went above and beyond normal levels of crime. They burned, pillaged, and destroyed—often to avenge themselves of male domination, as the doctors themselves conjecture. Although only a minority of Málaga's female prisoners were implicated in *necrofagia*, the psychiatrists discovered some type of degenerative mental illness in 72 percent of them; 24 percent were "social psychopaths" and an additional 20 percent were "social imbeciles"; 8 percent were "congenitally amoral" and 46 percent were entirely illiterate. Two thirds of the women were under thirty-five; there were ten virgins, seven prostitutes (whose loss of virginity had been precocious), and the rest had been married or living with a man. Vallejo-Nájera and Martínez were surprised to discover that despite the "Marxist" label, none of the women had forsaken their Catholic beliefs, although they were not practitioners. The two psychiatrists find cause for optimism in this, reinforced by their finding that it was not really any sort of coherent ideology but their simple animal passions that led to their crimes during the "chaotic Red era."[146]

Bloody reprisals against women had characterized the conflict in southern Spain. Gilmore reports that "the Rightists of Fuenmayor rounded up the wives, sisters, and mothers of the dead or exiled Leftists, shaved their heads, stripped them naked, and rode them about town tied onto the backs of donkeys. One pregnant woman had her legs fastened with esparto twine. She expired in agony as her tormentors watched impassively."[147] Following the Second Republic's downfall, special rituals of humiliation were arranged throughout Spain for anarchofeminists and other activist women, leaving them traumatized for decades. Rural women who had belonged to the Republic's broad-based Mujeres Antifascistas organization recalled getting their heads shaved and adorned with little red bows, or being forced to drink large doses of castor oil so that they would soil themselves uncontrollably as they were paraded through the streets.[148] If the reclusion of the counterrevolutionary woman in her mythic home was the foundation of community life, the public humiliations consummated after the war symbolically equated revolutionary women with prostitutes and filth.

For many women of the postwar era, life itself seemed like a giant reprisal. Their fathers, brothers, and husbands were dead or in Franco's prisons; they were reduced to eating cauliflower and carrot leaves, with an occasional onion, while sending their children out to pick through the garbage; the miserable diets provoked outbreaks of tuberculosis and typhus—epidemic in Málaga in 1941 because the government had allowed the crowded Holy Week celebrations to be held for propaganda purposes. A typhus epidemic decimated the poor neighborhoods of Madrid in April of the same year, killing scores of abandoned children. Throughout the 1940s the poorest people huddled together in bombed-out tenements on the outskirts of major cities, dressed in tattered clothes, often shoeless, with very little to eat.

The food was no more plentiful in the jails, and numerous prisoners depended on their womenfolk to bring them something extra. In what might seem a dramatic reversal of Spanish machismo, many imprisoned husbands tacitly encouraged their wives to trade sex for food. "The horns of a cuckold are like teeth," the new cynical wisdom had it. "They hurt a little when they first emerge, but later you can eat with them."[149] There were also numerous cases of women who surrendered their bodies in exchange for reduction of sentences and even commutation of death penalties for their husbands, brothers, or fathers. Manuel Barrios points a finger at Colonel Manuel Díez Criado, stationed in reconquered Seville, who repeatedly took advantage of his position in this way.[150]

In a country devastated by war, misery, and famine, many respectable women and girls were forced into prostitution to survive. As Rosa María Badillo and her colleagues point out, it was here that the Spain of the vanquished differed most sharply from the "home" mythology being promoted throughout the land by the victors.[151] Unlucky women of all ages went to work in the *casas de trato*, also known as *casas de tolerancia* because they were legal for the first seventeen years of the Franco regime (again, authoritarian sexuality does not mean puritanism). In the early 1940s Spain had some eleven hundred legal bordellos; in numerous provincial areas they were the only places men could go to evade social rigidity or their sanctimonious wives. But the greed of many a madam led numerous women to sell their bodies on the street; this illegal form of prostitution was occasionally subject to police persecution. The luckiest of the unlucky became the mistress of some newly rich black marketeer.[152]

All of this was going on while the Sección Femenina was urging women to quit their daytime jobs and get back to their homes. The existence of available fallen women, licensed or freelance, was paradoxically essential to the reimposition of authoritarian sexuality in the (middle-class) Spanish home and to the preservation of the virginity of the women being groomed for maternal roles.

The end of the civil war did not spell an end to the chances for young Spanish women to be the girlfriends and fiancées of heroes. Franco's decision to help Hitler on the Russian front led to the creation of the famous División Azul, or Blue Division (since blue was the color of the Falange and by extension that of the new-old Spain). Over a two-year period some 47,000 Spanish men would see combat duty in the Soviet Union, many of them with girlfriends waiting for them back home. The opportunities for the female version of heroism (long-suffering abnegation and patience) were thereby multiplied. In the words of Medina, an advice columnist, "Just remember that your boyfriend is one more on the enormous list of brave ones ready to crush communism, and that, like you, there are many women who are saying good-bye to a loved one but who know how to compensate their sorrow at his leaving with an immense pride in his manliness."[153] Spaniards would demonstrate their manliness on and off the battlefields of Eastern Europe. According to the diaries of Count Galeazzo Ciano, Mussolini's foreign affairs minister, the "anti-erotic pills" that were so effective for the German soldiers were useless on the first shipment of three thousand Blue Division troops.[154] Worse still, the young Spaniards ignored the Third Reich's prohibitions about fraternizing with Jewish women and other women of feared nationalities. A fondness for miscegenation was precisely what distinguished Spanish fascist thought from that of Nazism, as Jo Labanyi has pointed out in her excellent study.[155] One German commandant who had finally given his regiment of Spaniards permission to visit a bordello changed his mind after learning that the prostitutes were all Slavs. In protest the Spaniards inflated their regulation condoms and hung them from their rifles. Then they marched a thousand kilometers from Poland to the Russian front in forty days, singing songs composed for the occasion like

Tenemos que recorrer	We have to cover
mil kilómetros andando	a thousand kilometers walking
para luego demostrar	in order to demonstrate later
lo que llevamos colgando.	what we have hanging.[156]

Once fighting began, the Spaniards routinely unnerved and disconcerted their German allies with old-fashioned notions of personal heroism that contrasted sharply with German reliance on technical/material superiority. Warriors, yes; monks, not exactly, no more than the lusty *conquistadores* who accumulated large harems of indigenous women in the bad old days ushered in by Castilian expansionism in the New World. "To do what one feels like while serving God: this is the great dream of the Spaniard," one scholar wryly put it.[157]

Chapter 4
The Guardians of Morality

Sexual politics played a huge role in the conflicts that led to the Spanish Civil War. It is sometimes difficult for "liberated" people to recognize that the short-term effect of their sexual-freedom discourse is a net increase in sexual anxiety, readily exploited by authoritarian personalities and institutions. Following Franco's victory, numerous proponents of sex without guilt (intellectuals, professionals, leftist leaders) carried their provocative beliefs with them into exile; those unable to escape—the vast majority of Spaniards—would shoulder the burden of a greatly enhanced sexual authoritarianism for several decades thereafter.

Even as they grieved for their fallen comrades, Spanish clerics of the 1940s had reason to rejoice: they had won the custody battle. As good *padres* they understood that rescuing the people (the children) from pre-Franco laicist eroticism would not be easy; but they had some twenty thousand pulpits at their disposal and they were more respected and/or feared in the cities than at any time in Spain's history. In rural and provincial areas the clerics enjoyed an even greater sway over the minds and hearts of their flock; throughout Spain episcopal power was integrated with that of civil governors in formal and informal ways. Mussolini and Italian fascism had been forced to contend with the Catholic Church; Franco, by contrast, the savior and Caudillo of Spain, was transported in early-1940s religious processions under a canopy by the bishops themselves. The 1953 Concordato or treaty with the Vatican ratified arrangements and dispositions that had existed since 1938 at least (some dated back to the Counter Reformation). Catholicism was declared the official creed of Spain; other faiths were not permitted; religious instruction in the public schools was obligatory; the clergy enjoyed both state financing and judicial immunity, as well as control and censorship of the press, books, theater, and movies. So many clerics found employment in the Ministry of Education under Franco that it came to be known as the Monastery of Education.

In the meantime, Falangists who had fallen for the Nationalist cause were commemorated with plaques built into church walls in their home-towns. The seminaries were full again, and groups like Acción Católica, Congregaciones Marianas, and Hijas de María had hundreds of thou-sands of new members. Children born of agnostic parents during the war, now walking and talking, were brought in to be baptized and given saints' names, instead of "Bakunin," "Germinal," "Lenin," and the like.[1] Given the close identification of church and state, participation in reli-gious activities was almost a civil obligation. Former adherents of the Republic and atheists accepted it because they had no desire to call at-tention to themselves. There were even conflicts in pro-Franco homes, usually along the gender fault line. Legions of long-suffering fathers and sons, writes Eslava, had to put up with the sanctimonious tyranny of wives or mothers who were "more papist than the Pope."[2] Doña Perfecta had returned with a vengeance.

For more than three decades Spain was saturated with religious publi-cations, processions, novenas, pilgrimages, retreats, spiritual exercises, nocturnal adorations, midnight masses, sermons, and rosaries. Few could remember such an intense period of devotion. One of the biggest events was the International Eucharistic Congress celebrated in Barce-lona in 1952 with twelve cardinals, three hundred bishops, archbishops, and abbots, over fifteen thousand priests and seminary students, and one dictator. Pope Pius XII joined in by radio to congratulate "our be-loved son Francisco Franco." In the grandiose culminating act of the congress at Montjuïc stadium, 819 seminarians were ordained priests while half a million people took Holy Communion. The prostitutes of Barcelona had been "cordially invited" to leave the city for the duration of the saintly festivities. Franco was later made a knight of the Supreme Equestrian Order of the Militia of Our Lord Jesus Christ, the Vatican's highest lay honor.[3]

Warnings about dances, beaches, and women's fashions occupied a predictably disproportionate space in pastoral epistles. Swimsuits were designed to maximize modesty and minimize exposure, and in any case were permitted for water use only; sunbathing was not allowed without a bathrobe in place, and the names of transgressors were made public. In May 1951 the First National Congress of Beach and Swimming Pool Morality was held in Valencia; the objective of the organizers, the Epis-copal Commission on Morality and Orthodoxy in Spain, was segregation by gender at every beach and swimming pool in Spain.[4] Although this goal was not achieved, for many years Spanish bathers were to be care-fully observed by men with binoculars—not to save them from drowning but to enforce decency and decorum. The bishop of Barcelona fretted about the growing presence of foreign tourists on Spain's beaches with their "gravely sinful behavior" and their "exotic and immoral fashions that could not even be described without offending your modesty."[5] The Jesuit Father Laburu added that any "normally constituted man" watching a woman exhibit herself on the beach could not help but feel reckless lust growing within.[6] One type of sex was authorized: that of husband and wife specifically intended for procreation, and even this type was morally risky. Couples were urged to preface their coupling with the pious phrase, "Señor, no es por vicio ni fornicio, que es por dar hijos a tu servicio" [Lord, we do this not out of vice or lust, but to have children to serve you].[7] Some Catholic marriage manuals sought to resuscitate an ancient practice known as *las noches de Tobías* (Tobias nights) whereby a pair of newlyweds would deliberately refrain from consummating their marriage for three consecutive nights in order to appease the divinity.[8]

What happened with sexual morality under Franco was partly the revenge of the country mouse on his envied cousin of the city. Political scientist Juan Linz affirms that it was the clergy's lower-middle-class rural extraction and narrow seminary studies that made them "reverent toward those with money and power who had facilitated their upward mobility with scholarships and connections," but mistrustful of everyone else—women, intellectuals, proletarians.[9] Like Franco himself, many priests were fervently committed to late-nineteenth-century conspiracy theories that attributed all of Spain's problems to Freemasons, Jews, communists, and protestants. But we should also remember that the Church triumphant under Franco was an extremely traumatized church, still mourning for thousands of clergy and family members slaughtered in the late 1930s. Therefore it was hypervigilant. Unfortunately, the new regime was not set up to help people work through their rigidities, but to make rigidity state policy. Francoism facilitated what one psychoanalyst calls the "intergenerational transmission" of posttraumatic constructs, whereby new generations become "reservoirs of the mental representations of past generations victimized by some historical trauma."[10] Hence the irony: While the full force of *political* repression was reserved for the working classes, the big losers of the civil war, the weight of *sexual* repression was to be borne by the sons and daughters of the winning middle and upper middle classes, educated in private religious schools and inculcated with the posttraumatic paradigms of the priests, for example, that the civil war was caused by lewd behavior and pleasure-seeking.

What made this phobic religious message even worse was the liberal use of corporal punishment, practiced throughout the Catholic and public educational systems. In the schools run by religious orders the negative messages were easier to inculcate, obviously. As the ex-Carmelite nun Frances Lannon writes,

Few would contest and many thousands affirm that the schools of the Jesuits or Marists or Ursulines or Sisters of Mercy were much the same in the 1950s as they had been in the 1920s. It was probably clearer in the schools than in any other aspect of Church life how victory in the civil war had frozen and preserved attitudes that already in the 1920s seemed extreme in Catholic Europe. Imperviousness to cultural influences from beyond the frontiers, the subordination of women, a puritanical and obsessively negative view of sexuality, a highly authoritarian interpretation of politics and social relations were all dominant features of Catholic post-war education so well known—because so widely suffered—that they hardly need documenting.[11]

For their own good, to echo Alice Miller, Spanish schoolchildren of the epoch were segregated by gender and physically punished for the slightest breaches of classroom discipline. According to one female survivor, the constant liturgical activities

often engendered a secret repugnance, because they were inseparable from the presence and vigilance of religious personnel feared for their inflexibility or their brutality. In the case of boarding schools, the way pupils were treated could produce real traumas. Separated from their families, frightened by the fear of hell if they sinned against the sixth commandment, they would carry with them the imprint of an education that they would later reject but that left them marked forever.[12]

Here is the testimony of another member of the same unfortunate psychoclass:

We as children of that epoch looked on in astonishment at the deployment of Catholic fervor without really knowing what we had done to have to kneel down and implore heaven's forgiveness. Once a year we spent a week locked up in a *casa de ejercicios espirituales.* During the chapel sermonettes a severe Jesuit father would urge us to repent before it was too late. "You could all die tonight!" we heard him shout in the penumbra.[13]

Lannon relates that "autobiographical memoirs of childhood in Catholic bourgeois families and schools are pervaded by the ignorance, fear and guilt induced by omnipresent sexual and physical taboos."[14]

Wilhelm Reich argued that the creation of sexual anxiety over masturbation was the primary means of anchoring both religion and the authoritarian social order in Catholic youths; Foucault said something similar in his final New York lecture.[15] Let us explore this hypothesis with Spanish data from the Franco years, when masturbation was the schoolteacher's greatest obsession. Thanks to the (obligatory) sacrament of confession, prelude to the (obligatory) weekly communion in the schools, the priests were able to calculate that roughly eight out of ten boys and three out of ten girls were habitual masturbators.[16] To the prospect of hellfire the clergy added health warnings: children were told that masturbation was associated with heart problems, spinal debilities, brain tumors, and bowel obstructions. Even Spain's terrible postwar economic conditions were utilized by the priests to terrorize students. The following sermon was first delivered in 1942:

Forty meals! The energy of forty meals thrown overboard every time that you fall into the solitary vice! An energy that your growing bodies need for normal development. Haven't you seen those scrawny, feeble, weak, sickly, prematurely old men who beg for money on the street and dig in the trash cans? Haven't you felt sorry for them? Well: those are the ones who masturbated when they were young. Look at the sad state they're in, see how they've ended up! Note where solitary sin leads! Those dull eyes! Those flaccid muscles! Those drained bodies! All boys who masturbated! There they have the recompense for their sin: for one second of impure pleasure, a whole life of misery and a whole eternity of terrible torments in hell.[17]

Then the priest would move in for the kill, announcing that he need only examine the underside of each pupil's right eyelid to determine whether or not they had been playing with themselves. To augment feelings of guilt he would gesture at the crucifix on the wall and point out that every act of masturbation was the moral equivalent of a Jew spitting on Christ, a Sadducee striking him with a belt, a Pharisee lash with a whip, a slap by a rabbi of the Sanhedrin, and so on. The short- and long-term effects of this on young minds can be imagined.

The intensified shame-inducing morality renewed by priests under Franco was aided and abetted by a large population of shamed individuals eager to extend their own harsh introjects to others. In this process we can identify many levels and many spheres of influence: the enforcement of shame was carried out by archbishops and by pious old ladies, by the Ministerio de Información y Turismo and by small-town policemen, parish priests, confessors, and teachers, and by legions of bureaucrats anxious to please their superiors. Thousands of people took patriotism and moral vigilance to be one and the same thing, as indeed it was proclaimed to be. Even people in the smallest ponds could feel like big frogs.[18] Scores of energetic young Catholics joined up with the so-called Luises, the creation of the Jesuit Father Llanos, to go around separating couples or forcing newsstand vendors to remove offensive material from public view.[19] Zeal in the defense of morality was no vice; thus, another priest named Father Morales organized a large band of young followers and gave them the dizzying permission to commit property crimes for religious motives. In 1947 the adepts of Father Morales took up the glove symbolically cast down by Rita Hayworth (born Margarita Cansino) in the role of *Gilda*, angrily throwing ink bottles at her cleavage as displayed on movie posters or the big screen itself.[20]

The minister in charge of censorship, the ultra-Catholic Gabriel Arias Salgado, boasted that his efforts had saved countless souls from hell. He also believed that Stalin regularly traveled to a mine shaft in the Republic of Azerbaijan to receive instructions from Satan.[21] Although censors derived their moral authority and psychology from National Catholicism, they received their job security and pay from the government; thus it was in their own interest to make nit-picking and pettifogging demands on authors, artists, singers, dancers, producers, choreographers—anyone involved in the production of popular culture in Franco's Spain. These entertainment professionals included men and women whose Francoist credentials and allegiance to the regime were beyond dispute. In the end, people on the production side of Spanish popular culture learned to censor themselves first rather than engage in sterile battles.[22] Every newspaper and magazine in Spain had personnel in charge of retouching photos in order to disguise the real proportions of female stars. Words like *moño* or *caño* were discouraged, since by a typographical error they could easily become *coño* (a vulgar expression for the female pubic area). The song "Bésame mucho" was prohibited for obvious reasons, as was "Espinita," thought to foment adultery. All references to prostitution were deleted from the immortal "Ojos verdes." The censors who authorized Nat King Cole's "Ansiedad" were fired. The hit song "Raskayú" by composer Bonet de San Pedro barely made it past the censor, since one of its lyrics asks "Raskayú, cuando mueras, ¿qué harás tú? Tú serás un cadáver nada más" (Raskayú, when you die, what will you do? You'll be nothing but a cadaver). The censor correctly pointed out that such an affirmation was at variance with official church dogma regarding the afterlife.[23]

Carmen de Lirio, Spain's shapeliest vedette of the late forties and fifties, recalls a censor who sat in the front row during the final dress rehearsal for one of her shows. As soon as she began to sing her song, "Toma negro, toma café," the man jumped out of his seat and shouted, "Be so kind as to not shake your lower belly, Señorita!"[24] No show could go on without official approval, which in practice meant prolonged negotiations among the singers, dancers, director, producer, and censors. A guardian of morality could sometimes be persuaded to ease his demands by a sumptuous meal (very persuasive in those days of food rationing). One censor filed the following report in 1953:

In the show of the 20th of August the Inspection Service of this Delegation has made the following observations: In the first number, the chorus girls were not wearing the slips they had been ordered to, thereby allowing their buttocks to be seen. In the Cuban number, the chorus girls, though not all of them, allow the inner surface of their thighs to be seen and do not wear the little skirt as requested at the rehearsal. Señorita Loli is still using transparent chiffon near her lap, thereby allowing her panties to be seen. In the final number, the movements of the dancers are very exaggerated. Especially Señorita Susi, who while making an exit with her back turned to the public effects a rotating movement with her hips that is most indecorous. In the same number, the chorus girls do not simply file down the catwalk as ordered, but indulge in choreographically indecent wiggling.[25]

A hefty fine and even the closing of the show could be the result of such reports. An argument with a censor ended the career of the venerable theatrical director José Juan Cadenas. A dress rehearsal had been interrupted repeatedly by a censor who wanted the girls' costumes to cover more flesh; an angry Cadenas ordered the house lights turned up and faced the censor: " 'How old are you, young man?' 'I'm 27, Mr. Cadenas.' 'What a pity! When I was your age I spent my time undressing women, not dressing them. Lights out! The show is cancelled!' "[26]

Moral criteria were never applied with national uniformity. Shows that were permitted in cities of twenty thousand or more were prohibited in small towns; dancers in Barcelona could show their navels, those in Madrid could not. Often a show approved by the city censors ran afoul of the Church in the provinces. Cardinal Segura of Seville decreed that anyone in his flock who attended *La blanca doble* would be excommunicated, for it was "a diabolical spectacle in which the impudent exhibition of almost-naked women incites the lowest passions of concupiscence in men."[27] The result: long lines at the ticket office. When the show got to Las Palmas in the Canary Islands, Monsignor Antonio Pildain cleverly stationed a group of women dressed in mourning next to the ticket window; when anyone approached to buy a ticket, the women would clamor, "Let us pray a *padrenuestro* for the soul of this sinner who is about to commit a mortal sin by attending the show."[28] This reduced ticket sales much more effectively, and eventually Pildain was made a bishop. What one writer calls Pildain's "anathematizing activity" was still going strong in the early 1970s, when the prelate sought to block planned homages to authors Benito Pérez Galdós ("spokesman for the infamous *Electra* campaign") and Miguel de Unamuno ("maximum heretic and teacher of heretics").[29]

*   *   *

In every country, the Catholic Church reviews films and assigns them a moral "grade." In Spain it was able to do much, much more. At least one priest was guaranteed a seat on every board or commission involved in censorship in any way; he was known as the *vocal eclesiástico* and, unlike civilian members, possessed veto power. According to Teodoro González Ballesteros, an expert in the field, Spanish priests "participated directly, and with decisive efficacy, in the authorization or prohibition of films." Censorship was already in effect by 1937 in Nationalist-controlled areas and continued in an arbitrary manner until the eve of the promulgation of the Constitution of 1978. Some sixty thousand films were processed by censors during this period; González Ballesteros reproduces 1,710 *fichas* (record cards) of movies that had to be altered for political or moral reasons. Political reasons included any shot or scene that denigrated Franco's former allies, Hitler and Mussolini. In the case of movies censored for sexual content, the *fichas* afford us precious insights into the workings of the Spanish censor's mind, practically identical to the ecclesiastical mind of the time. In what follows I offer instructive examples drawn from the priceless catalog of González Ballesteros.[30]

In the first years of the regime, any scenes or shots that contained references to adultery or even potential adultery were removed or greatly shortened. The 1939 Spanish movie *Susana tiene un secreto* (dir. Benito Perojo) was required to "suppress in the fourth reel the scene in which Susana, dressed in her wedding-gown, says: 'Nowadays it's the fashion for women to know everything by the time they get married.' " The words "Never get married—marriage is torture" were cut out of another movie the following year. Even a soporific mining documentary, *Magnesium in Spain*, was obliged to "suppress all shots in which women appear working"—not because they were in provocative postures but because it contradicted official propaganda about woman's proper place (the home). The fact that all foreign movies had to be dubbed in Castilian Spanish enabled cultural repressors to eliminate or disguise objectionable plot elements. In an American movie of 1949, the actress says, "My father and mother were divorced when I was just a little girl," but in the Spanish version she says, "My father died when I was just a little girl." All this in order to explain the mother's remarriage at the end of the film. Does this mean that displays of normal, healthy marital affection were permitted? No. Since Augustine, the Church had held that sex was a necessary evil, even within marriage. An occasional peck on the cheek slipped through the early censorship, but a man picking up his new bride and carrying her into the bedroom was eliminated from the Spanish *De lo pintado a lo vivo* (dir. Antonio de Obregón, 1951). Even in Anthony Mann's *El Cid*, starring Charlton Heston and filmed on location in Spain, the amorous sequences between the Cid and his loving wife, Doña Jimena, were cut to a minimum. Heston's phrase "Why can't Moors and Christians live in peace with one another" was also excised.

French movies were carefully scrutinized to suppress not only the female busts but the ubiquitous busts of Voltaire—the deist philosophe anathema to Spanish clergy since the eighteenth century. Italian movies were an even bigger headache for Spain's censors, since they originated within a culture whose canons of arousal greatly resembled those of Spain. The Iberian distributor of the Italian *Seven Widows and a Bachelor* (dir. Mario Mattoli, 1950) was simply told to eliminate all of the "thigh scenes." There was something troubling (arousing) in nearly every reel of *Mundo de noche* (dir. Gianni Proia, 1963): "Suppress the ritual dance of Nairobi. Suppress the sequence of the girl inside a cage. Suppress the scene of the Japanese girl obliged to undress between balloons. Suppress the dance sequence in the jungle of the Bahamas. Suppress the Muscle-Boys sequence. Suppress the striptease in silhouette sequence. Suppress every one of the New Orleans sequences." In Hitchcock's *Psycho* the famous shower scene and subsequent murder were naturally cut to the bare minimum. In the American-made documentary *The Vatican of Pius XII*, all references to the Vatican's treasury of artistic nudes were omitted. It goes without saying that Goya documentaries did not include long shots of his famous *Naked Maja*—close-ups of her eyes were permitted. An American movie's reference to press censorship was censored. The Spanish version of *An American in Paris* (dir. Vincente Minnelli, 1952) had to "speed up" the kissing scenes and do entirely without the cancan dancers. The 1959 Walt Disney cartoon *A Duck's Imagination* had to drop a close-up shot of a woman's bust bursting from a book. Beginning with *From Russia with Love* (1964), the opening credits' suggestive female dancers or swimmers were edited out of James Bond movies. The 1970 Italian *Portrait of Dorian Gray* was instructed to "suppress the shot in the boat scene when a girl puts her hand on Dorian's crotch." *Little Big Man* was shown in Spain sans references to women copulating with horses, and the daring Spanish *Pecado mortal* (dir. Miguel Angel Díez, 1977) had to delete a scene in which a woman eroticizes herself with a cat.

Spain's censors strove to keep Catholicism and the clergy from falling into ridicule. Here are a few of the many shots and scenes cut from the American religious movie *The Keys of the Kingdom* (dir. John M. Stahl, 1955):

Reel 10. In the scene of the priest assisting the dying doctor, suppress the shot in which the nun turns on her heel and exits angrily.
Reel 11. Suppress the shots of the priest in the enemy camp when he crouches, picks up the torch, and throws it into the gasoline to provoke the explosion. With this cut the impression will be given that the explosion was caused by the Major's gunshots.

The phrase "as ugly as the widow of a clergyman" was removed from a 1952 British film, for obvious reasons. In reel 6 of *The Sinking of the Titanic* (dir. Jean Negulesco, 1953), the distributor was told to "revise the priest's story in such a way that he no longer seems a Catholic priest who was demoted by Rome for drunkenness." George Sidney's *Scaramouche* (1953) was required to insert a notice at the start of the film advising that dueling was forbidden by the Church. The Italian *Renunciación* (dir. Luigi Zampa, 1955) was forced to revise every dialogue in order to make it clear "that the priest did not know that the money sent by Agustina came from prostitution and crooked business deals." No films, foreign or domestic, were allowed to feature suicides, including the 1955 British version of *Romeo and Juliet*. Dozens of vampire movies reviewed by censors over the years were obliged to omit references to clergy, Catholic dogma, and extreme unction, with special instructions to remove shots in which characters are struck or burned with crucifixes or the Eucharist. In an American western of 1956, the town clergyman's advice to Johnny the Coward had to be "rectified so that it does not incite to revenge but to law and order and legitimate self-defense." In Charles Vidor's *The Swan* (1958), the order came down to "suppress the shots of the friar in his underwear putting his habit on in the hallway." The following year a Spanish film, *El inquilino* (dir. José Antonio Nieves Conde), was obliged to water down the implications of its theme (Spain's severe housing shortage) and "suppress the shot of the '*beata*' praying and blessing herself, and later the one of the table when it falls to the floor with all the holy cards and the woman shouts 'Ay, my saints!' " Rather more explosive was the potential of *The Prisoner*, a 1960 film by director Peter Glenville:

Reel 5. Suppress the phrase of the Cardinal when he affirms that he has never loved his mother.
Reel 8. In the trial scene, suppress any aspect of the Cardinal's confession related to treason or crimes of a religious nature, like using the confessional for blackmail.

The British were at it again in *Anne of the Thousand Days* (1970) with a titillating scene of the cardinal's housekeeper lying in his bed. The Spanish comedy *Vamos a contar mentiras* (1962) was required to drop the line "thieves, priests, monks" and water down the scene of the imposter priests. Two years later, the Italian *Camping* (dir. Franco Zeffirelli) was ordered to "suppress the shot in which they break an egg on the face of a priest." A 1964 movie made in Castro's Cuba was authorized only after the distributor agreed to "suppress shots of the priest eating chicken while the others shoot themselves to death." The next year Spanish director José Luis Madrid was obliged to do without the scene of nuns praying the rosary in a van in his film *La vuelta*. A shot ridiculing friars walking through their cloister was cut out of the Spanish comedy *Juguetes rotos*. Hitchcock's *Frenzy* (1972) had to drop a particularly dangerous line in the eleventh reel: "Religious and sexual manias are closely linked." For the following season's *Corazón solitario*, a French-Spanish production, the censor decreed that "In the confession sequence, it will be necessary to suppress everything that induces one to think that the priest takes delight in imagining how ardent she [the penitent] must be." A Spanish-Italian comedy of the same year had to remove "the sequence in which the priest is subjected to the amorous advances of a fat woman." A scene of a monk striking a soldier with a crucifix was removed from the Italian *Soldier of Fortune* in 1976, and in the same year Robert Altman's *M*A*S*H* had to do without the Last Supper parody.

Even with their power over the content of films shown in Spain, Catholic clergymen were never comfortable with the inherently spectacular paganistic medium. And if film scholar Marsha Kinder is correct, uncensored Spanish films with religious themes were as potentially erotic as anything suppressed by the censors. Even homoerotic, as exemplified by *Marcelino, pan y vino* (dir. Ladislao Vajda, 1954), which tells the story of a five-year-old orphan raised by a dozen "mothering" monks and his mystical encounters with an image of the crucified Christ in the monastery attic. This family movie was extremely popular throughout Spain and the Hispanic world, perhaps because the public remained blithely unaware of the "blatant masochism" and "pederastic overtones" that Kinder discovers.[31]

Be that as it may, Spanish culture under Franco allows us to observe large-scale effects of perverse ideations and behaviors brought into existence by the very techniques designed to quash them. Reich had argued that the Church's well-organized attempt to repress sexuality in general, and youthful masturbation in particular, often served to awaken a counterforce of pregenital infantile impulses in young people. With the help of psychotherapy, "the Christian youth will soon realize that his intensive exhibitionistic and perverse inclinations refer partly to a regression to early infantile forms of sexuality and partly to an inhibition of genital sexuality."[32] Without psychotherapy, vast masses of masturbators will feel perverse, or sinful, or evil to one degree or another, thereby locking the behavior in place. The consciousness of doing something bad is essential to perverse pleasure, as Stoller pointed out.[33]

Unlike certain literary critics of our day, the aging Iberian dictator and his technocrats came to realize that perversion was not subversion. When censorship was relaxed in the late sixties, Spain experienced a veritable explosion of theater productions and movies that in no way threatened the stability of the regime. Historian Rafael Torres does not disguise his disgust:

That cinema of 1970–1975, the product of thirty years of total repression, showed the result of that continual institutional bombardment: the moviegoing public was largely imbecile, randy, puerile, and salacious, laughing at the insane adventures of a Landa or a López Vázquez—scrawny insincere men obsessed with genitals, cheating on their wives with a horde of voluptuous Scandinavians. Sex, love, and eroticism turned out to be, in film and in the streets, something worse than sin: it was a nightmare.[34]

Alfredo Landa and José Luis López Vázquez, let me emphasize, were very talented actors whose only "crime" was to personify the perverse erotic imagination of their fellow Spaniards. Torres is no nostalgic apologist for sexual authoritarianism, but a critic of the sexual immaturity that results from it.

In effect, the Spanish public had gone in for what was called *pornoceltibérico* like a potent but naive bull charging the cape held by Manuel Fraga Iribarne, the minister in charge of relaxing censorship. What they were being offered, Reich could have told them, was "not the sexuality of the *future*, but *the pleasure born of the contradiction between morality and instinct*, the pleasure of a dictatorial society, *debased, sordid, pathological pleasure.*"[35] No amount of Left Bank wishful thinking can turn dehumanizing perversion into redemptive subversion. The smutty Spanish comedies of the 1970s were an imaginative but ultimately bogus solution to a failure of intimacy; like perverse ideation itself, they cannily portrayed themselves as part of the solution rather than part of the problem.[36]

Men and Women Under Franco

In keeping with the program promoted by the Margaritas and other traditionalist sectors, Spain's youngsters were told little about the recent past and far more than they wanted to know about Spain's glorious sacromilitary traditions of conquest and conversion. Teachers' lesson plans dealt obsessively with the far-off period of the Gothic kings, Spain's version of the Aryan mythology so popular and so deadly in other parts of Europe.[37] Children's comics glorified figures like Alonso Pérez de Guzmán, the thirteenth-century warlord who had been more than willing to sacrifice his son's life to maintain possession of a stronghold. In her evocative study of life in postwar Spain, Carmen Martín Gaite poignantly penned the reaction of Spain's children to such hoary lore.[38] For many girls of her generation, she writes, the lifestyles and mentalities of the "new" Spain seemed ancient by comparison with those they associated with the much maligned Republic. Regardless of their parents' ideological affiliations, teenagers of the 1940s harbored childhood memories of the more stimulating and colorful Republican period, when grandmothers with shawls and prayer books shared the street with milicianas, when women could attend political meetings, drive cars, smoke with their legs crossed, or get a divorce.

Good-bye to all that. In the new-old social system of 1940s Spain, a woman's identity was defined by her relationship with the sacrament of matrimony. That includes the formal public rejection of marriage with human men in favor of symbolic marriage with Christ. There was something mysterious and romantic about such a higher calling, Martín Gaite relates; a religious vocation could be disobeyed with secular society's tacit approval, but, if heeded, it empowered a young woman to smile condescendingly on those who dared to question it. When the one doing the questioning was the girl's mother, an intense Oedipal/spiritual battle was liable to ensue. The mother superior of a convent in Albacete saw fit to inform secular mothers of the consequences of thwarting their daughters' religious callings, citing the tragic outcomes of four cases with which she was personally acquainted: two girls forced to marry had died during childbirth; another caught tuberculosis and died on the day she would have entered the convent; the fourth went insane and cast herself into a well, "leaving her mother overcome with sorrow." All this appeared in a Catholic school bulletin.[39]

As respectable as nuns were the many women whose fiancés or husbands had been killed in the war and who had decided not to seek out another man. It was typical for such women to retain close ties with the mother and sisters of the absent one, and many dressed in black permanently. No one could call them old maids, since God himself had intervened to take away the loved one. Some four thousand men of the Blue Legion had died fighting for the Nazis in the early forties, converting many Spanish women into "eternal fiancées." After the wars the young female population of the country was significantly greater than the young male population. In 1952 there were still two hundred thousand more women in Madrid than men. The sharp increase in priestly and monkly vocations further reduced the number of available young males. It was therefore inevitable that a considerable number of women with no desire to be brides of Christ would not find human husbands either. By sheer demographic logic they were fated to be *solteronas*, or old maids.

Such terms still have the power to unsettle women in our day, and in Franco's Spain they inspired genuine terror. The government had adopted all sorts of policies designed to restore the country's population to prewar levels. The first fertility-rewarding *ley de protección a las familias numerosas* was promulgated in August 1941; henceforth women would be coerced in subtle and gross ways to stay out of the job market and stay in the marriage market until they fulfilled their highest mission to Spain: catch a husband and get pregnant (preferably in that order). The cruelest fate that could befall a woman was *quedarse para vestir santos*, to wind up dressing icons, supposedly the typical activity of lonely unmarried women with plenty of time on their hands and nothing better to do than help out at the local church.

The fear of winding up a solterona was possibly the most powerful informal agent of socialization, one reinforced by the government, institutions of all types, and popular songs. Submitting to a man was supposedly every woman's most cherished dream.[40] Special efforts were made to encourage less attractive girls to accentuate the positive and dissemble the negative to better compete with the comely. As one female journalist advised her readers following Franco's victory: "The hour of the homely ones has arrived. . . . Girls who are too beautiful are somewhat predisposed to foolishness. But our homely one reads, educates herself. Her features are a little irregular, that's true, but she has an intelligent look, well-cared-for skin, hair combed with simplicity and good taste, a little bit of makeup wisely applied. . . . The homely girl doesn't give up: she struggles and wins."[41] Another text describes a homely girl named Luisa who becomes disillusioned, then escapist and reserved, then bitter, finally "frequenting the church without true piety"—to dress saints, surely.[42] The most common and grating piece of advice given to girls was to smile. A man could have a severe or austere expression (like Franco); women had to be pleasant, friendly, smiling. Not to smile was strange, antisocial, and, Martín Gaite suggests, secretly rebellious—a good way to wind up dressing saints.

Strange as it may sound at first, the homely girl had a strong ally in Spanish machismo. In a country where men "copulate with their eyes," affirms Eslava, to marry a woman too attractive was to ask for the never-ending torment of jealousy and paranoia provoked by lascivious eyes and propositions from every macho in the street.[43] Such women were in demand as mistresses and one-night affairs by the very same men who preferred small, average-looking, brunette virgins for purposes of matrimony.

Ava Gardner's visit to Spain in 1950 to make a movie illustrates this psychology well. As Eslava relates, the people of Spain knew nothing of her promiscuity, nor would they have believed that a woman could use men for sex anyway. Thus, when Gardner bedded her Spanish costar, an elegant and cultured bullfighter named Mario Cabré, every man in the country identified with him and lived his romance vicariously. The well-publicized jealousy of Frank Sinatra only served to accentuate the prestige of the Spanish macho-designate. But when shooting was finished, Ava packed her bags and left, brushing Mario off like an annoying fly. Unable to believe that the actress abandoned the matador, the Spanish public bought the latter's version of events: "The truth is that I was afraid to marry her." She was both too beautiful, he pointed out, and not a virgin—two strikes against her in the Spanish marriage market.

Iberian machismo predates Franco, obviously, but it achieved special degrees of intensity under him, as did that quintessence of machismo, *donjuanismo*. Donjuanismo is more sophisticated than garden-variety machismo in that it requires the would-be seducer to possess a subtle knowledge of female paradigm scenarios; only by telling them what they secretly want to hear will the seducer be successful. A Don Juan is not interested in women per se, only as tokens of his social dominance or virility in a perpetual game of one-upmanship with rivals and father figures. George Devereux argued that "the successful resolution of oedipal ties and conflicts calls for a fantasized homosexual triumph over the father."[44] In the case of Don Juan, *no rival equals no desire*, in genuine Girardian fashion, and the conquest of a woman means nothing at all unless the whole masculine world knows about it. While in Spain, says Eslava, Ava Gardner also slept with José Luis Dominguín (Hemingway's favorite matador). She was startled when immediately after sex Dominguín jumped out of bed and hurriedly put his clothes on. "But, what are you doing? Where are you going?" The matador was surprised at her surprise. "Where do you think I'm going?" he responded. "To tell everyone about this!"

The enthusiasm Spanish males felt for foreign female sex symbols turned to resentment when they observed the attractions that international male stars held for Spanish women. Again, the macho touchiness in question predated Francoism. During the 1930s, the immortal Carlos Gardel made women weak in the knees all over the Spanish-speaking world with his sentimental tangos; jealous Spaniards retaliated by defining the tango as "the laments of a cuckold as sung by a pimp." An even bigger rival/role model was Jorge Negrete, the Mexican baritone whose delightful *corridos* celebrated machismo in general and his own in particular. When he pulled into Madrid's Atocha train station in 1948, scores of female fans ripped the buttons and zippers from his clothes. Fed up with the excesses of his female fans in Spain, Negrete loudly asked in a nightclub, "¿Qué pasa? Aren't there any men in this country?" A Spanish patriot avenged national honor right then and there, says Eslava, silencing the Mexican with a resounding slap on the face.

For a variety of reasons, Spanish men were not nearly so eager to tie the knot as women were. There was, for one thing, the fear of the opposite sex drummed into their heads as schoolchildren; in many cases the brainwashing was so successful that the youths simply opted out of the marriage game altogether to become priests and monks. Other young men weary of masturbation discovered they could achieve fast relief for their biological needs either in a *casa de tolerancia* or, if they belonged to the middle or upper classes, with a maidservant. The civil war had made Spain safe for this and many other benighted customs based on the abuse of social position. In fact, says Eslava, many pious mass-attending mothers kept this possibility in view when hiring a maid or cook, making sure that she was as clean and pleasant as possible; since boys will be boys, it was better for their son to relieve their urges with someone trustworthy rather than risk venereal disease with a streetwalker.[45] The knowledge of numerous unhappy marriages with no possibility of divorce, and the economic demands of a wife and children, also conspired to give Spanish men cold feet.

On the other hand, social forces arrayed against the bachelor were constant and unrelenting. There were far more women than men in Spain, constantly sharing information with one another regarding techniques and methods for snaring a husband. More important still, married men with dependents were considered more stable and more reliable as employees; raises and promotions were always meted out to married men, rarely to bachelors. There were, in addition, constant exhortations from the government for people to pair off and procreate for the good of the country. Francoist psychiatrist Vallejo-Nájera (the doctor who studied female Marxist delinquents), wrote that "The bachelor, as a general rule, is a bad patriot and a bad citizen, or a sick man."[46]

Fear of being thought a homosexual must be added to the list of good reasons to marry. Boys were watched anxiously by parents and teachers for unequivocal signs of their gender identity. Woe to the young man who showed too much fondness for flowers, housecleaning, or folk dancing and not enough enthusiasm for fundamental masculine pastimes. As one popular song put it:

El hijo que tiene Asunción   The son that Asunción has
ni fuma, ni bebe,   doesn't smoke, or drink,
ni juega al balón   or play soccer.
Asunción, Asunción,   Asunción, Asunción,
mira que tu hijo será maricón.   Look, your son will be a fairy.[47]

There was no worse fate for a man than to be gay in the self-consciously virile society ushered in by Franco's victory. Lynching homosexuals caught in flagrante delicto was condoned; stoning them in public parks "was one of the innocent pastimes of gangs of little rascals." The powerfully motivating cry of "¡Maricón el último!" (Last one there is a fairy!) resonated in streets and plazas all over Spain, whenever a given little rascal challenged his chums to an improvised foot race. For decades young men took much care not to hold their cigarettes in their right hands or use umbrellas; they were further expected to crane their necks to ogle passing women. Plumbers and repairmen who propositioned housewives and got indignantly turned down excused themselves by saying they had not wished the *señora* to think they were fairies. During Franco's time only a tiny minority of intellectuals had anything positive to say about nonheterosexual forms of love. Exiled gay author Juan Goytisolo's *Juan sin tierra* is a brilliant dissection of the "collective schizophrenia" that resulted from the Church's stand on sin and purity. Following Franco's demise, homosexual desire will come to be seen as the very antithesis of authoritarian sexuality in numerous Spanish novels and films.[48]

*   *   *

The chief outlet for unmarried Spanish women under Franco was the Seccion Femenina. Its leader was Pilar Primo de Rivera, daughter of General Miguel Primo de Rivera (Spain's dictator of the twenties) and sister to José Antonio, the charismatic founder of Falange Española executed by leftists in 1936 and elevated to martyr status by Franco. Although Pilar never married, Martín Gaite suggests that her public image had much in common with that of the "eternal fiancée," devoted to keeping alive the movement started by "el Gran Ausente"—the Great Absent One, as her dead brother was referred to in Falangist circles.[49] The extravagant fascist writer Giménez Caballero hatched a plan for her to wed Hitler and sire a superrace, but Goebbels politely informed him that the Führer had lost a testicle in the Great War.[50] Doña Pilar was to remain eternally faithful to her brother's memory, and to his view of the Spanish woman's true virtues. Chief among them were submission and abnegation, but they also included strength and dignity, gentleness, good manners, and . . . smiling. Alicia Alted describes Pilar's devoted followers as "lay nuns," inasmuch as the vast majority remained unmarried themselves while organizing home economics and childcare courses in nearly every city, town, and village of Spain.[51] These courses formed part of every young woman's "social service" obligation. Here is where the immense power of the Sección Femenina really made itself felt, reports Martín Gaite, because any woman who wished to attend college, work for the government, apply for a passport or driver's license, or belong to any sort of recreational or cultural association, needed to have the little blue S.S. button on her lapel.[52]

The monolithic unanimity achieved by *nacional-catolicismo* in Spain contrasts sharply with church-state relations under Mussolini. Victoria De Grazia affirms that, "Compared to Italian Catholicism, Italian fascism was riddled with contending attitudes about young women. Like the Church, the dictatorship was reacting against the emancipatory tendencies of interwar society. Yet unlike Catholicism, it exploited the desire to be modern as much as it curbed it. Thus at every level, fascist institutions sent out mixed messages."[53] In Spain there were no mixed messages. For nearly forty years the Church, the Army, and the Sección Femenina stood together against all forms of subversion. Women under Franco were expected to be carriers of babies and of the ideologies of the regime. Some women were more dedicated to this goal than others, Helen Graham notes:

> As far as urban working-class women were concerned, social control came chiefly through their total absorption in the battle for material survival rather than by dint of any internalization of regime norms of "womanhood." . . . By contrast, however, the thousands of middle-class women mobilized as providers of basic health and education provision in the cadres of the Sección Femenina were often much more consciously engaged on a project: sustaining the social fabric in the vast material crisis of the 1940s, helping to stabilize the regime in order to build the New State as a self-consciously middle-class enterprise.[54]

There was at least one talented middle-class girl (Carmen Martín Gaite) for whom the obligatory social service was a silly and futile waste of six months, as hateful and cumbersome as the culottes that girls had to wear while performing Falangist calisthenics.

The Sección Femenina's commitment to physical fitness, inspired by European fascism, had as its principal justification the preparation of female bodies for maternity. Pilar Primo de Rivera and her assistants did succeed in raising the general level of health and physical fitness of Spanish women, with exercises that bore a strange resemblance to another proven area of Falangist expertise—Spanish folk dancing.[55] But it was here, finally, that the Sección Femenina finally ran afoul of another pillar of the regime—the Church, or rather the most conservative sector of the church hierarchy, for whom the very thought of so many young women jumping up and down reeked of "a neo-paganism of incalculable consequences," as one bishop put it.[56] Martín Gaite affirms that in reality the clerics had nothing to worry about: adolescent girls dutifully performed their jumping jacks in their cumbersome culottes just as one day they would dutifully comply with their marital obligations without removing their nightgowns. Alted writes that the women of Valladolid had to give up riding bicycles because of the apprehensions of the provincial archbishop, while the schoolgirls of Seville had to wait for the death of Cardinal Segura in order to practice any sport whatsoever.[57] As Spanish sociologist María Teresa Gallego has argued, the history of the Sección Femenina is, in general, the history of women learning to submit to symbolic violence.[58]

The emphasis on physical fitness did not mean that Spanish women were in charge of their own bodies. Catholic moral theology was reinforced throughout the Franco years not only by priests but also by doctors with similar mental paradigms. Jesus de Miguel's study of sixteen medical school manuals and scores of medical journals published from 1939 through 1975 presents a chilling portrait of what we might call "authoritarian gynecology." The position of Spanish physicians was that woman was, first and foremost, a mother, designed and destined to procreate within the framework of an indissoluble marriage. It was recommended that she be of medium height, with hips slightly wider than her shoulders, smooth skin, and well-developed breasts.[59] Women were especially vulnerable to psychosomatic illnesses, most doctors agreed; weak, more or less passive, more or less perverse, clearly unstable. At the same time, however, a few fervently Francoist gynecologists maintained that woman was superior to man—not because of her intelligence or her capacity to work, but simply because the future of the nation (and therefore of civilization itself) depended upon her womb. Spanish gynecological treatises of the epoch resolutely opposed women working outside the home: not only did it contribute to the "corruption of customs" and the "destruction of the family," it was a cause of serious illnesses. The general tendency was to see anything that happened to women's bodies, including menstruation and menopause, in pathological terms. Activities to be avoided by menstruating women were bathing, drinking alcohol, eating ice cream, exercising, studying, and making love. Women were especially unsuited for the medical profession, the male doctors observed; they had also observed that prolonged involvement with either sports *or sex* led to an unfortunate "masculinization" of women.

Woman's maternal destiny had a serious corollary: under Franco any form of rational birth control was forbidden. Dr. José Botella and a number of other Spanish gynecologists explained that birth control was quickly leading to the degeneration of the human race (outside of Spain). If for some bizarre reason a Spanish married couple did not wish to have children, there was a simple solution: abstinence. As late as 1975 the so-called rhythm method was being condemned in the strongest terms by two gynecologists at the Universidad de Navarra (Opus Dei); for Juan Jiménez and Guillermo López, *el método Ogino* was a de facto abortive system, therefore criminal, whose misuse was scientifically implicated in cases of mongolism.[60] Abortion itself was the occasion for the most indignant utterances of Spanish gynecologists, many of whom saw it as a Red invention or tactic, practiced only by those depraved beings who wanted to destroy Spanish society. Not that birth control, abortion, masturbation, lesbianism, or even sex education were topics actually discussed in most of the older gynecological manuals. Francoist doctors prided themselves on their exemplary moral decorum, which usually meant that certain themes were simply not mentioned, even for purposes of condemnation.

Moral criteria were not to be abandoned at any time or for any reason, not even in the treatment of infertility. The Church held that any emission of semen outside of a woman's vaginal cavity was illicit. How then to acquire a sperm sample for examination in the laboratory? Masturbation and coitus interruptus were obviously out of the question. So most of Spain's Catholic gynecologists settled on the use of a perforated condom, "with the hole made in such a way that the majority of the sperm is deposited in the vaginal cavity and only a small amount remains in the condom; otherwise, the maneuver will be too similar to contraception and therefore illicit." [61] Dr. Botella, director of Madrid's prestigious Institute of Obstetrics and Gynecology, used another technique: "The woman is directed to sit up in bed immediately following the [sex] act and place a saucer underneath, with which the excess semen that falls can be collected and sent for analysis." Fortunately for their consciences, Spain's sterility specialists were morally authorized to analyze sperm even when they suspected that it had been obtained in a sinful way.

Female passivity and frigidity were considered normal by the authoritarian gynecologists. The president of the Spanish Royal Academy of Medicine advised women to dissemble their "natural" frigidity on their wedding nights lest they dampen the desire of their new husbands, who in turn were advised to be gentle and "behave in such a way that the woman submits almost without realizing it." [62] Even though a few women were discovered to be capable of orgasm, the clitoris continued to be underrated, or censored, by the Spanish medical establishment. Sex was not for pleasure anyway, and masturbation was "the vice of abnormal women only." In other countries, doctors endeavored to keep pace with the socioeconomic emancipation of women and the discoveries of Freud and Kinsey. A number of Spanish gynecologists not only rejected the notion that psychoanalysis could help women with their sexual problems, but considered it to be a form of "moral rape" that only served to burden virgin minds with "the tremendous complexes and obsessions with sexual monstrosity of the Jew Freud." [63]

These jaundiced views of women and their bodies held by Francoist gynecologists were a faithful reflection of their privileged bourgeois habitus and social dominance. The best way to balance the picture is by reference to Dr. Jaime Espinell, the physician charged with certifying the health of Madrid's prostitutes during the 1950s. This doctor dispensed large doses of compassion along with the antibiotics he prescribed for the various venereal diseases afflicting the women. "I have heard many bleak stories," writes Espinell, "from the lips of these priestesses of impure love, profoundly sad and cruel stories, that made me rebel inside myself against the mask of hypocrisy worn by those who exploit them and live at their expense." [64] The number of pimps and exploiters—and cases of venereal disease—increased dramatically when legalized prostitution came to an end in 1956. Dr. Espinell eventually adopted an orphan after the mother, a former patient, was murdered by her pimp. As Torres points out, the exemplary and truly Christian conduct of Espinell contrasts with that of another gynecologist employed at the Hospital de San Juan de Dios, who prided himself on his numerous sexual liaisons with women he had previously certified as free from disease.

The stick of authoritarian sexuality under Franco was accompanied by the carrot of economic incentives, as annually provided for in legislation favoring large families. Two years before his death, for example, Franco handed the National Natality Prize to Francisco Rojas Gómez and his wife, residents of the province of Jaén and progenitors of nineteen children, all still living at home, fourteen of whom were under the age of eighteen. First prize in "family promotion" went to Rafael González Sánchez and his wife. Of the thirteen children born to them, one had died, one was in a residence for the mentally retarded, and the others had gone on to higher education and distinguished careers. Asked by a journalist whether so many children had been a problem, the father replied, "The only problem was that we were unable to have more."[65]

Spain in Recovery

By the 1990s, the crisis of vocations and the general secularization of Spanish society had led the church hierarchy to adopt positions that two noted sociologists characterized as "schizophrenic."[66] While on the one hand advocating a fairly radical wealth-redistribution plan through groups like Cáritas, most bishops nevertheless stiffened their extremely conservative stance on family morality. They took to scapegoating the moderate Socialist government while it was in power—even though it was quite accommodating to the Church.

It was far too accommodating for political scientist Gonzalo Puente Ojea, who compares Spain's much-heralded transition to democracy in the late 1970s with the Bourbon Restauración of the late 1870s: both were engineered from on high, he argues, with minimal input from the people and maximum regard for the ongoing interests of the Catholic Church.[67] In Puente's view, the bishops and their "lackeys" in the Spanish parliament (Socialist leaders included) have sought to lobotomize the national memory in the matter of past abuses. Of the eight measures Puente recommends to achieve a true separation of church and state in Spain, five of them deal with the traditional terrain of the national custody battle, the educational system:

We emphasize the practical consequences of the Catholic straitjacket on education because it represents perhaps the fundamental key to the current situation of Spanish society. Forty years of implacable Catholic indoctrination—in schools that continue to receive fundamental protection under the current government (economic subventions and official recognition of diplomas and titles)—have incorporated and in considerable measure perpetuated the sectarian thinking and nationalist vocation of the Spanish right fostered by Francoism, thereby producing successive generations, born after 1936, who at the very least are insensitive to ideological and political debate or, worse, have assimilated the stereotypes of Catholic ideas that destroy critical judgment and paralyze the mind. The exceptions, and they exist, only confirm the rule.

Puente himself would presumably count as one of the exceptions: born and raised in a devout middle-class Catholic family, he has gone on to become a leading anticlerical intellectual.[68]

Rhetoric aside, it is clear that authoritarian sexuality and its cultural support systems retain a good deal of their former power. Defenses that enable exploitative events at a microlevel derive their dynamics and find their alibis in families, institutions, and theologies. These larger systems can be instigators, accessories after the fact, or both. Consensual or not, sex without commitment does not require a priest to transcend his meager repertory of role-relationship models. After physical consummation he can continue to regard women as basically bad, dirty, and threatening—therefore erotic enough to make it likely that the behavior will be repeated, or become habit-forming, or addictive. Following his dysfunctional script, a priest can go from affair to affair or from brothel to brothel his entire life. Drewermann affirms that, among the priests he has known, it is far more common for them to engage in repeated episodes of forbidden and degraded sex than to sincerely fall in love with one whole woman.[69] And as Father Sipe points out, the celibate/sexual system works by ignoring prior history and seeing sexual problems as isolated acts to be confessed, forgiven, and forgotten.[70] Consider the backgrounds of abusive American priests summarized by Richard Irons and Mark Laaser: "They came from family backgrounds characterized by rigidity and dysfunction, with themes of abuse and neglect present. . . . They had limited training or education in the adverse effects of transference and countertransference in pastoral counseling. They had virtually no training or education in the areas of sexual abuse, domestic violence, addictive disease, or healthy professional boundaries."[71] On either side of the Atlantic such traits and training deficiencies make it much harder for either the priest or his superiors to acknowledge clergy sexual misconduct as a *pattern* that derives its energy (and its shield) from the institutional mind-set itself. Hence biographies like that of a seventy-year-old Spanish priest, Miguel S.P., who is living out his days as *cura* of a tiny hamlet of 320 souls. He was transferred there ten years ago from a mountain village with a population of 729, where he had been sent from a coastal town of 2,949 inhabitants, where he had been sent after being shuffled from one parish to another in a large city. Every one of the transfers was to get him out of hot water for having sexual relations with his female parishioners, Rodríguez alleges.[72]

Sometimes an affair with a married woman that was supposed to be "just for sex" can evolve into something more mature, as the priest's punitive superego slowly cedes terrain to what, in the context of his life, is a healthier ego and a greater capacity for intimacy. Ironically, that is when things can really get out of hand, as they did in the most important parish on the island of Ibiza. As religion teacher in the local high school and director of the mandatory classes for couples engaged to be married, Father Bartolomé Roselló had never missed an opportunity to counsel young people on the dangers of illicit sex; but on the side he was the ardent lover of the wife of a wealthy businessman. In 1989 the husband opened his eyes and hired a detective; soon he was in possession of an audio tape of Father Bartolomé and his wife having sex. He played it for the bishop of Ibiza himself, Monsignor Manuel Ureña Pastor, and demanded that the adulterous priest be expelled from the Church, or at least the island. But while the bishop was parsimoniously mulling the matter over, the two lovers fled Ibiza for the mainland; the local high school students had a new religion teacher when they returned from their Christmas vacations in January 1990. Monsignor Ureña told the faithful that Father Bartolomé had gone to his sister's house to recover from job-related stress, but the clerical cover-up failed when the cuckolded husband's mother began playing the sex tape for her friends in high society circles. Father Roselló is now the parish priest of Novelda (Alicante).[73]

Although the United States is home to millions of Catholics, it is by no means a clerical society. Many countervailing systems are in motion in the United States as they are nowhere else in the world (psychotherapy, the recovery movement, the victims' movement)—easily mocked, perhaps, but certainly helpful and empowering to many people. In addition, legions of American lawyers have discovered the benefits involved in litigating the suits of former abuse victims. The Church can hire lawyers too, of course, and even in the United States numerous prosecuting attorneys shy away from legal action against priests or bishops beloved by local communities.

The judicial slowness that occasionally plagues American victims is endemic in Iberia. Spain has seen nothing remotely similar to the multimillion dollar damage awards that have bankrupted several American dioceses.[74] The Spanish population has yet to be empowered by psychotherapy or the victims' movement; there is even a relatively low level of consciousness about consumers' rights. The jury system is not in widespread use in Spain, and Spanish lawyers are insufficiently trained in the predatory skills of their American counterparts. And, on top of all this, many devoutly Catholic Spanish families are in denial about the realities of clergy sexual abuse—even when the victims are their own offspring.

The case that compelled numerous Spaniards to think about abuse issues for the first time occurred in Cuenca, a provincial capital and diocesan see two hours east of Madrid. On the night of 28 January 1990, a mentally retarded youth named Juan Andrés complained of rectal pains to his caretakers at the Asociación de Padres y Amigos de Deficientes Mentales de Cuenca (ASPADEC). He had spent the afternoon with Father Ignacio Ruiz Leal, age thirty-seven, the parish priest of Valdecabras and canon of the Cathedral of Cuenca. Juan Andrés said that Father Ruiz had approached him in the cathedral, promising to give him a watch and some second-hand clothing if he accompanied him back to the rectory following mass. It was later alleged that the priest had used the same modus operandi on two other young men—Daniel, with an IQ range of 50–60, and Andrés, with an IQ range of 34–44, luring both of them to his lodgings to bathe and try on different garments, caressing their genitals in the process. But Juan Andrés (IQ range, 47–57) suffered a different fate, according to testimony: after the de rigueur fashion show the priest bade him to get on his hands and knees, held tight his arms, "hurt him a lot in the butt," even while Juan Andrés screamed and cried, and threatened him with death if he told anyone about the incident. The woman in charge of ASPADEC, Matilde Molina, pressed charges against the priest and on 14 February he was arrested.

When word spread of the priest's detention, the conservative Catholic establishment of Cuenca swung into action. The bishop issued a statement in which he opined that the whole thing was either a fantasy or a malicious trick on the part of the retarded teenager. Matilde Molina began to be attacked in the local press. Father Ruiz was released from jail when the local tribunal's forensic doctor and his colleagues (all devout Catholics) discovered a genital disorder that supposedly made the priest physically incapable of rape. At the trial ten months later, a renowned Spanish urologist made the local doctors retract their hasty diagnosis. Psychiatrist Mariano Marcos then described Father Ignacio Ruiz as "a personality perennially subjected to his mother," with alarming gaps in his psychosexual development that did indeed make him capable of violent homosexual rape. This testimony was hotly contested by Dr. Martínez, the local forensic doctor, who "vehemently defended the absolute normality of Father Ignacio's sexual development" and also dismissed the psychodynamic approach to personality disorders. In the meantime, the Servicio Central de Policía Científica had found hairs from the three retarded individuals on the priest's pillow, along with semen stains corresponding to his blood type. But the three presiding magistrates (Señor Bahillo, Señor Teruel, and Señor Vesteiro), devout conservative Catholics to a man, were not impressed by the evidence and dropped all charges against the priest on 28 December 1990—the feast day of the Holy Innocents.[75]

At least in this case the parents of the youths paid attention to them. A thirteen-year-old altar boy of Polinyá (Barcelona) was not so fortunate. Pío's devout Catholic parents did not believe him any of the ten times that he complained to them about the town's parish priest, Father Jordi Ignasi Senabre Bernedo, until one day in May 1988 when the teenager became convinced that his pimples were the result of AIDS. School officials and the boy's mother took him first to the hospital and then to the headquarters of the Guardia Civil. There Pío testified that on more than twenty occasions the priest had arranged to be sodomized by his altar boy, first massaging the youth's penis and then assuming the position; many of these encounters had taken place just before Sunday mass. Other sessions, said the boy, had been devoted to mutual masturbation. In the end Father Jordi was awarded the benefit of the doubt by the church hierarchy and ultra-Catholic elements of the local populace.[76]

Numerous Spanish priests of liberal sympathies are angered by what they regard as cover-ups and attempted cover-ups. In the words of Father Diamantino García, "The truth shall make us free—the Gospel says—and the truth about our priests should be of the same category that binds all citizens. I have the impression that the Church, as an institution, comes out too quickly to protect, privilege, and rescue the priests accused of sexual scandals, by making imprudent public statements and finding them expensive, powerful defense lawyers—who are usually practicing Catholics—and thereby giving the worst example to society."[77] García extends his critique to the curia of the Vatican under Pope John Paul II, whose attitudes have much in common with those that prevailed in the Spanish Catholic Church under Franco.

The comparison is not far-fetched, especially when we consider the great power that the staunchly conservative Opus Dei has gained under Pope John Paul II. The youthful and still unknown Escrivá de Balaguer first aroused the interest of Archbishop Soldevila, the cardinal later assassinated by anarchists, with a poem for the rector of his seminary in which "he praised the security provided by obedience to a superior's will."[78] Escrivá de Balaguer miraculously escaped his would-be executioners in Madrid during the civil war. He embraced the cause of Franco and made influential friends quickly. Opus Dei members would soon fill the university posts vacated by fleeing *republicanos* and would eventually occupy high offices in Spain, at the Vatican, and all over the Catholic world; they would be influential in Latin American military governments for thirty years.[79]

The hierarchical matrix of authoritarian sexuality has been an "accessory after the fact" by its very nature. Men did not and do not rise to become cardinals, or archbishops, or bishops, or seminary rectors, by rocking the boat. Key promotions within the church hierarchy are usually reserved for conservative men who are trustworthy defenders of the status quo, committed to sweeping as much as possible under the rug. The case of Father Antonio Muñoz, an alleged sex addict and deadbeat dad, provides a clear example; in between numerous love affairs, says Rodríguez, the priest found time to father and mistreat five children with Josefa Romero Benítez of Málaga. To keep her from going public with the scandal, church higher-ups purportedly had a nun named Sor Agustina deliver monthly child support payments. Altogether three different bishops are alleged to have intervened at one point or another in the cover-up. The first, Emilio Benavent Escuin, retired in 1982 at the rank of archbishop. The second, Angel Suquía Goicoechea, became a cardinal in 1985 and is currently archbishop of Madrid; he is notorious for his authoritarian political views. The third, Ramón Buxarrais Ventura, resigned in 1991.[80] In case after case prelates do their duty as they see it, applying damage control to scandals, working to conserve Spain's dwindling supply of priests. Perceived institutional needs usually take pride of place over their subordinates' personal development.

Even within the same family, the hard-won distancing that one member might value as recovery from trauma might easily be seen by another as a threatening betrayal of traditions held most sacred. Internalized family systems are the only things that separate many people, or so they fear, from total personality disintegration.[81] That is why clergy accused of abuse find staunch supporters: the priests have been assigned stock roles in an inner/outer family drama. Among Catholic believers, notes Drewermann, the figure of the priest elicits "an enormous disposition to all kinds of paternal transferences."[82] Scurrilous rumors about the parish pastor can be very distressing for the devout; psychic overload is prevented by switching to comforting but defective modes of reality-testing. Sometimes defending a priest accused of sexual misconduct may be a way of defending against a repressed exploitative event in one's personal history.

If the "family" is such a perfect institution, one might ask, why would a young man wish not to have one, to remain childless and uncommitted? As it turns out, the broad strategic defense of "family values" is interwoven with numerous smaller tactical defenses designed to disavow desires of revenge or block out recognition of marital and parental failures. For many of the priests and nuns who wind up on Drewermann's couch, months or years of beating around the bush can suddenly give way to a torrent of repressed truths—"one finds out that the father or the mother was an alcoholic, that they spent days and days without speaking to each other, that they were often seized by uncontrollable bouts of rage, that there wasn't the least sign of tenderness between them," and so on, with the child situated between the two battlefronts for years on end, praying for a supernatural peace to put an end to the cold war.[83] Current studies reveal that repressive and unrealistic forms of Catholic moral theology actually stack the cards *against* family stability in the first place. The dysfunction that results—for example, the perverse connection between motherhood and priesthood—serves to give them new recruits. There is something vaguely vampiresque about this process, now fortunately in decline in Spain and all over the Catholic world.

Thousands of Spanish priests have successfully undergone a process of personal growth, choosing to follow their consciences instead of the advice of the hierarchy. In the waning years of the Franco regime, small collectives of *curas casados*, or married priests, began to appear, "celebrating mass assisted by their wives, immersed in a luminous consciousness of modernization and progress," recalls Spanish sociologist Gustavo Bueno.[84] In the bad old days the Inquisition would have stepped in and stamped out, but not in the contradictory but exhilarating years that followed the Second Vatican Council (1962). As Lannon points out, bishops and theologians from all over the world "demolished the theological and ecclesiastical underpinnings of National-Catholicism and state confessionalism, as they plotted a new, more liberal, and more tolerant course for the Church. This radical change left Catholic authoritarians in Spain, including Franco himself, disconcerted and suddenly displaced from the orthodox center they were sure they had always occupied."[85]

The official statistics almost speak for themselves: between 1954 and 1990, some twenty-five thousand Spanish men and women achieved "secularization," 25 percent of them during the sixties and another 54 percent during the seventies.[86] Many altruistic young people who might have entered the Church in an earlier epoch chose instead to become social workers, medical personnel, teachers, counselors, and so forth. According to Bueno, the marriage and/or secularization of so many former priests led to a "desacralization" of the clergy in general, a discrediting of conservative moral theology, and the opening of a serious breach in "one of the most efficient networks for the control of the population that the Catholic Church possessed, that is, the network of confessionals distributed all over the country." Bueno reasons that the sacrament of penance is based on the concept of a celibate confessor situated beyond human passions, therefore a safe repository for the worst secrets; the rapid rise of subjective conscience as the best moral guardian in post-Franco Spain is a kind of "Lutheranization" of the Spanish body politic.[87]

If true, this would be a great historical irony: Spain financed the Counter Reformation, hunted down its own Lutherans, and became a haven for the celibate/sexual power system. The personal merits of Ignatius of Loyola and other saints cannot be denied, but the terrible Golden Age schism underwrote the inner schisms of many priests and guaranteed that untold numbers of Catholics would be betrayed by them over the centuries. There would not have been a "golden age" of clergy sexual abuse had Spanish priests been permitted to have wives and taught to view human love and redemption in terms other than sacrificial angst. It is not a coincidence that exploitative events increased in the sixteenth and seventeenth centuries as the Spanish-financed church moved to suppress anything remotely connected to Erasmian or Protestant reforms, thereby reinforcing confessional power-knowledge. The result: a dramatic increase in scandalous *turpiloquia in confesione,* the confessors' groping questions and unrepressed words of lust.[88]

If the social and intellectual history of Spain were pictured as a chaotic system, then the inflexible, ultra-Catholic mentality locked in fatal symbiotic embrace with extremist anticlericalism would surely constitute the "strange attractor." But that was Spain at its worst, deprived of self-trust by its despots. "You cannot be left to your own devices," Franco reputedly said to his people ("No se os puede dejar solos"). Spain at its best was host to the continuous development of more enlightened, healthier spiritual concepts, within Catholicism and without. Under Franco numerous priests, and nuns became agents of social change—and some two hundred of them served jail time for it, more than all the Communist countries of Eastern Europe put together.[89] Most of their bishops collaborated with the peaceful Spanish transition to democracy following Franco's death that surely will be recalled as one of the most encouraging events of the twentieth century. If we cast our eyes anew at Spanish history, we can glimpse that the potential for recovery from spiritual devastation and social trauma has been there all along, faint but real. Against heavy odds, there have been Spaniards in every century who rejected despotic pessimism to embrace freedom, optimism, and an internal locus of control. This invincible Spanish capacity for rebirth shines in the autobiography of the priest Diego de Torres Villarroel (1693–1770), who recounts decades of browbeating at the hands of his ecclesiastical superiors. "I finally became so crazy," Torres wryly confesses, "that I started to trust myself."[90]

Notes

Introduction: Authoritarian Sexuality in Spain

1. *Eunuchs for the Kingdom of Heaven: Women, Sexuality and the Catholic Church*, 9, 99.

2. This on the authority of religious historian Peter R. Brown, *The Body and Society*. Fredric Jameson uses Brown to defenestrate what he calls "Foucault's abortive trilogy" (*The History of Sexuality*) in "On the Sexual Production of Western Subjectivity," 159.

3. "On the Sexual Production of Western Subjectivity," 174. Following quotations: 175, 177.

4. "Sexuality and Solitude," 371. As David Macey says in *The Lives of Michel Foucault*, "the lectures and interviews from this period [1980–83] prove to be very repetitious, as the same themes are addressed over and over again from slightly different perspectives" (417).

5. Dijkstra, *Idols of Perversity*, 253–57.

6. *The Kristeva Reader*, 24–33.

7. Self-directed cruelty or self-victimization is what gives fanatics their "terrible strength," in the view of Taylor, *The Fanatics: A Behavioural Approach to Political Violence*, 184–221. "Self-mutilation typically reflects unconscious identification with a hateful and hated object," writes Kernberg, "The Psychopathology of Hatred," 227. The best study on ritual and clinical mutilation remains Favazza, *Bodies Under Siege: Self-Mutilation in Culture and Psychiatry*.

8. *The Cult of the Virgin Mary: Psychological Origins*, 49–89. - Michael P. Carroll

9. These two legends are V256.3.1 and V256.4, respectively, in Goldberg's excellent *Motif-Index of Medieval Spanish Folk Narratives*. Yet another relevant tale: "V462.1.1.1. Aged monk advised not to go to city for medical help because of danger of fornication. Goes and fathers a child. Returns to monastery to tell his brethren to avoid occasion of sin. Returns to cell."

10. Many spiritually inclined psychotherapists assess the religiosity of their patients in terms of the developmental level reflected therein. Dr. Moshe Halevi Spero has constructed a most detailed picture of the types of religious beliefs and representations that correspond to internal object relations of lesser or greater maturity (*Religious Objects as Psychological Structures: A Critical Integration of Object Relations Theory, Psychotherapy, and Judaism*). Jesuit psychiatrist W. W. Meissner has penned a superb psychobiography of the Basque visionary's triumphant struggle with his punitive and regressive superego (*Ignatius of Loyola: The*

Psychology of a Saint). From this perspective, which I share, it becomes legitimate to speak of religious dysfunction without implying that all religious belief is dysfunctional.

11. *The Authoritarian Personality*, 391.

12. Stone et al., *Strength and Weakness*, 244.

13. *The Anatomy of Prejudices*, 184.

14. "Neurotic Downward Identification."

15. *The Anatomy of Prejudices*, 223, italics in original.

16. Laeuchli, *Power and Sexuality: The Emergence of Canon Law at the Synod of Elvira.*

17. From an ancient ballad included by Díaz Roig in her anthology, *El Romancero viejo*, 117 (my translation). For the classic study of Rodrigo and his legacy in Spanish culture, see Menéndez Pidal, *Floresta de leyendas heróicas españolas: Rodrigo, el último godo.*

18. *La ira sagrada*, 18, 68–69 (my translations).

19. *Aportes de la psicología a la vida religiosa*, 89–90 (my translation).

20. *Sex, Priests, and Power*, 33, 114, 156.

21. Hampden-Turner, "Authoritarianism, Schismogenesis, and the Self-Exciting System: Bateson and Nevitt Sanford" and "The Cybernetics of Mental Health" in *Maps of the Mind*, 174–81. The concept of schismogenetic systems was introduced by Bateson in *Steps to an Ecology of Mind*. See also Kramer and Alstad, *The Guru Papers: Masks of Authoritarian Power.*

22. Outstanding examples from among his five hundred publications include *Razas, pueblos y linajes; Las brujas y su mundo; El Carnaval; Ensayo sobre la literatura de cordel; Inquisición, brujería y criptojudaismo; Ritos y mitos equívocos; Los judíos en la España moderna y contemporánea; Ensayo sobre la cultura popular española; Introducción a una historia contemporánea del anticlericalismo español* (henceforth *Anticlericalismo español*); and *Las formas complejas de la vida religiosa.* For comparative studies by other authors, see Kamen, "Clerical Violence in a Catholic Society: The Hispanic World, 1450–1720," Moore, *The Formation of a Persecuting Society*, and Revuelta González, "La Iglesia española ante la crisis del Antiguo Régimen (1808–1833)."

23. *Aggression and Community*, 29–52.

24. "A belief system that describes people as inherently depraved can victimize and limit spiritual growth both individual and as a species" (Abraham, "The Significance of Religious Messages in Sexual Addiction," 162). When certain types of negative religious messages ally themselves with strong doses of parental punishment, the consequences for individuals and societies are endless. To historian Philip Greven we owe one of the best-documented studies of this longlived phenomenon among Puritans and Pentecostals in the United States (*Spare the Child*). The consequences include obsessional, paranoid, and other disorders of rigidity; dissociative disorders; sadomasochism; authoritarianism; and depression—"Though they cannot remember consciously what happened to them during the first 3 or 4 years of life, the ancient angers persist while the adult conscience directs rage inward upon the self." Greven notes that children come to accept the inevitability of punishment and are prone to protect their abusive parents by denying themselves; the urgency of the apocalyptic impulse among many American Protestants represents, he affirms, a living legacy of long forgotten punishment. Humiliation techniques lie at the heart of what Swiss psychotherapist Alice Miller calls "poisonous pedagogy" in one of her most in-

fluential works, *For Your Own Good*. Rita Brock refers to theological systems based on blame, escape from punishment, and longing for hierarchy as "the nostalgia of dominated and abused children" ("And a Little Child Will Lead Us," 51). In sum, shame is one of the crucial links connecting different types of abuse trauma with religious dysfunction and authoritarian sexuality.

25. "The Problem of Sexual Trauma and Addiction in the Catholic Church," 130–37. From p. 135: "This privileged and forced communication gives the priest an education and a power of almost unmanageable proportions. Hearing the confessions may expand his knowledge of human nature and compassion; it may also fuel self-justification for his own transgressions. Frequently a priest has used the system of confession to threaten and silence his victims and to reinforce the cycle of his own addictive behavior." Sipe, an ordained Roman Catholic priest now married and in psychotherapeutic practice, denies that scandals of priest pedophilia or adultery or rape are unfortunate anomalies in an otherwise wholesome, normal parishional mission. After thirty-five years of research and fifteen hundred interviews, he holds that the sexual exploitation of minors or women by priests "is primarily a symptom of an essentially flawed celibate/sexual system of ecclesiastical power" (*Sex, Priests, and Power*, 4).

26. "Devastated Spirituality: The Impact of Clergy Sexual Abuse on the Survivor's Relationship with God and the Church," 154.

27. As reproduced by Linz, "Religión y política en España," 7 (my translation).

28. See Jiménez Campo, *El fascismo en la crisis de la II República*, 140–46, and Losada Malvárez, *Ideología del Ejército Franquista*, 33–44.

29. *Clérigos*, 273.

Chapter 1. Institutionalized Sexual Predation

1. *Cuentos españoles de los siglos XVI y XVII*, 68.

2. *El hábito no hace al monje*, 71. Following citation: 69 (my translations).

3. Esteban, *Refranero anticlerical*, 34–35.

4. *Sexuality in the Confessional*, 207.

5. *The Spanish Character*, 211.

6. Kamen, *The Phoenix and the Flame*, 327.

7. Foucault, *The History of Sexuality, Volume 1: An Introduction*, 19.

8. Cited by Caro Baroja, *Anticlericalismo español*, 90, who affirms that writers like Sánchez, "hidden behind their Latin, probed deeply into the human conscience, and it's a shame that their discoveries have not been utilized more by psychologists and sociologists" (91, my translation).

9. *History of Sexuality*, 19.

10. Claramunt, *Modas y epidemias psíquicas en España*, 144–45.

11. Ibid., 187–99.

12. Manuel Amezcua, "La vida contradictoria de la beata," 33–43.

13. Claramunt, *Modas y epidemias psíquicas en España*, 195 (my translation).

14. *The Phoenix and the Flame*, 324.

15. Bennassar, *The Spanish Character*, 211.

16. *Anticlericalismo español*, 14.

17. *El hábito no hace al monje*, 76.

18. See Gilmore, "The Anticlericalism of the Andalusian Rural Proletarians," or Delgado Ruiz, "La antirreligiosidad popular en España."

check

19. E. Inman Fox, "Ortega y la cultura española (1910–1914): Vieja y nueva manera de mirar las cosas," in his *Ideología y política en las letras de fin de siglo*, 361–94.

20. "I shit on God" or "I shit on the Sacred Host."

21. *Metaphors of Masculinity*, 189. Hence the joke about the attractive woman whose plunging neckline so upsets the curate that he refuses to give her communion; she goes to the head priest and demands communion "because of my divine right." "Your left one is very nice, too," the ogling clergyman replies (191, my rendition). The men studied by Brandes avoided communion because of the submissive, unmanly posture required for it. Psychoanalyst and Freudian biographer Ernest Jones came to believe that the unconscious darkside of communion was a fantasy of receptivity structurally similar to fellatio. See Michael P. Carroll, "Ernest Jones on Holy Communion: Refurbishing an Early Psychoanalytic Insight," 307–15.

22. Mitchell, *Passional Culture*, 37–39.

23. "That fatalist God induces one to submission, but also to blasphemy (let us not forget that Andalusia is the region of Spain that blasphemes the most). In this intense affective ambivalence vis-à-vis God and in the attachment to the maternal can be found, we believe, the two fundamental keys for understanding traditional Andalusian religiosity." Carlos Domínguez Morano, "Aproximación psicoanalítica a la religiosidad tradicional andaluza," 141 (my translation).

24. Abascal y Sáinz de la Maza, *Brujería y magia*. Andalusia has been a net exporter of superstitions to other regions of Spain, reports Del Real, *Superstición y supersticiones*, 56.

25. *The Spanish Character*, 88–89.

26. As cited by Esteban, *Refranero anticlerical*, 18, 28 (my translations).

27. Caro, *Anticlericalismo español*, 87.

28. Ranke-Heinemann, *Eunuchs for the Kingdom of Heaven*, 266.

29. "Indeed, so wide was this chasm that a movement known as Richerism gained many adherents in France and northern Italy. This was a protest of the lower clergy against the hierarchy, against the higher clergy's control of ecclesiatical advancement, against the high incomes of bishops and abbots, with a demand for a more equitable distribution of clerical income." *Anticlericalism*, 59.

30. Alejandre, *El veneno de Dios: La Inquisición de Sevilla ante el delito de solicitación en confesión*; Dufour, *Clero y sexto mandamiento: La confesión en la España del siglo XVIII*; and Haliczer, *Sexuality in the Confessional*.

31. *The Anatomy of Prejudices*, 222–23.

32. Linton, *Culture and Mental Disorders*, 132.

33. *Sexuality in the Confessional*, 207.

34. *The Anatomy of Prejudices*, 195.

35. Bourdieu and Wacquant, *An Invitation to Reflexive Sociology*, 171–72, emphases in original.

36. *Clérigos*, 532.

37. "Sexual Behavior by Male Clergy with Adult Female Counselees: Systemic and Situational Themes," 103–18.

38. Quoted but not identified by Drewermann, *Clérigos*, 551.

39. Irons and Laaser, "The Abduction of Fidelity: Sexual Exploitation by Clergy," 126. Other types include the "False Lover," the "Naive Prince," and the "Dark King." The "Self-Serving Martyr" was the most frequent category. In practice, the narcissistic and dependent personality traits of the exploitative clergy vary little from one type to another.

40. *Clérigos*, 557.

41. Rodríguez, *La vida sexual del clero*, 221.

42. *Clérigos*, 556.

43. Delgado Ruiz, *De la muerte de un dios*, 150.

44. Galenson, "The Precursors of Masochism," 372.

45. *Cofradías y hermandades andaluzas*, 147–65.

46. *Aggression and Community*, 151. Ethnographers of Spain would certainly savor Camille Paglia's rich descriptions of anxious male identity formation under the influence of a patriarchal mother's "gravitational field" (*Sexual Personae*, 258 and passim).

47. *El drama del menor en España (cómo y por qué los adultos maltratamos a niños y jóvenes)* (1993) and *Tu hijo y las sectas. Guía de prevención y tratamiento para padres, educadores y afectados* (1994).

48. *La vida sexual del clero*, 78, 170.

49. *Clérigos*, 282, 286 (my translations, italics in original).

50. In the view of British psychiatrist Estela Welldon, "perverse motherhood must be seen as the product of emotional instability and inadequate individuation brought about by a process that spans at least three generations. But part of the problem lies with society. Our whole culture supports the idea that mothers have complete dominion over their babies; thus we encourage the very ideas the perverse mother exploits. We help neither her nor her children, nor society in general, if we glorify motherhood so blindly as to exclude the fact that some mothers can act perversely. . . . In my clinical experience, the opportunity that motherhood offers of being in complete control of a situation creates fertile ground for some women who have experienced injurious and traumatic events in their own lives to exploit and abuse their babies" (*Mother, Madonna, Whore*, 81, 74–75). For more information about mothers' deeply ambivalent feelings toward their children, see *Representations of Motherhood*, eds. Bassin et al.; or Eyer, *Mother-Infant Bonding: A Scientific Fiction*. For the breakthrough exploration of this topic, see Rheingold, *The Fear of Being a Woman: A Theory of Maternal Destructiveness*.

51. *For Your Own Good*, 85.

52. *Clérigos*, 267–68. In a book that I have always considered remarkably intuitive, Spanish psychohistorian Alvaro Fernández Suárez relates "ontological insecurity" in Spain to primitive emotionality, mysticism, a social structure dominated by families and clans, and the Catholic glorification of suffering, sacrifice, and death magic. *España, árbol vivo* (1961).

53. Rodríguez, *La vida sexual del clero*, 205–6.

54. Reproduced by Luis Carandell, *Celtiberia Show*, 54 (my translation).

55. *Observing the Erotic Imagination*, vii. See also his much-cited *Perversion*. Stoller's definition of perversion as "the erotic form of hatred" has been widely adopted by psychotherapists. See also David Shapiro, *Autonomy and Rigid Character*, 129: "The nature of rigid character—its regime of will, discipline, authority, its moralistic prejudices—has further consequences for the nature of sexual interests. Moralistic notions of sex as dirty, coarse, and degrading may have the effect not merely of inhibiting sexual interests but of making dirtiness, coarseness, and degradation especially erotic. . . . Above all, the rigid views of sexual responsiveness and sexual excitement as inimical to self-control, and of the sexual relationship as a surrender of one to the other, will have the effect of imbuing ideas and images of wantonness and subjugation—images of the prostitute and the slave, for example—with special erotic significance."

56. *The Anatomy of Prejudices*, 38.

Wm. Christian

— 57. *Visionaries: The Spanish Republic and the Reign of Christ.* The following indented quotation: 227, with citations from Madre Soledad's 1921 manual, *El libro
de las casitas.*

58. Ibid., 227–28.

59. Rougement, *El amor y Occidente*, 163, 343–44.

60. As cited by Gutiérrez Serrano, "San Antonio María Claret, nuestro hermano y maestro," 115 (my translation). Southern Spanish poets of the nineteenth
century have specialized in a similar pious sadomasochism, replete with requests
to be inflamed and penetrated by the same daggers of grief that pierce many a
maternal icon's breast. Even twentieth-century cosmopolitan poets like Federico
García Lorca remained ensnared within this worldview, as any number of his
writings attest. For example, his "Elegía a María Blanchard" (1932) in which he
portrays the tortured life of a hunchbacked woman painter (*Prosa*, 193–99). For
a fuller discussion of Lorca's magico-persecutory metaphors, see Mitchell, *Violence and Piety in Spanish Folklore*, 157–58. The emotions and even the language of
mystical Marianism often replicate those of mother worship in its earthiest and
most primitive varieties. See Preston, "New Perspectives on Mother Worship,"
325–43.

61. Kernberg, "The Psychopathology of Hatred," 227.

62. "[The martyrs] were *suprasensual men* who found enjoyment in suffering.
They sought out the most frightful tortures, even death itself, as others seek joy,
and as they were, so am I—*suprasensual*." [Wanda replies]: "Take care that in
being such you do not become a martyr to love, the martyr of a woman." *Venus
in Furs and Selected Letters*, 91 (emphases in original).

63. Walsh, *Opus Dei*, 15. The following quotations: 17, 30. For more on the kin-
based ecclesiastical culture of northern Spain and the manufacture of vocations
during this period, see Christian, *Visionaries*, 218–24, 230–31.

64. *Opus Dei*, 178–87.

65. As cited by Walsh, *Opus Dei*, 29.

66. "Female members of Opus were not, and are not, allowed to associate
with the more privileged males. Escrivá's fear of promiscuity was such that the
most rigorous rules were laid down to safeguard the prohibition against mixing.
At Netherhall House, the London University residence in Hampstead, double
doors separate the two houses and are ritually locked each night" (Walsh, *Opus
Dei*, 110).

67. *Sex, Priests, and Power*, 145.

68. Regarding the "superiority complex," consider the following from Father
Leo Booth: "Why did I really want to be a Jesuit? I was attracted to their power
image: intellectual giants, stormtroopers for Jesus, shrouded in mystery. Covet-
ing that elitist image I continued a quasi-Jesuit life-style in the Anglican tradition" (*When God Becomes a Drug*, 8).

69. Cited by Rodríguez, *La vida sexual del clero*, 85.

70. The forty-six-year-old priest was interviewed while accompanied by his
psychiatrist. In Rodríguez, *La vida sexual del clero*, 201–202 (my translation).

71. *Clérigos*, 515. The following quotation: 103 (my translations).

72. Rodríguez does not rule out that already gay youths might seek fellowship
in the seminary, "but it would probably be more exact to speak of pusillani-
mous and effeminate young Catholics who, molded by a castrating mother—and
therefore under pressure from a culture of machismo—end up finding refuge
in a protective and 'manly' clerical environment that with time will generate a

definitive homosexual orientation" (*La vida sexual del clero*, 170, my translation). Compare this with Sipe: "Do seminaries attract men who are inclined to the homosexualities, or does the homosocial organization of the clerical world foster and develop consciousness of and involvement in the homosexualties? Both questions merit an affirmative response" (*Sex, Priests, and Power*, 140).

73. *La vida sexual del clero*, 115. Following citation: 79.

74. In his best-selling *Subida al montesión* of 1535, the Spanish Franciscan friar Bernardino de Laredo gave detailed descriptions of the Blessed Mother's spiritual and physical participation in every one of Christ's passional torments; "body and soul, the Virgin was nailed to the cross with her tender heart and all of her being." Yet another friar had sung of Jesús and María "bound in one love, tormented in one pain, embraced on one cross" (as cited by García de la Concha, "La devoción a la Dolorosa en Sevilla," 35–36, my translations).

Chapter 2. The Anticlerical Imaginary, 1808–1901

1. *Spanish Catholicism*, 72.

2. *Anticlericalismo español*, 118.

3. Payne, *Spanish Catholicism*, 75–76.

4. Caro, *Anticlericalismo español*, 136 (my translation).

5. Callahan, *Church, Politics, and Society*, 125–25.

6. From the viscount of Martignac's eyewitness account, cited by Caro, *Anticlericalismo español*, 138.

7. *Church, Politics, and Society*, 143.

8. *Anticlericalism*, 51–52.

9. Benito Pérez Galdós, *Un faccioso más y algunos frailes menos*, 225. This is the final episode of the second series of *Episodios Nacionales*.

10. "Dios nos asista. Tercera carta de Fígaro a su corresponsal en París" [first pub. 1836], in *Artículos*, 200.

11. Callahan, *Church, Politics, and Society*, 168. The next three citations: 255, 267, 259.

12. *Spanish Catholicism*, 99.

13. *El nuevo pensamiento político español*, 50–51.

14. "La religiosidad integrista y la religiosidad ilustrada en el proceso de modernización de España" (1993).

15. *Anticlericalism*, 88.

16. Callahan, *Church, Politics, and Society*, 236, 239.

17. *Spanish Catholicism*, 105.

18. Gutiérrez Serrano, "San Antonio María Claret," 112. Thus was mind-numbing repetition allied with the activation of the magical maternal imago. Devotionalism's relentless insistence on the purity of mothers and especially of the Blessed Mother would lead to an iconoclastic backlash in 1936; during the sacking of some parish churches, prostitutes were paraded on platforms normally reserved for icons of the Virgen.

19. Cf. Velasco, "La religiosidad integrista," 359–65. See also Kurtz, *The Politics of Heresy: The Modernist Crisis of Roman Catholicism*.

20. *Anticlericalismo español*, 178.

21. For example, the work published in 1881 by Spanish socialist Fernando Garrido: *Poor Jesuits! Origins, doctrines, maxims, privileges and vicissitudes of the Com-*

pany of Jesus from its foundation until our times, including the secret code, or hidden instructions of the Jesuits, published for the first time in Castilian (as cited by Caro, *Anticlericalismo español*, 214, my translation).

22. *Sexuality in the Confessional*, 194–96.

23. Introductory studies include López Morillas, *El krausismo español*; Pérez de la Dehesa, *El pensamiento de Costa y su influencia en el 98*; or Tuñón de Lara, *Costa y Unamuno en la crisis de fin de siglo*.

24. *Anticlercalismo español*, 230. Following citations: 212–13.

25. Ibid., 213 (my translation).

26. As cited by Dendle, *The Novel of Religious Thesis in Spain, 1875–1936*, 63–65.

27. The account, by Juan Bravo Murillo, was entitled "La Internacional y las españolas," and it is glossed by Manuel Pérez Ledesma, "El miedo de los acomodados y la moral de los obreros," 30–36. For more on the origins of the "great fear," see Jover, *Realidad y mito de la Primera República*, 53–66.

28. Cited by Pérez Ledesma, 55. Following quotation: 58 (my translations).

29. Mainer, "Notas sobre la lectura obrera en España (1890–1930)," 64–65. For a whitewash of working-class culture in Spain that omits the hate-filled literature and skips over the anticlerical rage, see Luis, *Cincuenta años de cultura obrera en España, 1890–1940*.

30. Cf. Dinges, "Roman Catholic Traditionalism," esp. 87: "Traditionalist Catholics are the true 'soldiers of Christ' warring against theological modernists, against the 'scourges of the age,' and against the powers of evil and error that now occupy positions of power and authority in the Church."

31. *The Anatomy of Prejudices*, 352.

32. Dendle, *The Spanish Novel of Religious Thesis*, 67, 70, 71n., 73.

33. As cited by E. Inman Fox, *Ideología y política en las letras de fin de siglo (1898)*, 29 (my translation).

34. Ibid., 31–36.

35. *Anarchist Ideology and the Working-Class Movement in Spain, 1868–1898*, 191.

36. McFarlane and van der Kolk, "Trauma and Its Challenge to Society," 39.

37. As cited by Inman Fox, *Ideología y política*, 38 (my translation).

38. Ibid., 52.

39. *Anarchist Ideology*, 208.

40. *Anticlericalismo español*, 215.

41. Ibid., 126.

42. *Elia, o la España 30 años ha*, 12.

43. Dendle, *The Novel of Religious Thesis*, 65–67, 109–21. Following citation: 39.

44. Benito Pérez Galdós, *Doña Perfecta*, 31. Additional quotations are from pages 91, 87, 93, 104, 105, 34, 80, 88, 89, 58, 69, and 50 (my translations).

45. The name "María Remedios" is typically Spanish in that it refers to an advocation or sanctuary of the Mother of God. Other examples include Visitación, Concepción, Esperanza, Angustias, Amparo, Rocío, Natividad, Soledad, Maravillas, Candelas, Estrella, Pilar, Montserrat—"no other country of Western Europe could produce such a list of given names" (Bennassar, *The Spanish Character*, 89).

46. Garrido, *Grandeza y miseria del celibato cristiano*, 116.

47. *Autonomy and Rigid Character*, 145. We find a relatively more benign form of rigidity in Don Cayetano Polentinos, Perfecta's brother, an archaeologist and bibliophile obsessed with the task of vindicating his hometown's role in the most glorious accomplishments of Imperial Spain. In towns like Orbajosa, affirms Don Cayetano, "you can still see the national character in all its purity: upright, noble, incorruptible, pure, simple, patriarchal, hospitable, generous"

(54). He naively prides himself on having escaped the family neurosis, defined as "a lamentable propensity to the most absurd obsessions" (55). Don Cayetano represents an obsessive-compulsive style more stable and less extreme than the brittle paranoid style of his sister and the priest Don Inocencio (cf. Shapiro 138). Both neurotic styles will have a role to play in the formation of reactionary traditionalist thought in Spain.

48. *Autonomy and Rigid Character*, 120: "The identification of masochism as a female tendency reflects, not a female satisfaction in submission, but rather the tendency of women who are rigid characters to defend their autonomy and protect their dignity in this pseudo-submissive way." Shapiro argues that masochism is not always and not usually the erotic desire for pain but a much more familiar, even prosaic phenomenon: the chronic mulling over, nursing, and exaggeration of past humiliations and defeats. It is a mistake, in other words, to equate masochism with passivity. The actual goal of the chronically aggrieved, people obsessed with weakness or cowed by inner authority figures, who complain melodramatically about being hurt and victimized, is the compensatory attainment of a "moral victory," whereby a passively experienced shame or inferiority is transformed into an active stance, a "principled act of will" or a "martyr's pride" (119).

49. *Autonomy and Rigid Character*, 120.

50. "Remaining in the Bunker Long After the War Is Over: Deployment in the Individual, the Group, and the Nation," 167.

51. *Church, Politics, and Society*, 247.

52. Under the Spanish brand of disentailment known as *desamortización*, "serfs with land became free men without it," writes Nadal in *El fracaso de la revolución industrial en España, 1814–1913*, 62. See also Bernal, "La disolución del régimen señorial," 76–88. In northern Spain frustrated peasants poured into the ultra-Catholic Carlist movement; in southern Spain they turned to anarchism, smuggling, banditry, and bullfighting. See Mitchell, *Blood Sport*, 127.

53. Perfecta's conversation with María Remedios: "My nephew is no longer my nephew, woman: he is blasphemy, sacrilege, atheism, demagoguery. Do you know what demagoguery is?" "Something like when those people burned Paris with petroleum, and the ones that knock churches down and shoot icons." "Well, my nephew is all of that. . . . Don't you understand the immense size, the terrible extension of my enemy, who is not just a man but a sect? Don't you understand that my nephew, as he now stands against me, is not a single misfortune but a plague? Against it, dear Remedios, we will have a batallion of God to annihilate the infernal militia of Madrid." The two women agree that the only way to proceed is to adopt the tactics of Spain's Christians in their wars against the Moors in the good old days (88–89, my translation).

54. *Doña Perfecta* is the story of religious addiction blocking a marriage. In a novel published two years later, *La familia de León Roch* (1878), Galdós portrays religious addiction destroying a marriage from within. "At the instigation of her Italian Jesuit confessor, [María] kills all love in her heart for her husband, preferring trivial routine devotions to the warmth of human love." Dendle, *The Spanish Novel of Religious Thesis*, 44. Themes of sexual love and frigidity among married Catholic women will be developed more explicitly by anticlerical writers of the early twentieth century. For an excellent overview of anticlerical literature in both centuries, see Haliczer, *Sexuality in the Confessional*, 183–203.

55. Tussell Gómez, "The Functioning of the Cacique System in Andalusia, 1890–1931," 14.

56. *Liberals, Reformers, and Caciques in Restoration Spain, 1875–1909*, 120. José

Manuel Cuenca Toribio affirms that, despite the good done through *caciquismo* in some towns, "the only conclusion that can and must be extracted from its long and lamentable existence in Spanish life is that it was an authentic cancer. For as long as it lasted *caciquismo* was a continual source of civic degradation and a school of moral corruption, with absolute disregard for personal dignity. If our country was always lagging behind other more developed ones in the same geographic/cultural area, it is due in large part to *caciquismo*" (*El caciquismo en España*, 15, my translation). For the links between this abusive political system and cruel festive practices in Spain, see Mitchell, *Blood Sport*, 126–145.

57. Mariano Baquero Goyanes, introduction to his edition of Clarín's *La Regenta*, 15. The noted French scholar Jean Bécarud considered *La Regenta* to be "a first-class historical document covering a concrete moment of Spanish history" as well as "a veritable sociological study" (*De La Regenta al Opus Dei*, 11, 13). For Haliczer, "It is *La Regenta*, rather than any scholarly work written to date on the topic of confession, that provides us with the deepest insights into the moral dilemmas and sexual frustrations faced by confessors in the Counter-Reformation Church" (*Sexuality in the Confessional*, 200). See also Soledad Miranda, *Religión y clero en la gran novela española del s. XIX*.

58. Leopoldo Alas [Clarín], *La Regenta*, 5. Additional quotations and references are from pages 4, 151, 183, 199, 320, 230, 173, 363, 341, 167–69, 359–60, 403, and 518 (my translations).

59. *The Deceived Husband*, 215: "The intensity of Fermín's relationship with his mother is evidenced by the way it is principally expressed as a need for separation—a separation that, in [psychiatrist Robert] Stoller's terms, is a desperate need to differentiate. . . . At the same time, however, there is the lurking belief that, in emotional terms at least, the love of his mother is the one emotional security on which he can rely" (216).

60. *Clérigos*, 553 (my translation).

61. *Grandeza y miseria del celibato cristiano*, 128–35.

62. *Visionaries*, 245.

63. *When God Becomes a Drug*, 60.

64. Cf. Horowitz, *Introduction to Psychodynamics*, 227.

65. Ricardo Senabre, "Clarín y Galdós ante el público," 143–44.

66. *Spanish Catholicism*, 104.

67. Lannon, *Privilege, Persecution, and Prophecy*, 80.

68. Ullman, *La Semana Trágica*, 604–13.

69. Liberal newspapers speaking almost in unison included *El Globo, El Imparcial, La Correspondencia de España, El Liberal, Heraldo de Madrid* and *El País*); as cited by Fox, *Ideología y política*, 69.

70. Pérez Galdós, *Electra*, 37. Additional quotations are from pages 38, 107, and 130–133 (my translations).

71. Senabre, "Clarín y Galdós," 147–48 (my translation).

72. The phrase "parlor anarchist" is from Esenwein, *Anarchist Ideology*, 204, who uses it to refer to middle-class intellectuals more inspired by Friedrich Nietzsche than by true anarchist revolutionary thinkers like Ricardo Mella or José Prat. According to José-Carlos Mainer, Spain's "literary anarchism" dissolved between 1905 and 1910 as each radical young writer found stable, well-remunerated employment with newspapers and the publishing industry ("Notas sobre la lectura obrera en España," 73). See also Lily Litvak, *La musa libertaria: Arte, literatura y vida cultural del anarquismo español (1880–1913)*.

73. *Ideología y política*, 82.

74. Reproduced by Fox, *Ideología y política*, 89 (my translation).
75. Ibid., 76 (my translation).
76. From the article "Más frailes" (1902), reproduced by Fox, 76. Following citations: 60, 61.
77. *La ira sagrada*, 19–20.
78. *La Semana Trágica*, 155.
79. Cited by Delgado, *La ira sagrada*, 55.
80. My translation of the Spanish original: "Jóvenes bárbaros de hoy: Entrad a saco en la civilización decadente y miserable de este país sin ventura; destruid sus templos, acabad con sus dioses, alzad el velo de las novicias y elevadlas a la categoría de madres para virilizar la especie. No os detengáis ni ante los sepulcros ni ante los altares. No hay nada sagrado en la tierra. El pueblo es esclavo de la Iglesia. Hay que destruir la Iglesia. Luchad, matad, morid." Reproduced by Cárcel Ortí, *La persecución religiosa en España*, 93.
81. *Spanish Catholicism*, 133–34. The upper-class paternalists and ecclesiastics who normally preached social Catholicism were far less influential than the class-based Carlist "Libres" of Barcelona, which came to have 175,000 members and compete directly (and often bloodily) with the Confederación Nacional de Trabajo, or CNT. The Libres mixed left-wing economic ideas with their ultra-Catholicism, a strange hybrid that could not survive the legalization of the CNT in later years (144).
82. Cited by Delgado, *La ira sagrada*, 36 (my translation).
83. Payne, *Spanish Catholicism*, 134. See also Bruce Lincoln's "Revolutionary Exhumations in Spain," in his *Discourse and the Construction of Society*, 103–27.
84. "La razón de la fuerza," 111–13. See also Bernecker, "Acción directa y violencia en el anarquismo español."
85. *La Semana Trágica*, 162.
86. Young-Bruehl, *The Anatomy of Prejudices*, 245–46: "In 1920 the Klan hired organizers who built up the ranks by appealing to every prejudice. . . . More important than any other single prejudice for many of the Klan chapters of the Midwest and West was anti-Catholicism. Anti-Catholicism was a mode of obsessionality particularly important in areas such as Oregon, where few Negroes or Jews lived, where the public was generally well-educated, and where economic threats were seen as coming from without. Klan literature charged the Catholic Church with thought control, mind pollution, and division of loyalties (asking Americans to be loyal to 'the dago of the Tiber,' the Pope), but it is interesting to observe that Klan leaders construed Catholics in ways straight out of the book of antisemitism. They recruited 'escaped nuns' who went on lecture tours to inform Klansmen about Catholic priestly lustfulness, orgies in convents, and the Catholic practice of putting illegitimate babies in special leather bags and throwing them in furnaces. They peddled themes of sadistic perversity and infanticide — the old European antisemitic chestnuts, the staples of obsessional prejudice."

Chapter 3. Spanish Sexual Politics, 1901–1939

1. Lincoln, *Discourse and the Construction of Society*, 3–26.
2. Teresa Claramunt Adell and Angeles Ezama Gil, "El pensamiento reformista primisecular en *Alma Española*," 41–60. The authors point out that the only women who contributed to *Alma Española* were Emilia Pardo Bazán and Concepción Arenal (53). These are the same two female authors ransacked

by Havelock Ellis in his pseudoscientific survey of Spanish women, "La mujer española." Regarding the petit-bourgeois nature of early-twentieth-century reformist thought in Spain, see José-Carlos Mainer, "Literatura burguesa, literatura pequeño-burguesa en la España del siglo XX" and *Literatura y pequeña burguesía en España*. See also the cultural essays in Nigel Townson, ed., *El republicanismo en España (1830–1977)*.

3. In all this I gratefully follow Fernando García Lara, *El lugar de la novela erótica española*, 50–58.

4. As cited by García Lara, *Novela erótica española*, 115.

5. From a short autobiography published just before *Las ingenuas* and reproduced by García Lara, *Novela erótica española*, 139 (my translation).

6. As cited by Dendle, *The Spanish Novel of Religious Thesis*, 74.

7. For all this, see Lily Litvak, *Erotismo fin de siglo*, 158–227.

8. *Novela erótica española*, 74. In *The Dynamics of Literary Response*, 104–90, Holland argues that an author's style is always defensive in some way.

9. Serrano Poncela, *El secreto de Melibea*, 159; cited by García Lara, *Novela erótica española*, 73.

10. *Erotismo fin de siglo*, 1–2. Following citations: 185, 187, 191.

11. Trigo, *Jarrapellejos*, 211.

12. Why impoverished social conditions make people more prone to persecutory anxieties and actions is explained by Alford, *Melanie Klein and Critical Social Theory*, 42–45.

13. *Novela erótica española*, 148. See also his "Imágenes sexuales en la canción novecentista," 57–61.

14. *El cuplé*, 12. The following citations or quotations: 107, 115, 87, 95, 88, 115.

15. *El sexo de nuestros padres*, 27.

16. Salaün wryly notes that Joan Corominas, in his *Diccionario etimológico*, erroneously derives the word *sicalipsis* from *sykon* (Greek for vulva) and *aleiptikos* (Greek for rub or excite); the etymologist had greatly overestimated the cultural level of the *cuplé* world (127n). Following quotation: 125.

17. Salaün gets these and other examples from Alvaro Retana, *Historia del arte frívolo* (my translations). Retana was a prolific author of both erotic novels and erotic song lyrics.

18. *El cuplé*, 183.

19. Zueras Torrens, *Julio Romero de Torres y su mundo*, 86.

20. Ibid., 119–20. For the best global treatment of his work, see Mercedes Valverde Candil and Ana María Piriz Salgado, *Catálogo del Museo Julio Romero de Torres*.

21. Eslava, *El sexo de nuestros padres*, 16; Mainer, "Notas sobre la lectura obrera en España," 112–13.

22. I am grateful to Dr. Susan Verdi Webster for sending me several volumes in the series: *Los órganos genitales* (November 1932); *La virginidad* (January 1933); *Embarazo y parto anormales* (April 1933); *El matrimonio* (June 1935). For the complete publishing history of the series, see Gonzalo Santonja, "La Editorial Fénix (Madrid, 1932–1935): Notas sobre la literatura de quiosco durante la II República."

23. *El sexo de nuestros padres*, 28 (my translation).

24. As quoted by Vila-San Juan, *Vida cotidiana durante la dictadura de Primo de Rivera*, 312.

25. Eslava, *El sexo de nuestros padres*, 28.

26. *El cuplé*, 130–31.

27. Eslava, *El sexo de nuestros padres*, 29.
28. *Privilege, Persecution, and Prophecy*, 51–52.
29. *Visionaries*, 45. Following quotation: 7.
30. *Spanish Catholicism*, 147–48.
31. Thomas, *La guerra civil española*, 82–83.
32. *Spanish Catholicism*, 145.
33. Ibid., 60—as revealed by Azaña's own detailed diaries. A certain Father Montes seems to have particularly troubled the young Azaña.
34. As reproduced by Juan J. Linz, "Religión y política en España," 8 (my translation). Linz goes on to say that Azaña's speech sounds radical today, but in the context of the leftist debate on how best to defenestrate the Church it was actually "a constructive posture." This tells us a great deal about the context!
35. "El retorno de la hija pródiga: mujeres entre lo público y lo privado (1931–1936)," 121.
36. *The Family Romance of the French Revolution*, xv. She continues on the same page: "In many and sometimes surprising ways, family romances, both conscious and unconscious, helped organize the political experience of the Revolution; revolutionaries and counter-revolutionaries alike had to confront the issues of paternal authority, female participation, and fraternal solidarity. They had to tell stories about how the republic came to be and what it meant, and those stories always had an element of family conflict and resolution."
37. Bussy Genevois, "El retorno de la hija pródiga," 118.
38. Thomas, *La guerra civil española*, 91.
39. From an editorial published in the Madrid newspaper *El Sol* on 11 May 1931; cited by Delgado, *La ira sagrada*, 41 and 59 (my translation). For an exhaustive new study of these and other thinkers of the thirties, see Xavier Tussell Gómez and Genoveva Queipo de Llano, *Los intelectuales y la República*.
40. Cárcel Ortí, *La persecución religiosa en España durante la Segunda República*, 112–14, 163.
41. *Ser español*, 246.
42. Cited by Delgado, *La ira sagrada*, 28–30.
43. *La ira sagrada*, 101–15.
44. Ibid., 19 (my translation). For additional insights into the political psychology of anarchism in Spain, see Brademas, *Anarcosindicalismo y revolución en España: 1930–1937*; Kaplan, *Anarchists of Andalusia, 1868–1903*; Kern, *Red Years/Black Years: A Political History of Spanish Anarchism*; Mintz, *The Anarchists of Casas Viejas*; Winston, *Workers and the Right in Spain, 1900–1936*; and Esenwein, *Anarchist Ideology*, all of which make thorough use of the Spanish-language materials.
45. Cárcel Ortí, *La persecución religiosa*, 43–45. Other relevant studies or defenses of the Spanish Church during this period include Peers, *Spain, the Church and the Orders*; Comas, *Isidro Gomá-Francesc Vidal i Barraquer: Dos visiones antagónicas de la iglesia española de 1939*; Gomá y Tomás, *Por Dios y por España*; and Muntanyola, *Vidal i Barraquer: el cardenal de la paz*.
46. "La influencia de la religión en la España democrática," 52. For a global critique of Azaña's overly idealistic and "literary" approach to politics, see Arias, *Azaña o el sueño de la razón*.
47. *The Family Romance of the French Revolution*, 13–14. Following quotation: 106.
48. The example is from Christian, *Visionaries*, 37: "An older lady in Zumarraga told me that when as a girl she rode past on a bicycle, a priest called out that he hoped she would not have the nerve to go to Communion the next day.

One of her friends recalled Don Andrés Olaechea, one of the priests who led the rosary at Ezkioga, crossing the town square where a girl was riding a bicycle and muttering 'Sinvergüenza, sinvergüenza, sinvergüenza' [hussy, hussy, hussy] until he was out of sight."

49. *Observing the Erotic Imagination*, 90.

50. Cf. Horowitz, *Introduction to Psychodynamics*, 127.

51. As cited by Delgado, *La ira sagrada*, 54–55 (my translation).

52. Cárcel Ortí, *La persecución religiosa*, 95.

53. Lewis, *Spain, A Land Blighted by Religion*, 94.

54. Linz, "Religión y política en España," 5 (my translation).

55. The full story is now available for the first time in Verdoy's *La incautación de los bienes de los jesuitas durante la II República*.

56. Statistics cited by Cárcel Ortí, *La persecución religiosa*, 175.

57. Moreno, *La Semana Santa en Sevilla: Conformación, mixtificación y significaciones*, 180–214.

58. Melgar Reina and Marín Rújula, *Saetas, pregones y romances litúrgicos cordobeses*, 92 (my translation). While in Seville during Lent of 1988 I heard this saeta performed in the Basilica of the Macarena, eliciting wild applause and cheering from the mostly proletarian audience.

59. *Visionaries*, 7 and 287.

60. *Visionaries*, 301.

61. Dr. Bessel A. van der Kolk, "Trauma and Memory," 279–302.

62. *Spare the Child*, 155. "The most consistent thread connecting apocalyptics generation after generation has been the experience of pain, assault, and physical coercion resulting from harsh corporal punishments in childhood" (206).

63. *Visionaries*, 347–72. The following quotations are from pages 31, 48, 50, 275, 277, 280.

64. Ibid., 132.

65. Cf. Spero, *Religious Objects as Psychological Structures*, 50–92, or Meissner, *Ignatius of Loyola*, 361–68.

66. For a succinct overview and annotated bibliography, see Lawton, *The Psychohistorian's Handbook*, 123–59. See also the classic volume edited by Lloyd deMause, *The History of Childhood* (Psychohistory Press, 1974). I agree with anthropologists Ralph Linton and George Devereux that cultural schemata cannot be reduced to baby and infant care techniques. See Linton, "Culture and Normality," esp. 203–4, on the key role of adolescence. Human society might be pictured as a variable number of mostly automatic and unconscious schemata whose purpose is to write the psychocultural scripts, supply the props of rationalization, and motivate the appropriate acting out.

67. *Visionaries*, 232.

68. For an introduction to the effect of culture on mental disorders, see Ari Kiev, *Transcultural Psychiatry*, 46–94. There is a good overview in Bock, *Rethinking Psychological Anthropology*, 154–209. See also George Devereux, *Basic Problems of Ethnopsychiatry*; I. Al-Issa, ed., *Handbook of Culture and Mental Illness*; or Jürg Siegfried, "Culture and Mental Illness," 223–31. Postfreudian psychology now places the emphasis on trauma in the genesis of hysterical dissociation that classic Freudian psychology placed on incestuous fantasy and drive conflict. See Bessel A. van der Kolk et al., "History of Trauma in Psychiatry," 47–74. There is also a good discussion of these issues in Mitchell and Black, *Freud and Beyond. A History of Modern Psychoanalytic Thought*, 206–18. Cultural context retains its decisive role. Certain anomalies of western Irish mental health are inseparable

from what Scheper-Hughes refers to as the "ascetic Jansenist tradition of Irish Catholicism" (*Saints, Scholars, and Schizophrenics*, 133). The Jansenist tradition did not thrive in Spain, as discussed earlier. I am suggesting that, instead of Irish-type schizophrenia, we get Spanish-type dissociation, whereby items from the "psychic warehouse" of half-forgotten coercive experiences, filtered through a particular set of social relations, became supernatural visions.

69. Thomas, *La guerra civil española*, vol. 1, 89.

70. Walsh, *Opus Dei*.

71. Some sixty scholars made contributions to *Las mujeres y la Guerra Civil Española*, organized by Salamanca's Civil War Archives, edited by the Instituto de la Mujer del Ministerio de Asuntos Sociales, and published by the Ministerio de Cultura (Madrid, 1991). I am much indebted to this large collection of research findings.

72. Bussy Genevois, "El retorno de la hija pródiga," 126–28.

73. As cited by Delgado, *La ira sagrada*, 33.

74. Jesús Hernández, *Yo fui ministro de Stalin* (Mexico, 1953), 99; cited by Eslava, *El sexo de nuestros padres*, 36 (my translation). For her side of the story, see Dolores Ibárruri, *They Shall Not Pass*.

75. Thomas, *La guerra civil española*, 14.

76. Bussy Genevois, "Del otoño del 33 al verano del 34: ¿Los meses claves de la condición social femenina?" 18.

77. Bussy Genevois, "Del otoño del 33 al verano del 34," 18–19, and "El retorno de la hija pródiga," 131.

78. Discussed by Carmen Martín Gaite, *Usos amorosos de la postguerra española*, 53.

79. Preston, *Franco*, 100.

80. Bussy Genevois, "El retorno de la hija pródiga," 133.

81. Cárcel Ortí, *La persecución religiosa*, 180.

82. *Franco*, 105, 123.

83. *The Anatomy of Prejudices*, 224.

84. *Visionaries*, 258.

85. "Primitives are like children, the tropes say. Primitives are our untamed selves, our id forces—libidinous, irrational, violent, dangerous. Primitives are mystics, in tune with nature, part of its harmonies. Primitives are free. Primitives exist at the 'lowest cultural levels'; we occupy the 'highest,' in the metaphors of stratification and hierarchy commonly used by Malinowski and others like him" (Torgovnick, *Gone Primitive*, 8). My approach to such issues is based on Bourdieu, *La distinción*, 169–76. For an introduction to Bourdieu's constructivist structuralism and his theory of habitus, see Turner, *The Structure of Sociological Theory*, 508–517. See also *Bourdieu: Critical Perspectives*, ed. C. Calhoun, E. Li-Puma, and M. Postone. How one social class attempts to impose its moral and emotional paradigms on another is a prime interest of researchers in the social history of emotions. For a good overview, see Stearns and Stearns, "Emotionology: Clarifying the History of Emotions and Emotional Standards," 284–309.

86. "El derecho de la rebeldía," by Aniceto Castro Albarrán; cited by Juan Cano Ballesta, "Nuevo ensayo y retórica de la derecha en vísperas del Bienio Negro (1933)," 81.

87. *The Mass Psychology of Fascism*, 91.

88. *El cuplé*, 98.

89. *The Mass Psychology of Fascism*, 141 (emphases in original).

90. Statistics cited by Cárcel Ortí, *La persecución religiosa*, 194.

Howard Stein [handwritten marginal note]

91. *Ser español*, 256–58.

92. "Psychoanalytic Anthropology and Psychohistory: A Personal Synthesis," 385. The Austrian psychohistorian Josef Berghold speaks of a "social trance" whereby the success of charismatic leaders is tied to their ability to activate certain types of unconscious persecutorial schemata in people who at some punishing stage of their childhood learned to conform to arbitrary authority or, worse, incorporated the aggressor, panically denied many personal needs and desires, and panically accepted hostile exterior demands as their own—"the panic character of this denial and acceptance implying that subsequently they cannot be critically reviewed, changed, or compared with other experiences or demands." "The Social Trance: Psychological Obstacles to Progress in History," 236. See also the article by David Lotto, "On Witches and Witch Hunts: Ritual and Satanic Cult Abuse," esp. 380–82 where he discusses research findings about easily hypnotizable people, their natural occurrence in a population (5–10 percent), their "trance logic," and their "pathological level of compliance with the wishes and beliefs of those in their environment." For a good overview of group-fantasy research, see Lawton, *The Psychohistorian's Handbook*, 177–218.

93. *Anti-Oedipus*, 105.

94. Cárcel Ortí, *La persecución religiosa*, 214. Following quotations: 209–18 (my translations).

95. Both sides were quickly caught in the thrall of "an apocalyptic-Manichean mentality," says Sperber, *And I Remember Spain: A Spanish Civil War Anthology*, xx. See also Hernando, *Delirios de Cruzada* and Amando De Miguel, *Franco, Franco, Franco*. The definitive study from the Church's point of view is Alvarez Bolado, *Para ganar la guerra, para ganar la paz. Iglesia y Guerra Civil (1936–1939)*. For striking examples of mythico-religious symbolism in republican songs, see Carlos Palacio, ed., *Colección de canciones de lucha*.

José Sanchez [handwritten marginal note]

96. *The Spanish Civil War as a Religious Tragedy*, 2, 8.

97. *Historia de la persecución religiosa en España, 1936–1939*, 758–68.

98. *La persecución religiosa*, 234–46.

99. Ibid., 254.

100. These examples are drawn from Cárcel Ortí's "Anthology of Cruelty," *La persecución religiosa*, 254–67. Delgado argues that anticlerical violence could not help but reflect the general pattern and practices of Spanish ritual violence in general. Ceremonies of cruelty required "the presence of a public capable of evaluating the art and efficiency of the executioners." Moreover, "it had to be guaranteed that the suffering of the one slated to die turn out to be amusing. In Spain amusement is a sacralized entity because the sacred, apart from atrocious, was also obliged to be an occasion of public merriment. Before killing, really or figuratively, it is necessary to laugh a while. The general norm was always fulfilled: since the festival was always violent, violence could never not be festive" (*La ira sagrada*, 65–69).

101. As quoted by Cárcel Ortí, *La persecución religiosa*, 218–19 (my translation).

102. The horrendous details of their martyrdom can be read in Montero, *Historia de la persecución*, 521–23. Other studies that detail the righteous slaughter in diverse regions of Spain include Castro Albarrán, *La gran víctima. La Iglesia española, mártir de la revolución roja*; Borkenau, *The Spanish Cockpit: An Eyewitness Account of the Political and Social Conflicts of the Spanish Civil War*; Cirac Estopañán, *Martirologio de Cuenca* (800 pages); Gassiot Magret, *Apuntes para un estudio de la persecución religiosa en España*; Florindo de Miguel, *Un cura en zona roja*; Sanabre Sanromá, *Martirologio de la iglesia en la diócesis de Barcelona durante la persecución*

religiosa; Sebastián y Bandarán and Tineo Lara, *La persecución religiosa en la Ar-chidiócesis de Sevilla*; Carlos Vicuña, *Mártires agustinos de El Escorial*; and Zahonero Vivó, *Sacerdotes mártires* (600 pages). Although the word "persecution" figures prominently in her title, Frances Lannon devotes exactly one paragraph to the atrocities, making no attempt to explain or account for them (*Privilege, Persecution, and Prophecy*, 201–2).

103. Marty and Appleby, "Conclusion: An Interim Report on a Hypothetical Family," in *Fundamentalisms Observed*, 837–38, 819–20.

104. Puccini, ed., *Romancero de la resistencia española* Ramos-Gascón, ed., *El Romancero del Ejército Popular*; Rodríguez Moñino, ed., *Romancero General de la Guerra de España*; Salaün, *Romancero libertario* and *La poesía de la Guerra de España*; Geist, "Popular Poetry in the Fascist Front during the Spanish Civil War." Political psychologist Maxwell Taylor identifies the following symptoms of millenarianism: an analysis of the world in terms of a real or impending catastrophe; a revelation that explains this state of affairs, and which offers some form of salvation or redressing of ills; as part of the revelation, the possession of special knowledge that the disastrous state is the result of the action of malevolent forces (spiritual or secular) which conspire to corrupt and subvert the normal organs of society. *The Fanatics*, 121. Norman Cohn's *The Pursuit of the Millennium* remains indispensable.

105. *La poesía de la Guerra de España*, 367.

106. *The Spanish Civil War as a Religious Tragedy*, 25–27.

107. As quoted by Cárcel Ortí, *La persecución religiosa*, 248 (my translation).

108. *Seductions of Crime: Moral and Sensual Attractions in Doing Evil*, 9.

109. *Melanie Klein and Critical Social Theory*, 42.   — Alford

110. Ibid., 43–44. See also W. R. Bion, *Experiences in Groups*. Most of the initial concepts can be found in Melanie Klein, *Envy and Gratitude and Other Works: 1946–1963*.

111. Conway and Siegelman, *Snapping*, 216, 269.

112. *The Spanish Civil War as a Religious Tragedy*, 2, 56.

113. As cited by Cárcel Ortí, *La persecución religiosa en España durante la Segunda República (1931–1939)*, 55. The following citation: 48 (my translations).

114. For a complete accounting of Monsignor Tedeschini's dark view of clergy training in Spain, see Cárcel Ortí, "Pío XI y el clero español durante la Guerra Civil."

115. Esenwein, *Anarchist Ideiology and the Working-CLass Movement in Spain*, 212–13.

116. Katz, *Seduction of Crime*, 114–63.

117. *Snapping*, 264.

118. *Ser español*, 254 (emphasis in original).

119. "La miliciana: Otra opción de combatividad femenina antifascista," 97–99.

120. Torrente Ballester, *Javier Mariño: Historia de una conversación*; excerpted in Julio Rodríguez Puértolas, *Literatura fascista española*, vol. 2, 771–86 (my translation).

121. All this according to J. V. Puente, cited by Juan Ramón Azaola, "La chica topolino," 129.

122. From his 1937 pamphlet "Mensaje a la mujer obrera," cited by Nash, "La miliciana," 105.

123. *El sexo de nuestros padres*, 33 (my translation).

124. Ibid., 35, accompanied by a photographic reproduction of one of the union sex coupons.

125. From the diary of a miliciana in Mallorca named Teresa Pámies, who still felt guilty years later about turning him down; as cited by Nash, "La miliciana," 106.

126. "La miliciana," 100, 104–6. Following citation: 106.

127. R. Fraser, *Recuérdalo tú y recuérdalo a otros*, 400.

128. *El sexo de nuestros padres*, 38–39.

129. "La representación gráfica de las mujeres."

130. Calleja Martín, "Mujeres de la industria de espectáculos: Madrid (1936–1939)," 121.

131. "Mujeres Antifascistas Españolas: Trayectoria histórica de una organización femenina de lucha."

132. María José Sainz Bretón, Olga Morentin Arana, and Arantza Romano Igartua, "*Mujeres*: Organo de prensa del Comité de Mujeres Antifascistas," 49.

133. The pioneering works in this area are both by Mary Nash: *Mujeres Libres: España, 1936–1939* and *Mujer y movimiento obrero en España, 1931–1939*.

134. "Captación y capacitación: El problema de la autonomía en las relaciones de Mujeres Libres con el movimiento libertario."

135. Cobo Romero, "Los partidos políticos y las mujeres en la retaguardia republicana jiennense (1936–1939), 72.

136. Carmen Cardiño and Manuela Rodríguez, "Creación en 1937 de la Asociación Unión de Muchachas en Madrid."

137. *Literatura fascista española.*

138. "La Bestia y el Angel: Imágenes de las mujeres en la novela falangista de la Guerra Civil," 372.

139. Carrionero Salimero et al., "La mujer tradicionalista: Las Margaritas," 188. Following quotations: 190, 194.

140. "El Monje Guerrero," 208. Following quotation: 209.

141. Vizcaíno Casas, *La España de la posguerra, 1939–1953*, 54.

142. See Ferrer Benimeli, *El contubernio judeo-masónico-comunista*, 273–333, and Pérez Embid, "El símbolo de Santiago en la cultura española." In *The Structure of Spanish History*, Américo Castro argued that without Santiago "the history of Spain would have been entirely different" (130). Studying the myth we come to understand how, unlike the contemplative religiosity that prospered in other nations, "medieval Spanish Christianity was more productive of holy wars, propaganda, and thaumaturgy" (157). See also González-López, "The Myth of Saint James and Its Functional Reality." With his vindication of the Jewish and Moorish contributions to Spanish civilization, Castro (1885–1972) was to be a continual thorn in the side of the Franco regime's racialist propaganda. For a comparison of the myth of Santiago and the cult of Santa Teresa, see Di Febo's *La Santa de la Raza*, 23–59.

143. Juan Antonio Vallejo-Nájera (Head of the Servicios Psiquiátricos del Ejército) and Eduardo M. Martínez (Director of the Clínica Psiquiátrica de Málaga), "Psiquismo del fanatismo marxista. Investigaciones psicológicas en marxistas femeninos delincuentes," *Revista Española de Medicina y Cirugía de Guerra* II, No. 9 (May 1939); reproduced in *Las mujeres y la Guerra Civil Española*, 343–350. The study is introduced by an indignant Antonio Sánchez Nadal, "Experiencias psíquicas sobre mujeres marxistas malagueñas. Málaga 1939," 340–343.

144. *Aggression and Community*, 44.

145. Mercedes Formica, *Visto y vivido* (Barcelona, 1982), 214, cited by Sánchez Nadal, "Experiencias psíquicas sobre mujeres marxistas malagueñas," 342–43 (my translations).

146. Vallejo-Nájera and Martínez, "Psiquismo del fanatismo marxista," 344–47.

147. *Aggression and Community*, 44.

148. Real López et al., "Las mujeres en la inmediata postguerra," 320.

149. Eslava, *El sexo de nuestros padres*, 40.

150. *El último virrey. Queipo de Llano*, 34.

151. Badillo Baena et al., "La conjura de la miseria," 313.

152. Torres, *La vida amorosa en tiempos de Franco*, 119–41.

153. As cited by Martín Gaite, *Usos amorosos de la postguerra española*, 151 (my translation).

154. Gil, "La Legión Azul," 61.

155. "Women, Asian Hordes and the Threat of the Self in Ernesto Giménez Caballero's *Genio de España*."

156. Gil, "La legión azul," 56 (my translation).

157. Fernández Suárez, *España, árbol vivo*, 196 (my translation). By the end of 1943 the Blue Division (also known as the Blue Legion) had become an obstacle in Franco's path to a more accommodating relationship with the Allied Powers. But when it was officially dissolved in 1944, many Spaniards joined up with German troops, fought in Poland or Yugoslavia, and lost their lives defending Hitler's bunker. In the meantime, numerous Spaniards of the vanquished Republic had fought against the Axis Powers in France and Northern Africa; they accompanied the Normandy invasion and formed part of the first Allied troops to occupy downtown Paris in August 1944 (Gil, "La Legión Azul," 63).

Chapter 4. The Guardians of Morality

1. Abella, "La nueva España," 28.

2. *El sexo de nuestros padres*, 68–69.

3. Gil, "Religión, moral y costumbres a comienzos de los cincuenta," 37–40.

4. Vizcaíno Casas, *La España de la posguerra*, 103.

5. Peñafiel, "Un cierto deshielo," 26–27.

6. As cited by Gil, "Religión, moral y costumbres a comienzos de los cincuenta," 41.

7. Eslava, *El sexo de nuestros padres*, 73.

8. This is from Father Clavero's marriage manual, *Antes que te cases*, 38. See also Ranke-Heinemann, *Eunuchs for the Kingdom of Heaven*, 228–29, for an account of Saint Jerome's deliberate falsification of the Book of Tobit to express his own sexual pessimism.

9. "Religión y política en España," 19 (my translation).

10. Volkan, "Intergenerational Transmission and 'Chosen' Traumas: A Link Between the Psychology of the Individual and That of the Ethnic Group," 258–59.

11. *Privilege, Persecution and Prophecy*, 85.

12. Sánchez-Gijón, "Moral pública y vicios privados," 75 (my translation).

13. Carandell, "Golpes de pecho," 76 (my translation).

14. *Privilege, Persecution and Prophecy*, 50.

15. Reich, *The Mass Psychology of Fascism*, 151–69; Foucault, "Sexuality and Solitude," 372.

16. Eslava, *El sexo de nuestros padres*, 101. Word spread among unregenerate schoolboys that sirloin made an excellent vaginal substitute for masturbatory purposes, but steak was a luxury item in postwar Spain. A watermelon or canta-

loupe previously heated in the sun was an acceptable vegetarian substitute (112).

17. From Father Clemente's *La pureza y el joven cristiano* (Madrid, 1942), 50; reproduced by Eslava, *El sexo de nuestros padres*, 101 (my translation).

18. According to Eslava, the ideal profession for a voyeur was that of public park guard, easily identified in Franco's Spain by his brown corduroy uniform, whistle, and shotgun. These men specialized in hunting down young lovers' splendor in the grass. Hiding behind a tree or bush, the guard would allow the amorous couple to proceed with their lovemaking, never missing a detail; when orgasm seemed imminent, he would leap from his hiding place blowing his piercing whistle. As if this were not traumatic enough, the lovers were then required to hand over their identity cards while the guard took his time jotting down details and calculating the amount of the fine. As often as not the sinners could read their names in the newspaper the next day: "Julio Calvo and Soledad Pérez have been fined for immorality and public scandal," and so on. Could the amorous couple not go to a hotel? Presuming they could afford to do so, any hotel desk clerk could demand to see a *libro de familia*, as proof of marriage, before allowing a couple to share the same room. Here a profit motive supported the moral one: couples who did not have the document had to pay for two rooms, often at two different wings of the hotel so that the desk clerk could keep an eye on any "visiting," thereby earning a tip to look the other way (91–92, 206).

19. For these and similar incidents, see Blázquez, *La traición de los clérigos en la España de Franco*. In fairness to Father Llanos, it must be mentioned that he lived out his days helping residents of the poorest slum neighborhoods of Madrid.

20. Rumors spread throughout Spain that in the uncensored version of the movie, the glove scene had immediately led to a sex scene; tricked photos of a naked Gilda sold like hotcakes for five duros each. Eslava, *El sexo de nuestros padres*, 207, 220.

21. Gil, "Religión, moral y costumbres a comienzos de los cincuenta," 45.

22. How to decipher disguised antiauthoritarian sentiments in Spanish novels, plays, and movies is explained by Hans-Jörg Neuschäfer in *Adiós a la España eterna*, 44–294.

23. Vizcaíno Casas, *La españa de la posguerra*, 48, and Pardo, "Las canciones de una época," 12.

24. As quoted by Tejada, *La represión sexual en la España de Franco*, 139 (my translation).

25. Abella, "Evasiones cotdianas," 115–16 (my translation).

26. Llovet, "¡Que apaguen la sala!" 21 (my translation).

27. As quoted by J. M. Amilibia, *El día que perdí aquello*, 95.

28. Vizcaíno Casas, *La España de la posguerra*, 107.

29. Carandell, *Celtiberia Show*, 63.

30. *Aspectos jurídicos de la censura cinematográfica en España*, 31, 212, 214, 227, 240, 244, 277, 242, 287, 278, 225, 237, 227, 290, 315, 320, 233, 234, 249, 251, 254, 258, 262, 271, 272, 313, 289, 293, 299, 323, 327, 328, and 343 (my translations). The year cited for a foreign film is the year it was released in Spain, not necessarily the year of original release.

31. *Blood Cinema*, 241–44: "In *Marcelino*, the naked body of Jesus is fetishized with the same fragmenting close-ups that are conventionally used to eroticize the female body for the male gaze in Hollywood classical cinema. Despite the rigid material form of the statue, the successively larger close-ups animate his androgynous body, allowing us to savor the sensuality of its rippling lines and fleshlike texture. Though the spectacle is somewhat desexualized by being pre-

sented to the gaze of an innocent child, the context creates pederastic overtones. . . . In this case, Marcelino and Jesus are united in an erotic exchange: the
boy lures the beautiful young man off the cross with tempting food and drink,
and the boy is lured to his death with the divine pleasures of original plenitude."

32. *The Mass Psychology of Fascism*, 181.

33. *Observing the Erotic Imagination*, 3–43.

34. *La vida amorosa en tiempos de Franco*, 36–37.

35. *The Mass Psychology of Fascism*, 141 (emphases in original).

36. Cf. Chasseguet-Smirgel, *Creativity and Perversion*. For a searching critique
of authors who sought to enlist psychoanalysis in the service of utopian ideology or some other well-rationalized attempt to recover primary narcissism, see
Chasseguet-Smirgel and Grunberger, *Freud or Reich?* At least Reich sought to
make the world safe for genital orgasmic fulfillment; this made him a sexual reactionary for Herbert Marcuse, who taught that polymorphous perversity was
the royal road to individual and social liberation; then came Norman O. Brown
to denounce Marcuse for his timidity (Robinson, *The Freudian Left*, 228–29). See
also the excellent collection of essays edited by Fogel and Myers, *Perversions and
Near-Perversions in Clinical Practice*.

37. See Poliakov, *The Aryan Myth*.

38. "What we postwar children really wanted was to go to the movies or be
bought a bicycle; we were fed up with the abnegated, vigilant, and virile life of
those hirsute ancestors, whose feats that we studied next to the precarious home
brazier had no connection whatsoever with our latent needs for affection, adventure, and well-being." *Usos amorosos*, 23 (my translation). The following citations:
26, 49, 36–37.

39. Carandell, *Celtiberia Show*, 47.

40. Martín Gaite, *Usos amorosos*, 45, 42.

41. Josefina Xaudaró: "Las feas con estilo," *Destino*, 30 December 1939; cited
by Martín Gaite, *Usos amorosos*, 42 (my translation).

42. From a 1952 issue of *Chicas*; cited by Martín Gaite, *Usos amorosos*, 43.

43. *El sexo de nuestros padres*, 140–41. The following anecdotes: 277–78, 131, 26,
221.

44. "Retaliatory Homosexual Triumph over the Father: A Clinical Note on
the Counteroedipal Sources of the Oedipus Complex" (orig. 1960), in Devereux, *Basic Problems of Ethnopsychiatry*, 144.

45. *El sexo de nuestros padres*, 80.

46. "Política racial del Nuevo Estado," 55 (my translation).

47. Cited by Eslava, *El sexo de nuestros padres*, 77 (my translation). Following
quotation: 78.

48. See the excellent work by Smith, *Laws of Desire*. See also Six, *Juan Goytisolo:
The Case for Chaos*, 39–72.

49. *Usos amorosos*, 57. For her side of the story, see Pilar Primo de Rivera, *Cuatro discursos*, 34–35.

50. Eslava, *El sexo de nuestros padres*, 60: "A la luz del dato impresiona la tozudez
del *Führer*: la primera guerra mundial le costó un huevo y, lejos de escarmentar,
reincidió en una segunda."

51. "Las mujeres en la sociedad española de los años cuarenta," 297–99.

52. *Usos amorosos*, 59–60.

53. *How Fascism Ruled Women*, 147. So far no study of Spanish women under
Franco can rival De Grazia's work in terms of comprehensiveness and scholar-
ship.

54. "Gender and the State: Women in the 1940s," 194.

55. "Coros y Danzas" was the brainchild of Maruja Sampelayo, associated before the war with the secularizing Institutión Libre de Enseñanza, afterward dedicated to the recovery of traditional Spanish folk music and dances with the Sección Femenina. References to the positive labors of Falangist women abound in *El folklore español*, ed. J. M. Gómez-Tabanera (1968).

56. The bishop of Madrid, Eijo Garay, writing in *Ecclesia* (December 1941); cited by Martín Gaite, *Usos amorosos*, 61. Following citation: 62.

57. Alted Vigil, "Las mujeres," 297–98.

58. *Mujer, Falange y Franquismo*, 175–201.

59. De Miguel, *El mito de la inmaculada concepción*, 20. Following citations: 31, 44, 49, 52, 57.

60. As cited by de Miguel, *El mito*, 62.

61. Dr. Alfredo Mendrín, writing in 1956, as quoted by de Miguel, *El mito*, 88. Following quotation: 89 (my translations).

62. Dr. Federico Corominas in a 1956 speech; as quoted by de Miguel, *El mito*, 79 (my translation).

63. So wrote Dr. Víctor Cónill Montobbio and his son Dr. Víctor Cónill Serra in *Tratado de ginecología*, 5th ed. (Barcelona: Labor, 1967), 244, as quoted by de Miguel, *El mito*, 93 (my translation).

64. *Memorias de un médico de la lucha antivenérea* (1963); as quoted by Torres, *La vida amorosa en tiempos de Franco*, 137 (my translation). The following citation: 138.

65. Del Campo, *La nueva familia española*, 89.

66. Giner and Sarasa, "Religión y modernidad en España," 85.

67. "Del confesionalismo al criptoconfesionalismo," 101–3. The following indented quotation: 94–95 (my translation).

 68. His relentlessly critical books include *Ideología e historia: La formación del cristianismo como fenómeno ideológico* (1993) and *Fe cristiana, Iglesia, poder* (1991).

69. *Clérigos*, 559.

70. *Sex, Priests, and Power*, 141.

71. "The Abduction of Fidelity," 125.

72. *La vida sexual del clero*, 103.

73. Ibid., 231–34.

74. For details, see the groundbreaking book by Berry, *Lead Us Not into Temptation* (1992).

75. Rodríguez, *La vida sexual del clero*, 189–97 (my translations).

76. Rodríguez, *La vida sexual del clero*, 181–88.

77. As cited by Rodríguez, *La vida sexual del clero*, 68 (my translation).

78. Walsh, *Opus Dei*, 17.

79. Lewis, "The Right and Military Rule, 1955–1983," 163–65.

80. Rodríguez, *La vida sexual del clero*, 335–42.

81. Cf. Laing, *The Politics of the Family*, 14.

82. *Clérigos*, 245.

83. *Clérigos*, 283, 489 (my translations).

84. "La influencia de la religión," 55.

85. "Catholicism and Social Change," 278.

86. As cited by Rodríguez, *La vida sexual del clero*, 23–25.

87. "La influencia de la religión," 55–57.

88. Dufour, *Clero y sexto mandamiento*, 124–27.

89. Pérez Iruela, "La Iglesia se desmarca," 73.

90. *Vida, ascendencia, nacimiento, crianza y aventuras*, 118 (my translation).

Bibliography

Abascal y Sáinz de la Maza, José Rafael de.
1984   *Brujería y magia: Evasiones del pueblo andaluz.* Seville: Fundación Blas Infante.
Abella, Rafael.
1990   La nueva España *and* Evasiones cotidianas. In *Vida cotidiana en la España de los 40,* ed. Juan María Martínez, 23–33 and 109–17. Madrid: Ediciones del Prado.
Abraham, W. Nicholas.
1994   The Significance of Religious Messages in Sexual Addiction: A Literature Review. *Sexual Addiction and Compulsivity: The Journal of Treatment and Prevention* 1:159–84.
Ackelsberg, Martha.
1991   Captación y capacitación: El problema de la autonomía en las relaciones de Mujeres Libres con el movimiento libertario. In *Las mujeres y la Guerra Civil Española,* ed. Instituto de la Mujer, 35–40. Madrid: Ministerio de Cultura.
Adorno, T. W., Else Frenkel-Brunswik, Daniel J. Levinson, and R. Nevitt Sanford.
1950   *The Authoritarian Personality.* New York: Harper & Row.
Aguilar, Encarnación.
1983   *Las hermandades de Castilleja de la Cuesta: Un estudio de antropología cultural.* Seville: Servicio de Publicaciones del Ayuntamiento de Sevilla.
Alas, Leopoldo [Clarín].
1990   *La Regenta.* México: Editorial Porrúa. [Orig. 1884–1885.]
Alejandre, Juan Antonio.
1994   *El veneno de Dios: La Inquisición de Sevilla ante el delito de solicitación en confesión.* Madrid: Siglo XXI de España.
Alford, C. Fred.
1989   *Melanie Klein and Critical Social Theory.* New Haven: Yale University Press.
Al-Issa, I., ed.
1995   *Handbook of Culture and Mental Illness: An International Perspective.* Madison, Conn.: International Universities Press.
Alted Vigil, Alicia.
1991   Las mujeres en la sociedad española de los años cuarenta. In *Las mujeres y la Guerra Civil Española,* ed. Instituto de la Mujer, 293–303. Madrid: Ministerio de Cultura.

Alvarez Bolado, Alfonso.
1995 *Para ganar la guerra, para ganar la paz: Iglesia y Guerra Civil (1936–1939)*. Madrid: Publicaciones de la Universidad Pontificia de Comillas.
Amezcua, Manuel.
1991 La vida contradictoria de la beata. *Demófilo: Revista de Cultura Tradicional* 7:33–43.
Amilibia, J. M.
1975 *El día que perdí aquello*. Madrid: Sedmay.
Anderson, Walter.
1974 J. L. Moreno and the Origins of Psychodrama. In *Psychodrama. Theory and Therapy*, ed. Ira A. Greenberg, 205–11. New York: Behavioral Publications.
Arias, Luis.
1995 *Azaña o el sueño de la razón*. Madrid: Nerea.
Aróstegui, Julio, ed.
1994 *Violencia y política en España*. Madrid: Marcial Pons/Asociación de Historia Contemporánea.
Azaola, Juan Ramón.
1990 La chica topolino. In *La vida cotidiana en la España de los 40*, ed. Juan María Martínez, 128–29. Madrid: Ediciones del Prado.
Badillo Baena, Rosa María, Carmen Ramos Fernández, and Manuel Ponte.
1991 La conjura de la miseria: La lucha de las mujeres contra el hambre en los barrios obreros malagueños durante los primeros años de postguerra. In *Las mujeres y la Guerra Civil Española*, ed. Instituto de la Mujer, 311–16. Madrid: Ministerio de Cultura.
Baquero Goyanes, Mariano.
1985 Introducción. In *La Regenta*, ed. M. Baquero Goyanes, 9–117. Madrid: Espasa-Calpe.
Barnes, Andrew E.
1989 *Ces sortes de Pénitence Imaginaires*: The Counter-Reformation Assault on Communitas. In *Social History and Issues in Human Consciousness: Some Interdisciplinary Connections*, ed. A. E. Barnes and P. N. Stearns, 61–83. New York: New York University Press.
Barrios, Manuel.
1990 *El último virrey: Queipo de Llano*. Seville: Rodríguez Castillejo.
Bassin, Donna, Margaret Honey, and Merle M. Kaplan, eds.
1994 *Representations of Motherhood*. New Haven: Yale University Press.
Bateson, Gregory.
1975 *Steps to an Ecology of Mind*. New York: Ballantine.
Bécarud, Jean.
1977 *De La Regenta al Opus Dei*. Madrid: Taurus.
Bennassar, Bartolomé.
1979 *The Spanish Character: Attitudes and Mentalities from the Sixteenth to the Nineteenth Century*. Trans. B. Keen. Berkeley: University of California Press.
Benson, Gordon.
1994 Sexual Behavior by Male Clergy with Adult Female Counselees: Systemic and Situational Themes. *Sexual Addiction and Compulsivity: The Journal of Treatment and Prevention* 1:103–18.

Berghold, Josef.
1991   The Social Trance: Psychological Obstacles to Progress in History. *Journal of Psychohistory* 19:221–43.
Berke, Joseph H.
1988   *The Tyranny of Malice: Exploring the Dark Side of Character and Culture.* New York: Summit Books.
Bernal, Antonio Miguel.
1977   La disolución del régimen señorial, la propiedad de la tierra y la conformación del actual sistema agrario andaluz. In *Crisis del Antiguo Régimen e industrialización en la España del siglo XIX,* 76–88. Madrid: Cuadernos para el Diálogo.
Bernal, Manuel.
1994   *El hábito no hace al monje: Clero y pueblo en los refraneros españoles del siglo de oro.* Seville: Padilla Libros.
Bernecker, Walther L.
1994   "Acción directa" y violencia en el anarquismo español. In *Violencia y política en España,* ed. Julio Aróstegui, 147–88. Madrid: Marcial Pons/ Asociación de Historia Contemporánea.
Berry, John.
1992   *Lead Us Not into Temptation: Catholic Priests and the Sexual Abuse of Children.* New York: Doubleday.
Bion, W. R.
1974   *Experiences in Groups.* New York: Ballantine.
Blázquez, Feliciano.
1991   *La traición de los clérigos en la España de Franco: Crónica de una intolerancia, 1936–1975.* Madrid: Editorial Trotta.
Bock, Philip K.
1995   *Rethinking Psychological Anthropology: Continuity and Change in the Study of Human Action.* Prospect Heights, Ill.: Waveland Press. [Orig. 1988.]
Böhl de Faber, Cecilia, a.k.a. Fernán Caballero.
1963   *Elia, o la España de 30 años ha.* Madrid: Biblioteca de Autores Españoles. [Orig. 1857.]
Booth, Leo.
1991   *When God Becomes a Drug: Breaking the Chains of Religious Addiction and Abuse.* New York: Putnam.
Borkenau, Franz.
1937   *The Spanish Cockpit: An Eyewitness Account of the Political and Social Conflicts of the Spanish Civil War.* London: Faber & Faber.
Boruah, Bijoy.
1988   *Fiction and Emotion: A Study in Aesthetics and the Philosophy of Mind.* Oxford: Clarendon Press.
Bourdieu, Pierre.
1988   *La distinción: Criterio y bases sociales del gusto.* Trans. María del Carmen Ruiz de Elvira. Madrid: Taurus. [Orig. 1979.]
Bourdieu, Pierre, and Loïc J. D. Wacquant.
1992   *An Invitation to Reflexive Sociology.* Chicago: University of Chicago Press.
Brademas, John.
1974   *Anarcosindicalismo y revolución en España: 1930–1937.* Trans. J. Romero Maura. Barcelona: Ariel.

Brandes, Stanley.
  1980 *Metaphors of Masculinity: Sex and Status in Andalusian Folklore.* Philadelphia: University of Pennsyvlania Press.
Brenan, Gerald.
  1960 *The Spanish Labyrinth: An Account of the Social and Political Background of the Spanish Civil War.* Cambridge: Cambridge University Press. [Orig. 1943.]
Brock, Rita Nakashima.
  1989 And a Little Child Will Lead Us: Christology and Child Abuse. In *Christianity, Patriarchy, and Abuse: A Feminist Critique,* eds. Joanne C. Brown and Carole R. Bohn, 42–61. Cleveland: Pilgrim Press.
Brown, Peter R.
  1988 *The Body and Society: Men, Women, and Sexual Renunciation in Early Christianity.* New York: Columbia University Press.
Bueno, Gustavo.
  1994 La influencia de la religión en la España democrática. In *La influencia de la religión en la sociedad española,* ed. Javier Sádaba, 37–80. Madrid: Libertarias/Prodhufi.
Bussy Genevois, Danièle.
  1991 Del otoño del 33 al verano del 34: ¿Los meses claves de la condición social femenina? In *Las mujeres y la Guerra Civil Española,* ed. Instituto de la Mujer, 15–22. Madrid: Ministerio de Cultura.
  1993 El retorno de la hija pródiga: Mujeres entre lo público y lo privado (1931–1936). In *Otras visiones de España,* ed. Pilar Folguera, 111–38. Madrid: Editorial Pablo Iglesias.
Calhoun, C., E. LiPuma, and M. Postone, eds.
  1993 *Bourdieu: Critical Perspectives.* Chicago: University of Chicago Press.
Callahan, William J.
  1984 *Church, Politics, and Society in Spain, 1750–1874.* Cambridge, Mass.: Harvard University Press.
Calleja Martín, Rosario.
  1991 Mujeres de la industria de espectáculos. Madrid (1936–1939). In *Las mujeres y la Guerra Civil Española,* ed. Instituto de la Mujer, 118–124. Madrid: Ministerio de Cultura.
Cano Ballesta, Juan.
  1993 Nuevo ensayo y retórica de la derecha en vísperas del Bienio Negro (1933). *España Contemporánea* 6:75–85.
Carandell, Luis.
  1978 *Celtiberia Show.* Madrid: Editora Nacional.
  1990 Golpes de pecho. In *La vida cotidiana en la España de los 40,* ed. Juan María Martínez, 76. Madrid: Ediciones del Prado.
Cárcel Ortí, Vicente.
  1986 Pío XI y el clero español durante la Guerra Civil. In *Italia y la Guerra Civil Española,* 33–54. Madrid: Consejo Superior de Investigaciones Científicas.
  1990 *La persecución religiosa en España durante la Segunda Republica (1931–1939).* Madrid: Ediciones Rialp.
Cardiño, Carmen, and Manuela Rodríguez.
  1991 Creación en 1937 de la Asociación Unión de Muchachas en Madrid. In *Las mujeres y la Guerra Civil Española,* ed. Instituto de la Mujer, 60–61. Madrid: Ministerio de Cultura.

Caro Baroja, Julio.
1957   *Razas, pueblos y linajes.* Madrid: Revista de Occidente.
1961   *Las brujas y su mundo.* Madrid: Alianza.
1965   *El Carnaval. Análisis histórico-cultural.* Madrid: Taurus.
1969   *Ensayo sobre la literatura de cordel.* Madrid: Revista de Occidente.
1970   *Inquisición, brujería y criptojudaismo.* Barcelona: Ariel.
1974   *Ritos y mitos equívocos.* Madrid: Istmo.
1978   *Los judíos en la España moderna y contemporánea.* 3 vols. 2d ed. Madrid: Istmo.
1979   *Ensayo sobre la cultura popular española.* Madrid: Dosbe.
1980   *Introducción a una historia contemporánea del anticlericalismo español.* Madrid: Istmo.
1985   *Las formas complejas de la vida religiosa: Religión, sociedad y carácter en la España de los siglos XVI y XVII.* Madrid: Sarpe.
Carrionero Salimero, Florencia, Antonio Fuentes Labrador, María Angeles Sampedro Talabán, and María Jesús Velaso Marcos.
1991   La mujer tradicionalista: Las Margaritas. In *Las mujeres y la Guerra Civil Española,* ed. Instituto de la Mujer, 188–201. Madrid: Ministerio de Cultura.
Carroll, Michael P.
1986   *The Cult of the Virgin Mary. Psychological Origins.* Princeton: Princeton University Press.
1991   Ernest Jones on Holy Communion: Refurbishing an Early Psychoanalytic Insight. *Journal of Psychohistory* 18:307–15.
Castro, Américo.
1954   *The Structure of Spanish History.* Princeton: Princeton University Press.
Castro Albarrán, Aniceto de.
1940   *La gran víctima: La Iglesia española, mártir de la revolución roja.* Salamanca: Editorial Sígueme.
Chasseguet-Smirgel, Janine.
1984   *Creativity and Perversion.* Foreword by Otto Kernberg. New York: Norton.
Chasseguet-Smirgel, Janine, and Béla Grunberger.
1986   *Freud or Reich? Psychoanalysis and Illusion.* London: Free Association Books. [Orig. 1976.]
Chevalier, Maxime.
1982   *Cuentos españoles de los siglos XVI y XVII.* Madrid: Gredos.
Christian, William A., Jr.
1996   *Visionaries: The Spanish Republic and the Reign of Christ.* Berkeley: University of California Press.
Cirac Estopañán, Sebastián.
1947   *Martirologio de Cuenca.* Barcelona: Editorial Librería Religiosa.
Claramunt Adell, Teresa, and Angeles Ezama Gil.
1993   El pensamiento reformista primisecular en *Alma Española. España Contemporánea. Revista de Literatura y Cultura* 6:41–60.
Claramunt López, Fernando.
1991   *Modas y epidemias psíquicas en España.* Madrid: Ediciones Temas de Hoy.
Clavero Núñez, A.
1946   *Antes que te cases.* Valencia: Editorial Espiritualidad.
Cobo Romero, Francisco.
1991   Los partidos políticos y las mujeres en la retaguardia republicana jien-

nense (1936–1939). In *Las mujeres y la Guerra Civil Española*, ed. Instituto de la Mujer, 67–73. Madrid: Ministerio de Cultura.

Cohler, Bertram J.
1992 Intent and Meaning in Psychoanalysis and Cultural Study. In *New Directions in Psychological Anthropology*, ed. T. Schwartz, G. M. White, and C. A. Lutz, 269–93. Cambridge: Cambridge University Press.

Cohn, Norman.
1970 *The Pursuit of the Millennium: Revolutionary Millenarians and Mystical Anarchists of the Middle Ages*. New York: Oxford University Press.

Comas, Ramón.
1977 *Isidro Gomá-Francesc Vidal i Barraquer: Dos visiones antagónicas de la iglesia española de 1939*. Salamanca: Editorial Sígueme.

Conway, Flo, and Jim Siegelman.
1995 *Snapping*. 2d ed. New York: Stillpoint Press.

Cuenca Toribio, José Manuel.
1989 *El caciquismo en España*. Barcelona: Cuadernos "Historia 16," no. 188.

De Grazia, Victoria.
1992 *How Fascism Ruled Women: Italy, 1922–1945*. Berkeley: University of California Press.

Del Campo, Salustiano.
1991 *La nueva familia española*. Madrid: Ediciones de la Universidad Complutense de Madrid.

Deleuze, Gilles, and Félix Guattari.
1983 *Anti-Oedipus: Capitalism and Schizophrenia*. Trans. Robert Hurley, Mark Seem, and Helen R. Lane. Minneapolis: University of Minnesota Press. [Orig. 1972.]

Delgado Ruiz, Manuel.
1986 *De la muerte de un dios*. Barcelona: Nexos.
1989 La antirreligiosidad popular en España. En *La religiosidad popular*. Vol. 1, Antropología e historia, ed. C. Alvarez Santaló, M. J. Buxó, and S. Rodríguez Becerra, 499–516. Barcelona: Anthropos.
1992 *La ira sagrada: Anticlericalismo, iconoclastia y antirritualismo en la España contemporánea*. Barcelona: Editorial Humanidades.

Del Real, Carlos Alonso.
1971 *Superstición y supersticiones*. Madrid: Espasa-Calpe.

Delumeau, Jean.
1990 *Sin and Fear: The Emergence of a Western Guilt Culture, 13th-18th Centuries*. New York: St. Martin's Press.

DeMause, Lloyd.
1974 The Evolution of Childhood. *History of Childhood Quarterly* 1:503–606.
1974 *The History of Childhood*. New York: Psychohistory Press.
1991 The Universality of Incest. *Journal of Psychohistory* 19:123–64.

De Miguel, Amando.
1976 *Franco, Franco, Franco*. Madrid: Ediciones 99.

De Miguel, Florindo.
1956 *Un cura en zona roja*. Barcelona: Casals.

De Miguel, Jesús M., with Carmen Domínguez-Alcón.
1979 *El mito de la inmaculada concepción*. Barcelona: Editorial Anagrama.

Dendle, Brian J.
1966 *The Novel of Religious Thesis in Spain, 1875–1936*. Ann Arbor, Mich.: University Microfilms. Ph.D. diss., Princeton University.

Deschner, Karlheinz.
1993   *Historia sexual del cristianismo.* Trans. M. Ardid Lorés. Zaragoza: Yalde.
De Sousa, Ronald.
1987   *The Rationality of Emotion.* Cambridge, Mass.: MIT Press.
Devereux, George.
1965   Neurotic Downward Identification. *American Imago* 22:75–95.
1980   *Basic Problems of Ethnopsychiatry,* trans. B. M. Gulati and G. Devereux. Chicago: University of Chicago Press.
Díaz del Moral, Juan.
1991   *Historia de las agitaciones campesinas andaluzas.* Madrid: Alianza. [Orig. 1928.]
Díaz Roig, Mercedes, ed.
1981   *El Romancero viejo.* Madrid: Cátedra.
Di Febo, Giuliana.
1988   *La Santa de la Raza: Teresa de Avila, un culto barroco en la España franquista (1937–1962),* trans. Angel Sánchez-Gijón. Barcelona: Icaria.
1991   El Monje Guerrero: Identidad de género en los modelos franquistas durante la Guerra Civil. In *Las mujeres y la Guerra Civil Española,* ed. Instituto de la Mujer, 202–10. Madrid: Ministerio de Cultura.
Dijkstra, Bram.
1986   *Idols of Perversity: Fantasies of Feminine Evil in Fin-de-Siècle Culture.* New York: Oxford University Press.
Dinges, William D.
1991   Roman Catholic Traditionalism. In *Fundamentalisms Observed,* ed. Martin E. Marty and R. Scott Appleby, 66–101. Chicago: University of Chicago Press.
Domínguez Morano, Carlos.
1985   Aproximación psicoanalítica a la religiosidad tradicional andaluza. In *La religión en Andalucía: Aproximación a la religiosidad popular,* ed. CETRA, 131–75. Seville: Editoriales Andaluzas Unidas.
Drewermann, Eugen.
1995   *Clérigos: Psicograma de un ideal.* Trans. Dionisio Mínguez. Madrid: Editorial Trotta.
Dufour, Gérard.
1996   *Clero y sexto mandamiento: La confesión en la España del siglo XVIII.* Valladolid: Ambito Ediciones.
Edgerton, Robert D.
1992   *Sick Societies: Challenging the Myth of Primitive Harmony.* New York: Free Press.
Edmunds, Lowell.
1985   *Oedipus: The Ancient Legend and Its Later Analogues.* Baltimore: Johns Hopkins University Press.
Ellis, Havelock.
1972   La mujer española. In *La España del siglo XX vista por extranjeros,* ed. Francisco Flores Arroyuelo, 231–61. Madrid: Cuadernos para el Diálogo. [Orig. 1908.]
Esenwein, George R.
1989   *Anarchist Ideology and the Working-Class Movement in Spain, 1868–1898.* Berkeley: University of California Press.
Eslava Galán, Juan.
1993   *El sexo de nuestros padres.* Barcelona: Planeta.

Espinell, Jaime.
1963   *Memorias de un médico de la lucha antivenérea.* Barcelona: Rodegar.
Esteban, José.
1994   *Refranero anticlerical.* Madrid: VOSA.
Eyer, Diane E.
1992   *Mother-Infant Bonding: A Scientific Fiction.* New Haven: Yale University Press.
Favazza, Armando R.
1987   *Bodies under Siege: Self-Mutilation in Culture and Psychiatry.* Baltimore: Johns Hopkins University Press.
Fernández Suárez, Alvaro.
1961   *España, árbol vivo.* Madrid: Aguilar.
Ferrer Benimeli, J. A.
1982   *El contubernio judeo-masónico-comunista.* Madrid: Istmo.
Fogel, G. I., and W. A. Myers, eds.
1991   *Perversions and Near-Perversions in Clinical Practice: New Psychoanalytic Perspectives.* New Haven: Yale University Press.
Foucault, Michel.
1985   Sexuality and Solitude [James Lecture at the New York Institute for the Humanities, 1980]. In *On Signs*, ed. M. Blonsky, 365–72. Baltimore: Johns Hopkins University Press.
1990   *The History of Sexuality. Volume 1: An Introduction.* Trans. Robert Hurley. New York: Vintage Books. [Orig. 1976.]
Fox, E. Inman.
1988   *Ideología y política en las letras de fin de siglo (1898).* Madrid: Espasa-Calpe.
Fraser, R.
1979   *Recuérdalo tú y recuérdalo a otros.* Barcelona: Crítica.
Freud, Sigmund.
1963   Notes upon a Case of Obsessional Neurosis. In *Three Case Histories*, ed. Philip Rieff, 15–102. New York: Macmillan. [Orig. 1909.]
Galenson, Eleanor.
1988   The Precursors of Masochism. In *Fantasy, Myth, and Reality: Essays in Honor of Jacob A. Arlow*, ed. H. P. Blum et al., 371–80. Madison, Conn.: International Universities Press.
Gallego Méndez, María Teresa.
1983   *Mujer, Falange y Franquismo.* Madrid: Taurus.
García de la Concha, Federico.
1988   La devoción a la Dolorosa en Sevilla: Las cofradías y la Dolorosa. *ABC*, 21 March, 35–36.
García Lara, Fernando.
1978   Imágenes sexuales en la canción novecentista. *Letras del Sur*, 57–61.
1986   *El lugar de la novela erótica española.* Granada: Excma. Diputación Provincial de Granada.
García Lorca, Federico.
1969   Elegía a María Blanchard [1932]. In *Prosa*, 193–99. Madrid: Alianza.
Garrido, Javier. *– a priest*
1987   *Grandeza y miseria del celibato cristiano.* Santander: Sal Terrae.
Gassiot Magret, José.
1961   *Apuntes para un estudio de la persecución religiosa en España.* Barcelona: Ariel.

Geist, Anthony.
1985   Popular Poetry in the Fascist Front during the Spanish Civil War. In *Fascismo y experiencia literaria*, ed. H. Vidal, 145–53. Minneapolis: Institute for the Study of Ideologies and Literature.

Gies, David T.
1994   Introducción biográfica y crítica. In *Don Juan Tenorio*, ed. David T. Gies, 7–69. Madrid: Castalia.

Gilmore, David D.
1987   *Aggression and Community: Paradoxes of Andalusian Culture.* New Haven: ✓ Yale University Press.
1989   The Anticlericalism of the Andalusian Rural Proletarians. In *La religiosidad popular.* Vol. 1, Antropología e historia, ed. C. Alvarez Santaló, M. J. Buxó, and S. Rodríguez Becerra, 478–98. Barcelona: Anthropos.

Gil Pecharromán, Julio.
1990   Religión, moral y costumbres a comienzos de los cincuenta and La Legión Azul. In *Vida cotidiana en la España de los 50*, ed. Juan María Martínez, 37–40 and 52–63. Madrid: Ediciones del Prado.

Giner, Salvador, and Sebastián Sarasa.
1993   Religión y modernidad en España. In *Religión y sociedad en España*, eds. R. Díaz-Salazar and S. Giner, 51–92. Madrid: Centro de Investigaciones Sociológicas.

Goffman, Erving.
1963   *Stigma.* Englewood Cliffs, N.J.: Prentice-Hall.

Goldberg, Harriet.
1996   *Motif-Index of Medieval Spanish Folk Narratives.* Binghamton, N.Y.: Medieval and Renaissance Texts and Studies.

Gomá y Tomás, Isidro.
1940   *Por Dios y por España.* Barcelona: Rafael Casulleras.

Gómez-Tabanera, José Manuel, ed.
1968   *El folklore español.* Madrid: Instituto Español de Antropología Aplicada.

González Ballesteros, Teodoro.
1981   *Aspectos jurídicos de la censura cinematográfica en España con especial referencia al período 1936–1977.* Madrid: Editorial de la Universidad Complutense de Madrid.

González Calleja, Eduardo.
1994   La razón de la fuerza: Una perspectiva de la violencia política en la España de la Restauración. In *Violencia y política en España*, ed. Julio Aróstegui, 85–113. Madrid: Marcial Pons/Asociación de Historia Contemporánea.

González Gómez, Juan Miguel.
1985   Sentimiento y simbolismo en las representaciones marianas de la Semana Santa en Sevilla. In *Las cofradías de Sevilla.* Seville: Servicio de Publicaciones de la Universidad de Sevilla y del Excmo. Ayuntamiento de Sevilla.

González-López, Emilio.
1976   The Myth of Saint James and Its Functional Reality. In *Américo Castro and the Meaning of Spanish Civilization*, ed. J. Rubia Barcia, 91–111. Berkeley: University of California Press.

González Martínez, Carmen.
1991   Mujeres Antifascistas Españolas: Trayectoria histórica de una organi-

zación femenina de lucha. In *Las mujeres y la Guerra Civil Española*, ed. Instituto de la Mujer, 54–59. Madrid: Ministerio de Cultura.

Goytisolo, Juan.
   1982   *Juan sin tierra*, 3d ed. Barcelona: Biblioteca Breve.

Graham, Helen.
   1995   Gender and the State: Women in the 1940s. In *Spanish Cultural Studies, an Introduction: The Struggle for Modernity*, ed. H. Graham and J. Labanyi, 182–96. New York: Oxford University Press.

Greenberg, Ira A.
   1974   Moreno: Psychodrama and Group Process. In *Psychodrama: Theory and Therapy*, ed. Ira A. Greenberg, 11–28. New York: Behavioral Publications.

Greven, Philip.
   1992   *Spare the Child: The Religious Roots of Punishment and the Psychological Impact of Child Abuse.* New York: Vintage Books.

Gutiérrez Serrano, Federico.
   1988   San Antonio María Claret, nuestro hermano y maestro. *Boletín de las Cofradías de Sevilla*, March, 111–15.

Haliczer, Stephen.
   1996   *Sexuality in the Confessional: A Sacrament Profaned.* Oxford: Oxford University Press.

Hampden-Turner, Charles.
   1981   *Maps of the Mind.* New York: Collier.

Hernando, Bernardino M.
   1977   *Delirios de Cruzada.* Madrid: Ediciones 99.

Hobsbawm, Eric J.
   1959   *Primitive Rebels.* Manchester: University of Manchester Press.

Holland, Norman N.
   1989   *The Dynamics of Literary Response.* 3d ed. New York: Columbia University Press.

Horowitz, Mardi J.
   1979   *States of Mind.* New York: Plenum Press.
   1988   *Introduction to Psychodynamics: A New Synthesis.* New York: Basic Books.

Horowitz, Mardi, Bram Fridhandler, and Charles Stinson.
   1992   Person Schemas and Emotion. In *Affect: Psychoanalytic Perspectives*, eds. T. Shapiro and R. Emde, 173–208. Madison, Conn.: International Universities Press.

Hunt, Lynn.
   1992   *The Family Romance of the French Revolution.* Berkeley: University of California Press.

Ibárruri, Dolores [Pasionaria].
   1966   *They Shall Not Pass.* New York: International Publishers.

Irons, Richard, and Mark Laaser.
   1994   The Abduction of Fidelity: Sexual Exploitation by Clergy. Experience with Inpatient Assessment. *Sexual Addiction and Compulsivity: The Journal of Treatment and Prevention* 1:119–29.

Jameson, Fredric.
   1996   On the Sexual Production of Western Subjectivity; or, Saint Augustine as a Social Democrat. In *Gaze and Voice as Love Objects*, ed. R. Salecl and S. Zizek, 154–78. Durham, N.C.: Duke University Press.

Jiménez, Alvaro.
1993   *Aportes de la psicología a la vida religiosa*. Bogotá: Editorial San Pablo.
Jiménez Campo, J.
1979   *El fascismo en la crisis de la II República*. Madrid: Centro de Investigaciones Sociológicas.
Jover, José María.
1991   *Realidad y mito de la Primera República*. Madrid: Espasa-Calpe.
Julián, Inmaculada.
1991   La representación gráfica de las mujeres. In *Las mujeres y la Guerra Civil Española*, ed. Instituto de la Mujer, 353–58. Madrid: Ministerio de Cultura.
Kamen, Henry.
1983   Clerical Violence in a Catholic Society: The Hispanic World, 1450–1720. In *The Church and War*, ed. W. J. Sheils, 201–16. London: Basil Blackwell.
1993   *The Phoenix and the Flame: Catalonia and the Counter Reformation*. New Haven: Yale University Press.
Kaplan, Temma.
1977   *Anarchists of Andalusia, 1868–1903*. Princeton: Princeton University Press.
Katz, Jack.
1988   *Seductions of Crime: Moral and Sensual Attractions in Doing Evil*. New York: Basic Books.
Kern, Robert W.
1974   *Liberals, Reformers, and Caciques in Restoration Spain, 1875–1909*. Albuquerque: University of New Mexico Press.
1978   *Red Years/Black Years: A Political History of Spanish Anarchism*. Philadelphia: Institute for the Study of Human Issues.
Kernberg, Otto.
1992   The Psychopathology of Hatred. In *Affect: Psychoanalytic Perspectives*, eds. T. Shapiro and R. Emde, 209–38. Madison, Conn.: International Universities Press.
Kiev, Ari.
1972   *Transcultural Psychiatry*. New York: Macmillan.
Kinder, Marsha.
1993   *Blood Cinema: The Reconstruction of National Identity in Spain*. Berkeley: University of California Press.
Klein, Melanie.
1975   *Envy and Gratitude and Other Works: 1946–1963*. New York: Delacorte.
1986   *The Selected Melanie Klein*, ed. J. Mitchell. Harmondsworth, U.K.: Penguin.
Kramer, Joel, and Diana Alstad.
1993   *The Guru Papers: Masks of Authoritarian Power*. Berkeley: Frog.
Kristeva, Julia.
1986   *The Kristeva Reader*, ed. T. Moi. Oxford: Blackwell.
Kurtz, Lester.
1986   *The Politics of Heresy: The Modernist Crisis of Roman Catholicism*. Berkeley: University of California Press.
Labanyi, Jo.
1996   Women, Asian Hordes and the Threat of the Self in Ernesto Giménez Caballero's *Genio de España*. *Bulletin of Hispanic Studies* 73: 378–87.

Laeuchli, Samuel.
1972   *Power and Sexuality: The Emergence of Canon Law at the Synod of Elvira.*
Philadelphia: Temple University Press.
Laing, R. D.
1972   *The Politics of the Family and Other Essays.* New York: Vintage Books.
Lannon, Frances.
1987   *Privilege, Persecution, and Prophecy: The Catholic Church in Spain, 1875–
1975.* Oxford: Clarendon Press.
1995   Catholicism and Social Change. In *Spanish Cultural Studies, an Introduction: The Struggle for Modernity,* ed. H. Graham and J. Labanyi, 276–82.
New York: Oxford University Press.
Larra, Mariano José de.
1990   *Artículos.* México: Porrúa. [Orig. 1836.]
Lawton, Henry.
1988   *The Psychohistorian's Handbook.* New York: Psychohistory Press.
Lewis, Joseph.
1933   *Spain, A Land Blighted by Religion.* New York: Freethought Press Association.
Lewis, Paul.
1993   The Right and Military Rule, 1955–1983. In *The Argentine Right. Its History and Intellectual Origins, 1910 to the Present,* ed. S. M. Deutsch and
R. H. Dolkart, 147–80. Wilmington, Del.: Scholarly Resources.
Lincoln, Bruce.
1989   *Discourse and the Construction of Society.* New York: Oxford University
Press.
Linton, Ralph.
1956   *Culture and Mental Disorders.* Springfield, Ill.: Charles C. Thomas.
1988   Culture and Normality. In *High Points in Anthropology,* 2d ed., ed. P. Bo-
hannan and M. Glazer, 199–205. New York: McGraw-Hill. [Orig. 1956.]
Linz, Juan J.
1993   Religión y política en España. In *Religión y sociedad en España,* ed.
R. Díaz-Salazar and S. Giner, 1–50. Madrid: Centro de Investigaciones
Sociológicas.
Litvak, Lily.
1979   *Erotismo fin de siglo.* Barcelona: Antoni Bosch.
1981   *La musa libertaria: Arte, literatura y vida cultural del anarquismo español
(1880–1913).* Barcelona: Antoni Bosch.
Llovet, Enrique.
1990   ¡Que apaguen la sala! In *La vida cotidiana en la España de los 50,* ed.
Juan María Martínez, 21. Madrid: Ediciones del Prado.
Loewenstein, R.
1955   A Contribution to the Psychoanalytic Theory of Masochism. *Journal of
the American Psychoanalytic Association* 5:197–234.
López Morillas, Juan.
1956   *El krausismo español.* México: Fondo de Cultura Económica.
López Sánchez, Félix.
1994   *Abusos sexuales a menores: Lo que recuerdan de mayores.* Madrid: Publicaciones del Ministerio de Asuntos Sociales.
Losada Malvárez, Juan Carlos.
1990   *Ideología del Ejército Franquista (1939–1959).* Madrid: Istmo.

Lotto, David.
1994   On Witches and Witch Hunts: Ritual and Satanic Cult Abuse. *Journal of Psychohistory* 21:373–96.

Luis, Francisco de.
1994   *Cincuenta años de cultura obrera en España, 1890–1940.* Madrid: Editorial Pablo Iglesias.

Macey, David.
1993   *The Lives of Michel Foucault.* New York: Pantheon.

Machthild, Albert.
1991   La Bestia y el Angel. Imágenes de las mujeres en la novela falangista de la Guerra Civil. In *Las mujeres y la Guerra Civil Española,* ed. Instituto de la Mujer, 371–78. Madrid: Ministerio de Cultura.

Madariaga, Salvador de.
1972   *Mujeres españolas.* Madrid: Espasa-Calpe.

Mainer, José-Carlos.
1972   *Literatura y pequeña burguesía en España.* Madrid: Edicusa.
1974   Literatura burguesa, literatura pequeño-burguesa en la España del siglo XX. In *Creación y público en la literatura española,* 162–80. Madrid: Castalia.
1986   Notas sobre la lectura obrera en España (1890–1930). In *Literatura popular y proletaria.* Seville: Servicio de Publicaciones de la Universidad de Sevilla.

Marías, Julián.
1987   *Ser español. Ideas y creencias en el mundo hispánico.* Barcelona: Planeta, 1987.

Marichal, Juan.
1974   *El nuevo pensamiento político español.* México: Finisterre.

Martín Gaite, Carmen.
1987   *Usos amorosos de la postguerra española.* Barcelona: Anagrama.

Marty, Martin E., and R. Scott Appleby.
1991   Conclusion: An Interim Report on a Hypothetical Family. In *Fundamentalisms Observed,* ed. Martin E. Marty and R. Scott Appleby, 814–42. Chicago: University of Chicago Press.

May, Rollo.
1960   The Significance of Symbols. In *Symbolism in Religion and Literature,* ed. R. May. New York: Braziller.

McFarlane, Alexander C., and Bessel A. van der Kolk.
1996   Trauma and Its Challenge to Society. In *Traumatic Stress: The Effects of Overwhelming Experience on Mind, Body, and Society,* ed. B. A. van der Kolk, A. C. McFarlane, and L. Weisaeth, 24–46. New York: Guilford.

McLaughlin, Barbara.
1994   Devastated Spirituality: The Impact of Clergy Sexual Abuse on the Survivor's Relationship with God and the Church. *Sexual Addiction and Compulsivity: The Journal of Treatment and Prevention* 1:145–58.

Meissner, W. W.
1992   *Ignatius of Loyola: The Psychology of a Saint.* New Haven: Yale University Press.

Melgar Reina, Luis, and Angel Marín Rújula.
1987   *Saetas, pregones y romances litúrgicos cordobeses.* Córdoba: Publicaciones del Monte de Piedad y Caja de Ahorros de Córdoba.

Menéndez Pidal, Ramón.
1925   *Floresta de leyendas heróicas españolas. Rodrigo, el último godo.* 3 vols. Madrid: La Lectura.
Miller, Alice.
1990   *For Your Own Good: Hidden Cruelty in Child-Rearing and the Roots of Violence.* Trans. Hildegard Hannum and Hunter Hannum. 3d ed. New York: Noonday Press.
Mintz, Jerome R.
1982   *The Anarchists of Casas Viejas.* Chicago: University of Chicago Press.
Miranda, Soledad.
1982   *Religión y clero en la gran novela española del s. XIX.* Madrid: Pegaso.
Mitchell, Stephen A., and Margaret J. Black.
1995   *Freud and Beyond: A History of Modern Psychoanalytic Thought.* New York: Basic Books.
Mitchell, Timothy.
1988   *Violence and Piety in Spanish Folklore.* Philadelphia: University of Pennsylvania Press.
1990   *Passional Culture: Emotion, Religion, and Society in Southern Spain.* Philadelphia: University of Pennsylvania Press.
1991   *Blood Sport: A Social History of Spanish Bullfighting.* Philadelphia: University of Pennsylvania Press. Appendices by Rosario Cambria.
1994   *Flamenco Deep Song.* New Haven: Yale University Press.
Montero Moreno, Antonio.
1961   *Historia de la persecución religiosa en España, 1936–1939.* Madrid: Biblioteca de Autores Cristianos.
Moore, R. I.
1987   *The Formation of a Persecuting Society.* Oxford: Basil Blackwell.
Moreno, Isidoro.
1982   *La Semana Santa en Sevilla: Conformación, mixtificación y significaciones.* Seville: Publicaciones de la Universidad de Sevilla.
1985   *Cofradías y hermandades andaluzas: Estructura, simbolismo e identidad.* Seville: Editoriales Andaluzas Unidas.
Moreno, Jacob Levi.
1959   *Psychodrama.* 2 vols. Boston: Beacon House.
1974   Mental Catharsis and the Psychodrama. In *Psychodrama: Theory and Therapy,* ed. Ira A. Greenberg, 157–98. New York: Behavioral Publications.
Morrison, Andrew P.
1996   *The Culture of Shame.* New York: Ballantine.
Moses-Hrushovski, Rena.
1996   Remaining in the Bunker Long after the War Is Over: Deployment in the Individual, the Group, and the Nation. In *Psychoanalysis at the Political Border: Essays in Honor of Rafael Moses,* ed. L. Rangell and R. Moses-Hrushovski, 165–88. Madison, Conn.: International Universities Press.
Muntanyola, Ramón.
1971   *Vidal i Barraquer: El cardenal de la paz.* Barcelona: Estela.
Nadal, Jordi.
1975   *El fracaso de la revolución industrial en España, 1814–1913.* Barcelona: Ariel.
Nash, Mary.
1975   *Mujeres Libres: España, 1936–1939.* Barcelona: Tusquets.

1981   *Mujer y movimiento obrero en España, 1931–1939.* Barcelona: Fontamara.
1991   La miliciana: Otra opción de combatividad femenina antifascista. In *Las mujeres y la Guerra Civil Española,* ed. Instituto de la Mujer, 97–108. Madrid: Ministerio de Cultura.
Neuschäfer, Hans-Jörg.
1994   *Adiós a la España eterna: La dialéctica de la censura. Novela, teatro y cine bajo el franquismo.* Trans. Rosa Pilar Blanco. Barcelona: Anthropos.
Ney, Philip G.
1987   Does Verbal Abuse Leave Bigger Scars? A Study of Children and Parents. *Canadian Journal of Psychiatry* 32:371–78.
Paglia, Camille.
1990   *Sexual Personae: Art and Decadence from Nefertiti to Emily Dickinson.* New Haven: Yale University Press.
Palacio, Carlos, ed.
1939   *Colección de canciones de lucha.* Valencia: Tipografía Moderna.
Pardo, José Ramón.
1990   Las canciones de una época. In *La vida cotidiana en la España de los 50,* ed. Juan María Martínez, 12, 24, 36, 48. Madrid: Ediciones del Prado.
Payne, Stanley G.
1984   *Spanish Catholicism: An Historical Overview.* Madison: University of Wisconsin Press.
Peers, E. Allison.
1945   *Spain, the Church and the Orders.* London: Burns, Oates, and Washbourne.
Peñafiel, Jaime.
1990   Un cierto deshielo. In *La vida cotidiana en la España de los 50,* ed. Juan María Martínez, 5–36. Madrid: Ediciones del Prado.
Pérez de la Dehesa, Rafael.
1966   *El pensamiento de Costa y su influencia en el 98.* Madrid: Sociedad de Estudios y Publicaciones.
Pérez Embid, Florentino.
1954   El símbolo de Santiago en la cultura española. In *Santiago en la historia, la literatura y el arte,* ed. Colegio Mayor Universitario de la Estila, II, 167–183. Madrid: Editora Nacional.
Pérez Galdós, Benito.
1902   *Electra.* Ed. O. G. Bunnell. New York: ABC. [Orig. 1901.]
1991   *Doña Perfecta.* México: Editorial Porrúa. [Orig. 1876.]
1994   *Un faccioso más y algunos frailes menos.* Madrid: Historia 16/ Caja Madrid. [Orig. 1879.]
Pérez Iruela, José.
1990   Calificación moral de espectáculos. In *La vida cotidiana en la España de los 50,* ed. Juan María Martínez, 39. Madrid: Ediciones del Prado.
1990   La Iglesia se desmarca. In *La vida cotidiana en la España de los 60,* ed. Juan María Martínez, 73–75. Madrid: Ediciones del Prado.
Pérez Ledesma, Manuel.
1993   El miedo de los acomodados y la moral de los obreros. In *Otras visiones de España,* ed. Pilar Folguera, 27–64. Madrid: Editorial Pablo Iglesias.
Peristiany, J. G., ed.
1965   *Honour and Shame: The Values of Mediterranean Society.* London: Weidenfeld and Nicolson.

Piers, Gerhart, and Milton Singer, eds.
1971　*Shame and Guilt.* New York: Norton. [Orig. 1953.]
Poliakov, Léon.
1974　*The Aryan Myth: A History of Racist and Nationalist Ideas in Europe.* Trans.
E. Howard. New York: Basic Books.
Preston, James J.
1982　New Perspectives on Mother Worship. In *Mother Worship: Themes and Variations,* ed. J. J. Preston, 325–43. Chapel Hill: University of North Carolina Press.
Preston, Paul.
1994　*Franco: A Biography.* New York: Basic Books.
Primo de Rivera, Pilar.
1939　*Cuatro discursos.* Madrid: Editora Nacional.
Puccini, Dario, ed.
1960　*Romancero de la resistencia española.* México: Editorial Porrúa.
Puente Ojea, Gonzalo.
1991　*Fe cristiana, Iglesia, poder.* Madrid: Siglo XXI.
1993　*Ideología e historia: La formación del cristianismo como fenómeno ideológico.* 6th ed. Madrid: Siglo XXI.
1994　Del confesionalismo al criptoconfesionalismo: Una nueva forma de hegemonía de la Iglesia. In *La influencia de la religión en la sociedad española,* ed. Javier Sádaba, 81–146. Madrid: Libertarias/Prodhufi.
Ramos-Gascón, Antonio, ed.
1978　*El Romancero del Ejército Popular.* Madrid: Editorial Nuestra Cultura.
Ranke-Heinemann, Uta.
1990　*Eunuchs for the Kingdom of Heaven: Women, Sexuality, and the Catholic Church.* Trans. Peter Heinegg. New York: Doubleday.
Real López, Soledad, Margarita Abril, and Isabel Vicente.
1991　Las mujeres en la inmediata postguerra. In *Las mujeres y la Guerra Civil Española,* ed. Instituto de la Mujer, 317–21. Madrid: Ministerio de Cultura.
Reich, Wilhelm.
1970　*The Mass Psychology of Fascism.* Trans. Vincent R. Carfagno, ed. M. Higgins and C. M. Raphael. New York: Noonday Press. [Orig. 1933.]
Retana, Alvaro.
1964　*Historia del arte frívolo.* Madrid: Tesoro.
Revuelta González, Manuel.
1969　La Iglesia española ante la crisis del Antiguo Régimen (1808–1833). In *Historia de la Iglesia en España,* vol. 5, ed. Vicente Cárcel Ortí, 3–113. Madrid: Biblioteca de Autores Cristianos.
Rheingold, Joseph C.
1964　*The Fear of Being a Woman: A Theory of Maternal Destructiveness.* New York: Grune and Stratton.
Robinson, Paul.
1990　*The Freudian Left: Wilhelm Reich, Geza Roheim, Herbert Marcuse,* 2d ed. Ithaca: Cornell University Press.
Rodríguez, Pepe.
1993　*El drama del menor en España.* Barcelona: Ediciones B.
1994　*Tu hijo y las sectas. Guía de prevención y tratamiento para padres, educadores y afectados.* Madrid: Temas de Hoy.
1995　*La vida sexual del clero.* Barcelona: Ediciones B.

Rodríguez Moñino, Antonio, ed.
 1977   *Romancero General de la Guerra de España.* Madrid: Hispamérica.
Rodríguez Puértolas, Julio.
 1987   *Literatura fascista española.* 2 vols. Madrid: Akal.
Ross, John Munder.
 1992   A Psychoanalytic Essay on Romantic, Erotic Love. In *Affect: Psychoanalytic Perspectives,* ed. T. Shapiro and R. Emde, 439–74. Madison, Conn.: International Universities Press.
Rougement, Denis de.
 1984   *El amor y Occidente.* 3d ed. Trans. Antoni Vicens. Barcelona: Kairós. [Orig. 1938; revised 1956, 1970.]
Ruether, Rosemary Radford.
 1974   Misogynism and Virginal Feminism in the Fathers of the Church. In *Religion and Sexism,* ed. R. R. Ruether, 150–54. New York: Simon and Schuster.
Sacher-Masoch, Leopold von.
 1989   *Venus in Furs and Selected Letters.* Ed. Sylvère Lotringer and Chris Kraus. New York: Masquerade Books. [Orig. 1870.]
Sainz Bretón, María José, Olga Morentín Arana, and Arantza Romano Igartua.
 1991   *Mujeres.* Organo de prensa del Comité de Mujeres Antifascistas. In *Las mujeres y la Guerra Civil Española,* ed. Instituto de la Mujer, 48–53. Madrid: Ministerio de Cultura.
Salaün, Serge.
 1971   *Romancero libertario.* Paris: Seghers.
 1985   *La poesía de la Guerra de España.* Madrid: Castalia.
 1990   *El cuplé (1900–1936).* Madrid: Espasa-Calpe/Colección Austral.
Salinas, Pedro.
 1985   *Ensayos completos.* 3 vols. Madrid: Taurus.
Sanabre Sanromá, José.
 1943   *Martirologio de la Iglesia en la diócesis de Barcelona durante la persecución religiosa.* Barcelona: Editorial Librería Religiosa.
Sánchez, José.
 1972   *Anticlericalism: A Brief History.* Notre Dame, Ind.: University of Notre Dame Press.
 1987   *The Spanish Civil War as a Religious Tragedy.* Notre Dame, Ind.: University of Notre Dame Press.
Sánchez-Gijón, Aitana.
 1990   Moral pública y vicios privados. In *La vida cotidiana en la España de los 40,* ed. Juan María Martínez, 73–80. Madrid: Ediciones del Prado.
Sánchez Nadal, Antonio.
 1991   Experiencias psíquicas sobre mujeres marxistas malagueñas. Málaga 1939. In *Las mujeres y la Guerra Civil Española,* ed. Instituto de la Mujer, 340–43. Madrid: Ministerio de Cultura.
Santonja, Gonzalo.
 1986   La Editorial Fénix (Madrid, 1932–1935): Notas sobre la literatura de quiosco durante la II República. In *Literatura popular y proletaria,* 209–46. Seville: Servicio de Publicaciones de la Universidad de Sevilla.
Scheper-Hughes, Nancy.
 1982   *Saints, Scholars, and Schizophrenics: Mental Illness in Rural Ireland.* Berkeley: University of California Press.

Schneider, Carl D.
1992 *Shame, Exposure, and Privacy.* 2d ed. New York: Norton.
Schwartz, Theodore, Geoffrey M. White, and Catherine A. Lutz, eds.
1992 *New Directions in Psychological Anthropology.* Cambridge: Cambridge University Press.
Sebastián y Bandarán, José, and Antonio Tineo Lara.
1938 *La persecución religiosa en la Archidiócesis de Sevilla.* Seville: El Correo de Andalucía.
Senabre, Ricardo.
1986 Clarín y Galdós ante el público. In *Literatura popular y proletaria,* 141–54. Seville: Servicio de Publicaciones de la Universidad de Sevilla.
Serrano Poncela, Segundo.
1959 *El secreto de Melibea.* Madrid: Taurus.
Shapiro, David.
1981 *Autonomy and Rigid Character.* New York: Basic Books.
Siegfried, Jürg.
1996 Culture and Mental Illness. *Culture and Psychology* 2:223–31.
Sinclair, Alison.
1993 *The Deceived Husband: A Kleinian Approach to the Literature of Infidelity.* Oxford: Clarendon Press.
Sipe, A. W. Richard.
1994 The Problem of Sexual Trauma and Addiction in the Catholic Church. *Sexual Addiction and Compulsivity: The Journal of Treatment and Prevention* 1:130–37.
1995 *Sex, Priests, and Power: Anatomy of a Crisis.* New York: Brunner/Mazel.
Six, Abigail Lee.
1990 *Juan Goytisolo: The Case for Chaos.* New Haven: Yale University Press.
Smith, Paul Julian.
1992 *Laws of Desire: Questions of Homosexuality in Spanish Writing and Film, 1960–1990.* New York: Oxford University Press.
Sperber, Murray A., ed.
1974 *And I Remember Spain: A Spanish Civil War Anthology.* New York: Macmillan.
Spero, Moshe Halevi.
1992 *Religious Objects as Psychological Structures: A Critical Integration of Object Relations Theory, Psychotherapy, and Judaism.* Chicago: University of Chicago Press.
Stearns, Peter N., and Carol Z. Stearns.
1987 Emotionology: Clarifying the History of Emotions and Emotional Standards. In *Psycho/History. Readings in the Method of Psychology, Psychoanalysis, and History,* ed. G. Cocks and T. L. Crosby, 284–309. New Haven: Yale University Press.
Stein, Howard F.
1987 Psychoanalytic Anthropology and Psychohistory: A Personal Synthesis. In *From Metaphor to Meaning: Papers in Psychoanalytic Anthropology,* eds. Howard F. Stein and Maurice Apprey, 377–90. Charlottesville: University Press of Virginia.
Stoller, Robert J.
1975 *Perversion.* New York: Pantheon.
1985 *Observing the Erotic Imagination.* New Haven: Yale University Press.

Stone, William F., Gerda Lederer, and Richard Christie, eds.
1993   *Strength and Weakness: The Authoritarian Personality Today.* New York: Springer-Verlag.
Taylor, Maxwell.
1991   *The Fanatics: A Behavioural Approach to Political Violence.* London: Brassey's.
Tejada, Luis Alonso.
1977   *La represión sexual en la España de Franco.* Barcelona: Luis de Caralt.
Theweleit, Klaus.
1987   *Male Fantasies.* Trans. Stephen Conway. Minneapolis: University of Minnesota Press.
Thomas, Hugh.
1987   *La Guerra Civil española.* Vol. 1. *Los orígenes de la guerra.* Madrid: Urbión.
Torgovnick, Marianna.
1990   *Gone Primitive: Savage Intellects, Modern Lives.* Chicago: University of Chicago Press.
Torrente Ballester, Gonzalo.
1943   *Javier Mariño: Historia de una conversación.* Madrid: Editora Nacional.
Torres, Rafael.
1996   *La vida amorosa en tiempos de Franco.* Madrid: Temas de Hoy.
Torres Villarroel, Diego de.
1987   *Vida, ascendencia, nacimiento, crianza y aventuras.* Ed. Guy Mercadier. Madrid: Castalia. [Orig. 1743–1758.]
Townson, Nigel, ed.
1994   *El republicanismo en España (1830–1977).* Madrid: Alianza Universidad.
Trigo, Felipe.
1991   *Jarrapellejos,* ed. Angel Martínez San Martín. Madrid: Espasa-Calpe/ Colección Austral. [Orig. 1914.]
Tuñón de Lara, Manuel.
1974   *Costa y Unamuno en la crisis de fin de siglo.* Madrid: Cuadernos para el Diálogo.
Turner, Jonathan H.
1991   *The Structure of Sociological Theory.* 5th ed. Belmont, Calif.: Wadsworth.
Tussell Gómez, Xavier.
1976   The Functioning of the Cacique System in Andalusia, 1890–1931. In *Politics and Society in Twentieth-Century Spain,* ed. Stanley Payne, 1–27. New York: New Viewpoints.
Tussell Gómez, Xavier, and Genoveva Queipo de Llano.
1995   *Los intelectuales y la República.* Madrid: Nerea.
Ullman, Joan Connelly.
1972   *La Semana Trágica: Estudio sobre las causas socioeconómicas del anticlericalismo en España (1898–1912).* Barcelona: Ariel.
Unamuno, Miguel de.
1968   Vida de don Quijote y Sancho. In *Visión de España en la Generación del 98,* ed. J. L. Abellán. Madrid: Editorial Magisterio Español. [Orig. 1905.]
Vallejo-Nájera, Juan Antonio.
1938   *Política racial del Nuevo Estado.* San Sebastián: Editorial Española.
Vallejo-Nájera, Juan Antonio, and Eduardo M. Martínez.
1991   Psiquismo del fanatismo marxista. Investigaciones psicológicas en

marxistas femeninos delincuentes. In *Las mujeres y la Guerra Civil Española*, ed. Instituto de la Mujer, 343–50. Madrid: Ministerio de Cultura. [Orig. 1939.]

Valverde Candil, Mercedes, and Ana María Piriz Salgado.
1989   *Catálogo del Museo Julio Romero de Torres.* 2d ed. Córdoba: Servicio de Publicaciones del Ayuntamiento de Córdoba.

Van der Kolk, Bessel A.
1996   Trauma and Memory. In *Traumatic Stress: The Effects of Overwhelming Experience on Mind, Body, and Society*, ed. B. A. van der Kolk, A. C. McFarlane, and L. Weisaeth, 279–302. New York: Guilford.

Van der Kolk, Bessel A., Lars Weisaeth, and Onno van der Hart.
1996   History of Trauma in Psychiatry. In *Traumatic Stress: The Effects of Overwhelming Experience on Mind, Body, and Society*, ed. B. A. van der Kolk, A. C. McFarlane, and L. Weisaeth, 47–74. New York: Guilford.

Velasco, Fernando.
1993   La religiosidad integrista y la religiosidad ilustrada en el proceso de modernización de España. In *Religión y sociedad en España*, ed. R. Díaz-Salazar and S. Giner, 333–74. Madrid: Centro de Investigaciones Sociológicas.

Verdoy, Alfredo.
1995   *La incautación de los bienes de los jesuitas durante la II República.* Madrid: Editorial Trotta.

Vicuña, Carlos.
1945   *Mártires agustinos de El Escorial.* El Escorial: Monasterio de El Escorial.

Vila-San Juan, José Luis.
1984   *Vida cotidiana durante la dictadura de Primo de Rivera.* Barcelona: Argos-Vergara.

Vizcaíno Casas, Fernando.
1978   *La España de la posguerra, 1939–1953.* Barcelona: Planeta.

Volkan, Vamik D.
1996   Intergenerational Transmission and "Chosen" Traumas: A Link Between the Psychology of the Individual and That of the Ethnic Group. In *Psychoanalysis at the Political Border*, ed. L. Rangell and R. Moses-Hrushovski, 257–82. Madison, Conn.: International Universities Press.

Walsh, Michael.
1992   *Opus Dei: An Investigation into the Secret Society Struggling for Power within the Roman Catholic Church.* New York: HarperCollins.

Welldon, Estela V.
1992   *Mother, Madonna, Whore: The Idealization and Denigration of Motherhood.* New York: Guilford.

Winnicott, D. W.
1989   *Psychoanalytic Explorations*, ed. C. Winnicott. Cambridge, Mass.: Harvard University Press.

Winston, Colin M.
1985   *Workers and the Right in Spain, 1900–1936.* Princeton: Princeton University Press.

Wollheim, Richard.
1984   *The Thread of Life.* Cambridge, Mass.: Harvard University Press.

Worthman, Carol.
1992   Cupid and Psyche: Investigative Syncretism in Biological and Psycho-

social Anthropology. In *New Directions in Psychological Anthropology*, ed. T. Schwartz et al., 150–78. Cambridge: Cambridge University Press.

Young-Bruehl, Elisabeth.

1996   *The Anatomy of Prejudices*. Cambridge, Mass.: Harvard University Press.

Zahonero Vivó, José.

1951   *Sacerdotes mártires*. Alcoy: Marfil.

Zueras Torrens, Francisco.

1987   *Julio Romero de Torres y su mundo*. Córdoba: Publicaciones del Monte de Piedad y Caja de Ahorros de Córdoba.

Index

abuse trauma: and psychological rigidity, 45–47, 137(n55), 141(n48); and religious belief, 80–81, 134–35(n24), 146(n62, n68)

addiction: religious, 53, 57, 141(n54); sexual, 135(n25)

anarchists, 8, 41–42, 55, 58–61, 74–78, 82, 87–93, 96, 142(n72), 145(n44)

Augustine, 2–3, 16–17, 111

Alas, Leopoldo. *See* Clarín

Azaña, Manuel, 8, 74–77, 83, 145(n33,n34)

beatas, 11, 13–14, 18, 49, 88, 113

Blasco Ibáñez, Vicente, 8, 40–41, 62, 64

caciquismo, 142(n56)

Carroll, Michael P., 3–4

Castro, Américo, 150(n142)

Catholic education in Spain, 9, 49, 52–53, 55–56, 72–73, 77, 79, 82, 104, 106–8, 115–16, 124–25

censorship under Franco, 109–15

Christian, William A., Jr., 26–27, 52, 73, 80–81, 84, 145(n48)

Claramunt, Fernando, 18

Claret, Antonio María, 27–29, 36–37, 44

Clarín, 21, 48–55

cofradías, 16

Council of Trent, 11, 50

Counter Reformation, 12, 104, 131

Delgado, Manuel, 6, 76, 148(n100)

Dendle, Brian, 40

doctors. *See* gynecology and sexual attitudes; Trigo, Felipe

Drewermann, Eugen, 9, 20–21, 23–24, 30–31, 52, 125, 129–30

eroticism in popular culture, 63–73, 109–15

Escrivá de Balaguer, José María, 28–29, 82, 128, 138(n66)

Fernando VII, 32–34, 37

folk Catholicism, 3, 5, 10–11, 15, 23, 133(n9)

Foucault, Michel, 2–5, 13, 49, 107, 133(n2, n4)

Francis of Assisi, Saint, 27

Franco, Francisco, 8–9, 72, 84, 97, 104–6, 124, 130–31

Galdós, 40, 44–49, 55–60, 63, 90, 110

García Lorca, Federico, 138(n60)

gender roles under Franco, 116–21

Gilmore, David D., 7, 22, 100

Graham, Helen, 121

guerrilla priests, 32–35

gynecology and sexual attitudes, 64–67, 71, 121–23

Haliczer, Stephen, 11, 18, 38, 141(n54), 142(n57)

homosexuality, 14, 119–20, 138–39(n72)

hysterical prejudices, 5, 18–19, 26, 40, 84, 147(n85)

Ignatius of Loyola, Saint, 4, 97, 131, 133(n10)

Inquisition (Holy Office), 7, 12–15, 32–34, 36, 41–42, 47, 130

Jameson, Fredric, 2, 133(n2)

Jesuits, 12, 17, 32–35, 38–41, 50–51, 53,

Jesuits (*continued*)
55–59, 64, 73–74, 79, 81, 83, 91, 97,
106–8, 133(n10), 138(n68), 139(n21)

Kamen, Henry, 14
Kern, Robert, 48

Lerroux, Alejandro, 60–62, 75–76, 79
Labanyi, Jo, 103
Litvak, Lily, 66

Martín Gaite, Carmen, 115–17, 120–21,
153(n38)
masochistic priests, 3, 22, 24–31, 46,
138(n60)
masturbation, 30–31, 51, 107–8, 114,
122–23, 151(n16)
Miller, Alice, 24, 49
mothers. *See* perverse motherhood

obsessional prejudices, 40, 42, 62, 140(n30,
n47), 143(n86)
Opus Dei, 28–29, 82, 122, 128, 138(n66)
Ortega y Gasset, José, 15, 75

Payne, Stanley G., 32, 36–37, 55, 61, 73–74
pedophile priests, 14–15, 19, 30–31, 114,
127–28, 135(n25), 152(n31)
Pérez Galdós, Benito. *See* Galdós
perverse priests, 25–28, 137(n55)
perverse motherhood, 22–25, 137(n50),
142(n59)
prostitution, 25, 67–68, 94–95, 97, 101–3,
119, 123–24, 139(n18)

Reich, Wilhelm, 9, 64, 85, 107, 114–15,
153(n36)

republicanism in Spain, 74–83
Rodríguez, Pepe, 21, 23, 25, 31, 138(n72)
Romanticism, 37, 58
Romero de Torres, Julio, 70

Sánchez, José, 17, 34, 36, 87, 89, 91
Santiago, myth of, 9, 150(n142)
Sección Femenina, 98–99, 102, 120–21,
154(n55)
Second Vatican Council, 130
seminaries, 23, 29–31, 91, 105
Sipe, A. W. Richard, 6–7, 29, 125, 135(n25),
139(n72)
social trance, 86–93, 148(n92)
solicitation in the confessional, 11–13,
17–18, 50, 131, 135(n25), 142(n57)

Teresa of Avila, Saint, 1, 4, 16, 99
Trigo, Felipe, 63–67, 74, 77

Virgin Mary, 1, 3, 16, 23–24, 27–28, 44,
72–73, 80–81, 139(n74,n18), 140(n45)

Webster, Susan Verdi, 144(n22)
women: and politics, 82–85; and priests,
11, 19–27, 51–55, 125- 26, 136(n21),
145(n48); and show business, 67–71, 85,
95, 109–10; and the Spanish Civil War,
93–101. *See also* beatas; gynecology and
sexual attitudes; gender roles under
Franco; prostitution; Sección Femenina

Young-Bruehl, Elisabeth, 5, 9, 18–19, 26,
40, 84, 143(n86)